with best wishes

July 1989.

Learning
from the
Written Word

The Schools Council Project Reading for Learning in the Secondary School was based at Nottingham University from 1978–1982.

Project Directors:	Eric Lunzer, Keith Gardner
Project Officers:	Florence Davies, Terry Greene
Evaluator:	Roy Fawcett
Consultants:	Bob Moy, Margaret Berry

SCHOOLS COUNCIL

Learning from the Written Word

Eric Lunzer
Keith Gardner
Florence Davies
Terry Greene

Oliver & Boyd

Cover
C McNab & R Mackenzie, *From Waterloo to the Great Exhibition 1815–1851*,
Oliver & Boyd, 1982

Oliver & Boyd
Robert Stevenson House
1–3 Baxter's Place
Leith Walk
Edinburgh EH1 3BB

A Division of Longman Group Ltd

© Schools Council Publications 1984
First published 1984

ISBN 0 05 003771 4 (cased)
ISBN 0 05 003767 6 (paperback)

Set in Linotron Times Roman 10 on 13 pt

Printed in Great Britain by Butler & Tanner Ltd, Frome and London

Foreword

Learning from the Written Word is one of two volumes arising out of the work of a project carried out at Nottingham University on behalf of the Schools Council during the period 1979–1982. It is addressed to teachers in all subjects, especially in secondary schools, and is designed as a comprehensive guide to the principles and methods elaborated by the project, covering three major areas of the curriculum: English, Humanities and the Sciences.

The other publication, *Reading for Learning in the Sciences* is a shorter and more specialised book, prepared by the project officers with the collaboration of scientists engaged in education and adapted to the specific need of teachers of science.

The project on 'Reading for Learning in the Secondary School' was commissioned and designed as a contribution to curricular development and teaching methods. It stands or falls by the message that it conveys to all teachers in schools. The book *Learning From the Written Word* is its principal publication. Now it is conventional for the names of project directors to appear first in publications of this kind, and I would like to take this occasion to pay tribute to the very sterling work of my colleague Keith Gardner as organiser, inspirer and indefatigable publicist for the work of the project throughout its duration and since. I have had the task of preparing this book for publication, and this I have done, aided and abetted – sometimes rescued – by Maria Dicks. That means, too, that I myself bear the responsibility for all inaccuracies and omissions.

But it remains that *Learning From the Written Word* is not the work of one man, or of two, but that of a team. The team should include those many teachers and advisers who have collaborated with us, and some of their names we have listed in our acknowledgements, trying (but perhaps not always succeeding) not to omit those to whom we are most in debt. However, the principal contributors to the work of the project were, inevitably, the project officers themselves: Florence Davies and Terry Greene, for it is they who organised most of the work reported in these pages, who contributed so many of the ideas, and who prepared the first draft of the present volume. They are co-authors in the fullest sense. The remaining member of the team was the evaluator, Roy Fawcett. He is not a co-author, nor was it appropriate that he should be. For his job was partly to stand back from the work, to form his own evaluation of our trial materials, and to obtain the fullest kind of feedback from different users. This he did and did supremely well. If this version of our work communicates to teachers and answers their problems it is very largely because it incorporates so many valuable suggestions that came to us from Roy.

Eric Lunzer

Contents

Part II Reconstruction of Text

Acknowledgements

Learning from the Written Word owes its existence to the teachers who participated in the Reading for Learning project. If the project team were responsible for initiating and integrating the approach, it is the teachers who developed it. It is they who brought it to life in the classroom and who created the variety of forms in which it is manifest.

We are first and foremost indebted to those teachers who allowed us to describe their lessons, and to those who so generously allowed us to work with their classes.

Dave Andrews,　Elliott Durham School, Nottingham
Stuart Ballantyne,　Newfield School, Sheffield
A Barnes,　Forest Hill School, ILEA
Brenda Barratt,　Castle Donington High School, Castle Donington
Roger Beswick,　Priory School, Barnsley, Yorkshire
R Bradford,　formerly of Priory School, Barnsley, Yorkshire
P Bennett and P Blant,　Pingle School, Swadlincote, Derbyshire
Diane Blomfield and Richard Clammer,　High Green School, Sheffield
M Clarke,　Newfield School, Sheffield
Peter Coatham,　Castle Donington Community College, Castle Donington
　Leicestershire
A Conner,　Pingle School, Swadlincote, Derbyshire
Terry Cook,　Priory School, Barnsley, Yorkshire
M Goldthorpe,　Ferneley High School, Melton Mowbray, Leicestershire
Chris Hasty,　formerly of City School, Sheffield
Sue Hibbert,　Castle Donington Community College, Castle Donington
　Leicestershire
Sue Horner,　High Green School, Sheffield
J Holden,　formerly of St Ivo School, St Ives, Huntingdon
J Houlding,　Ecclesbourne School, Derbyshire
Stan Hutchings,　Priory School, Barnsley, Yorkshire
Mike James,　formerly of Toot Hill School, Nottinghamshire
Dave Jackson,　Toot Hill School, Nottinghamshire
Ian Littlehays,　Glenbrook Junior School, Nottingham
Peter McLeod and Derek May,　High Green School, Sheffield
Michelle McMichael,　formerly of Stratton Upper School, Biggleswade,
　Bedfordshire
Geoff Mitchell,　formerly of St Ivo School, St Ives, Huntingdon
R Roy,　Lewisham Teachers' Centre
A Nichol,　formerly of Norfolk School, Sheffield
Chris Reeves,　Ferneley High School, Melton Mowbray, Leicestershire
Jean Rodgers,　Priory School, Barnsley, Yorkshire
J Shimwell,　Kirk Hallam School, Derbyshire
Dr Maurice Spenceley,　Southwell Comprehensive, Nottinghamshire
J Stroy,　Frank Wheldon School, Nottingham
Brian Talbot,　Pingle School, Swadlincote, Derbyshire
John Taylor,　Lydgate Middle School, Sheffield
Vic Taylor,　Christ the King School, Nottingham
Rod Valentine,　Herries School, Sheffield

Peter Wade, Priory School, Barnsley, Yorkshire
Martin Whittle, Herries School, Sheffield
Elizabeth Wylie, formerly of Bushloe High School, Leicestershire
Sue White, formerly of Priory School, Barnsley, Yorkshire

In selecting the material for inclusion in this book, we had to provide examples which would inspire others to try out the approach; sufficient information about practical organisation implementation in the classroom, material which would illustrate pupil response, and a representative selection of lessons across the curriculum.

Because of these constraints, a wealth of valuable materials has not been included. Thus we owe a debt not only to those teachers whose work is documented, but also to those whose work is not. Their work has provided encouragement and support for the project team and for other teachers. Most of all they have given us confidence in the value and feasibility of the approach and have at the same time sharpened our awareness of the problems involved in the classroom implementation of the approach.

Likewise, the role of heads and senior colleagues in furthering curriculum is critical to the success of any project. Those who provided this kind of support are too numerous to name, but there are a few schools in which a project presence was warmly accepted over a long period of time, to which we are especially indebted. Accordingly, we wish especially to thank these headteachers:

D Emery, Priory School, Barnsley, Yorkshire
P Sykes, Castle Donington Community College, Leicestershire
M T Brewis, High Green School, Sheffield
P Usher, Herries School, Sheffield
P Threlfall, Newfield School, Sheffield
G N Precious, Ferneley High School, Melton Mowbray, Leicestershire.

Again, those responsible for initiating development at L.E.A. level are too numerous to list. Special thanks must go to those who were involved in the project over a long period:

Dave Allen, Mike Binks, Trevor Higginbottom and Brian Wilcox of the
    Sheffield Advisory Service
Brian Harris, H.M.I. for Science
Graham Frater, H.M.I. for English
Jack Taylor, Len Jones, Mary Jefferson and Alan Nutton of Barnsley L.E.A.
Bob Moy, Bob Stammers, Mike Raleigh and Michael Simons of Lewisham
    L.E.A.
Derek Cronshaw, Jack Ouseby and Jim McLaren of Nottingham L.E.A.
Dennis Brook and Reg Hardwick of Derbyshire L.E.A.
Helen Arnold, Giles Job and Les Smith of Suffolk L.E.A.
Anne Thomas, Tony Locke and Jeff Kirkham of Leicestershire L.E.A.
John Pearce, Don Cameron and Tom Lyons of Cambridgeshire L.E.A.

We are also indebted to the many colleagues who have given us valuable comment and criticism. Special thanks are due to Margaret Berry and Mike Stubbs in the Department of English, to Colin Harrison and Terry Dolan in the

School of Education, and to Norah Byron and Steve Munslow, formerly research students attached to the project.

As to the form of the present volume, the writers will shoulder the blame, but any credit must be shared with Dennis Pepper and Sue MacIntyre of the Schools Council who read and commented on every previous draft as well as the final MS, to the Schools Council Monitoring Group and its chairman Peter Coakley, and above all to our indefatigable ever-willing secretaries: Kay Lunzer, Paula Hill, Maria Dicks and Jill Cleaver.

We wish to thank those concerned for permission to reproduce extracts from the following books:

Richard Adams, *Shardik*, Rex Collings Ltd (permission granted by David Higham Associates Ltd)

Isaac Asimov, 'The Fun They Had'. Adaptation by Christopher Walker. Reprinted from *Earth Is Room Enough*. © 1957 by Isaac Asimov. Reprinted by permission of Doubleday and Company Inc. and NEA Services Inc.

B S Beckett, *Biology: A Modern Introduction*, second edition, Oxford University Press, © B S Beckett 1972, kidney diagram

L J Campbell and R J Carlton, *Foundation Science*, Routledge & Kegan Paul Ltd, 1973, extract from 'The Aneroid Barometer' and Figure 3

Children's Britannica 'Transmission of Sound' reproduced by permission of Encyclopaedia Britannica International Ltd

R J Cookes, *The Middle Ages*, Longman, 1972, pages 167–8

A Darlington, *Pollution and Life*, Blandford Press, 1974, extract from 'The first revolution and the second', page 7

D M Desoutter, *Your Book of Sound*, Faber & Faber, 1971

T Duncan, *Exploring Physics* Book 2, John Murray Ltd, 1963, 1970

Haydn Evans, *The Young Geographer* Books 2 and 4, A Wheaton & Co Ltd, 1978, Chapter 6 and pages 45 and 47 respectively

E J Ewington and D F Moore, *Human Biology and Hygiene* (*Secondary Science Biology* Book 2), Routledge & Kegan Paul Ltd, 1971, pages 72–74

V E Graham, *Activities for Young Naturalists*, Hulton Educational Publishers Ltd., 1969, extract from 'Making a Compost Heap, page 116

P Grayson, 'Stonehenge' in *Derbyshire Antiquities*, Grayson Publications, Chesterfield, 1971, page 4

Richard Hart, *Chemistry Matters*, Oxford University Press, 1978, pages 154–5

Elizabeth Jennings, 'My Grandmother' from *Collected Poems*, Macmillan London and Basingstoke, 1967 (permission granted by David Higham Associates Ltd)

D G Mackean, *Introduction to Genetics*, John Murray Ltd, 1977

M Macefield, *The House of History*, Thomas Nelson & Sons Ltd, 1931 extract from 'Sir Thomas More' in *The Second Storey*, pages 72–81

Man: A Course of Study © 1969, Education Development Center, Inc., Newton, Ma., extract from 'Salmon Survival Problems', page 56

E H Markman, 'Realising that you don't understand: elementary school children's awareness of inconsistencies' in *Child Development, Quarterly Journal of the Society for Research in Child Development*, **50**, 1979, pages 643–655, (Department of Psychiatry, Stamford University School of Medicine)

A Mee, *Nottinghamshire* (editor G E Denison), Hodder & Stoughton, 1970, page 184 (permission granted by A M Heath & Co. Ltd)

Nuffield Biology 4, Introducing Living Things, Longman, 1974, extract from 'Cycles of Reproduction'

Nuffield Biology 1, Introducing Living Things, Longman 1974, extract from 'Man and Microbes'

D B O'Callaghan, *Roosevelt and the United States* (Modern Times series), Longman, 1966, extract from Chapter 6, 'The Roaring Twenties'

R Pitcher & A Harris, *The Developing World: History One, Man Makes His Way*, Longman, 1970, extract from 'Building a Nation', page 49

Clive Rowe *et al., Railways Today* and *Building a Polder* (*Oxford Geography Project 2, European Patterns*) Oxford University Press, 1974

J G Rushby, J Bell & M W Dybeck, *Study Geography* Stage 1, Longman, 1975

John Steinbeck, *The Pearl*, Wm Heinemann Ltd, 1954 and Viking Penguin Inc. (Copyright 1945 by John Steinbeck. Copyright renewed © 1973 by Elaine Steinbeck, Thom Steinbeck and John Steinbeck IV)

R Stone & R Dennien, *Longman Physics Topics: Energy*, Longman, 1974

I M Tenen, *This England from the Earlier Times to 1485*, Macmillan, London & Basingstoke, 1952

R W Thomas, *Metals and Alloys*, Arnold & Wheaton, 1975, (now out of print – permission granted by author), page 24

R J Unstead, 'Medieval Castles', from *Castles*, Adam & Charles Black (Publishers) Ltd, 1970, pages 3, 4

C Windridge, *General Science* Book 1, extract from 'The Expansion of Solids' and *General Science* Book 2, 'Making a Constellation Viewer', both Schofield & Sims Ltd., 1976

E W Young & J H Lowry, *A Course in World Geography* Book 2, *People Around the World*, Edward Arnold, 1964, extract from 'Coniferous Trees'.

While every effort has been made to trace copyright owners, we apologise for any errors or omissions in the above list.

Note on copyright
Our objective is to further more extensive use of text books. One of the means towards this end is the marking by pupils of extracts copied from texts used in the classroom. Copyright clearance for the use of texts in this way is always required, as it is for any other form of copying.

Standard pro-formas for obtaining copyright permission are provided by many Education Authorities – or they may have special copyright licensing arrangements and a laid down procedure which should, of course, be followed.

If this is not the case, permission for copying should be sought from the publishers concerned. (See Appendix, page 241, for the details publishers usually require.) Our experience is that publishers are quick to respond to requests for permission to reproduce copyright material and are most often positive in their response.

EAL, KG, FID, TG

Background to the Project

The beginnings of our work on the ideas that are developed in the following pages go back to an earlier project directed by Eric Lunzer and Keith Gardner which investigated the extent and effectiveness of the teaching of reading in the secondary school. The results of that enquiry were published in a book that appeared in 1979, *The Effective Use of Reading* (Heinemann Educational).

The main findings reported in that volume can be put under three headings: comprehension, the use of reading in schools and the improvement of reading for learning.

When and how children fail to comprehend

There is little evidence to justify the teaching of reading comprehension as a set of separate sub-skills like drawing inferences, interpreting metaphors and understanding the meanings of words in context. These are not different processes in the reader. They are simply different tasks required of the reader to 'prove' that s/he has understood. When reading for learning, the actual process can be thought of as comprising five phases: decoding, making sense of what is said, comparing this with what one knows already, making judgements about the material and, finally, revising one's ideas.

In many ways the phase that proves decisive is the third: does the reader trouble to compare what is read with what is known already? When readers do this, the fourth and fifth phases will normally follow, and that means learning will happen – 'ideas are revised'. But all too often the process stops at the second phase: the reader does impose a kind of *local sense* on the phrases and sentences as they occur, but does not trouble to establish their *overall* sense and their coherence.

In *The Effective Use of Reading*, the authors define differences in comprehension as a function of 'the ability and willingness to reflect', which is really the same thing as saying that when pupils obtain different scores on a comprehension test they differ in the extent to which they go beyond making local sense to comparing what they read with what they know and with what went before.

A growing body of evidence shows that one of the reasons for failure to go beyond local sense is that children often take it for granted that to read correctly is to understand, as if recognising the words and what they mean is all there is to it. Indeed, when one is reading a gripping story for pleasure, understanding does come without effort. This style of reading is often called 'receptive', and what this means is that the reader does not pause at frequent intervals to reflect about the overall sense. The story carries him or her along and stimulates the right questions without any conscious effort. Apparently most pupils in the early years of schooling expect the same thing to apply to, say, reading about just why different kinds of farming are found in different conditions. Such a text is repro- duced on page 21 and it will be fairly obvious that unless the material is already well known to the readers they will need to pause for reflection. Reading with pauses is often called 'reflective reading' and a number of writers have shown that able readers do pause in this way, and also go back to check on coherence from time to time, while poorer readers do not. (See L. Thomas and S. Harris-Augstein, *The Self-organised Learner and the Printed Word*, Report to the Social Science Research Council, 1976, and cf. Chapter 7 in *The Effective Use of Reading*.) In a word, if most pupils were 'reflective readers' when necessary, then they would be better able to use reading for learning. As things stand, they are not. Often, when children do not understand they do not realise it. (See the note on page 28.)

Teachers do not often use reading as a teaching device

This conclusion rests on two sorts of evidence: observation and interview.

During the 'Effective Use of Reading' project in 1974–1975, observa- tions were recorded for a total of 202 lessons conducted with children aged 10–15 years, considerable care having been taken to ensure a represent- ative sample of schools and lessons. It was found that in one sense reading occupied a considerable portion of the pupils' lesson time.

But that is only half the story. It was also found that most of the reading occurred in very short episodes; very little of it took the form of continuous study. The reason for this was clear both from the rest of the lesson obser- vations and from talking to the teachers who conducted them: most reading is reading for writing. Pupils are asked to answer questions which they read from the blackboard or from a worksheet, or they are asked to copy relevant passages in answer to a list of questions, or simply to copy a summary. In other words, reading is used as a source for revision exer- cises, but not as a valuable auxiliary means of instruction.

Much the same picture was given by interviews conducted in many schools and regions of the country. It was apparent that even in those schools where the problems raised by 'language across the curriculum' were receiving most attention, attitudes to reading were divided. Many teachers preferred to rely on explanation, demonstration, and practical work. Understandably, teachers of science laid particular stress on the latter, but they were not alone. Moreover, while most teachers were well aware that the average pupil is relatively incompetent at learning from the written word, little was done to remedy the situation until the sixth form. Even here, the effort is often spasmodic and, as shown in a recent survey conducted by the NFER, study skills teaching is far from universal; nor is there agreement about how to teach and what to teach for greatest effect (R. Tabberer and J. Allman, *Study Skills at Sixteen Plus: An Interim Report*, NFER, Windsor, 1981).

Reading for learning can be improved

This was shown in two studies conducted as part of the 'Effective Use of Reading' project. One was an ambitious and carefully controlled enquiry on the effectiveness of reading laboratories. This was directed by Roy Fawcett and involved the use of SRA reading programmes in three secondary and five junior schools. When compared to others who had followed the regular school English programme, pupils who followed a one-term intensive SRA programme were shown to have gained significantly in speed of reading and in comprehension as measured by a variety of tests. This was especially true of those in the lower half of the ability range.

It must also be allowed, however, that the use of reading laboratories can involve a substantial inroad into the English timetable. It does entail expenditure on kits, and its relevance to subject learning is not always apparent to teachers or indeed to pupils. Moreover, many of the questions that children are made to answer in the course of reading laboratory work are factual 'looking up' tasks, requiring response to just one section in the passage that is supposed to have been read.

The second enquiry took the form of a series of developments generally based on the idea of group discussion centred on a text which everyone in the group can look at, read, and talk about. In one form or another, this idea is probably quite old. In the USA it gained currency through the work of Stauffer (*Teaching Reading as a Thinking Process*, Harper and Row, 1969) who devised the label 'directed reading thinking activities' (or DRTAs). Stauffer showed infant teachers how to get their pupils to predict what would be happening on the next few pages of their readers after looking at sections from the text, headings and illustrations. This seemed to have the effect not only of heightening motivation but of fostering active reading in relation to the text being studied.

Stauffer worked initially with six- and seven-year-olds. Later the work was extended and taken up in this country by Christopher Walker (*Reading Development and Extension*, Ward Lock Educational, 1974) who was also able to draw on similar procedures being developed in primary schools in the UK. Among the procedures described by Walker are 'group deletion' based on systematic deletion of words in a passage and group SQ3R, similar in many ways to the original work of Stauffer. The rubric stands for 'Survey, Question, Read, Recite, Review', these being the steps involved in a technique for promoting reflective reading that was developed by F. P. Robinson in *Effective Study*, Harper and Row, 1946.

Ideas such as these formed the basis for a fairly extensive programme of work developed by the 'Effective Use of Reading' team, and most notably by Terry and Elizabeth Dolan with their colleagues in what was called 'Pilot School 1'. Particular stress was laid on the role of discussion in small groups with minimal teacher intervention. This kind of activity, however, was only one part of the lesson plan and more often than not this took the form of a class introduction followed by small group work with a plenary report back and class discussion to complete the study. The techniques used by the team included an adaptation of 'Group SQ3R', 'group cloze' and 'group sequencing' as well as 'group prediction'.

The cloze procedure consists of omitting every fifth word in a passage (or every seventh or every tenth) and requiring the pupil reader to guess what the missing word is. This was first developed as an instrument for assessing the readability of a text (see C. Harrison, *Readability in the Classroom*, Cambridge University Press, 1981) and subsequently adapted to serve as a measure of comprehension. As used in Pilot School 1, the choice of words for deletion was freer, the aim being to provoke a fruitful discussion and not necessarily to find the exact words used by the original writer.

Sequencing was a technique invented by the project team on the analogy of the re-ordering of items used in tests of intelligence. This, too, proved to be highly successful in stimulating thoughtful discussion and evaluation of the meaning of a passage. Indeed, it forces the reader to go beyond local coherence.

Prediction was found to be excellent, given the right sort of passage. But this appeared to be the least generalisable of the techniques used.

Finally, SQ3R was adapted in such a way as to enable the pupil group to work independently under the guidance of a tape-recorded set of cues prepared by the teacher beforehand.

Introduction

Outline and general principles

The investigations published in *The Effective Use of Reading* clearly indicated the need for further work, in particular the development and refining of techniques that encouraged reading for learning. The present project is the result. During the course of it, we have been able to build on the earlier work by extending the range of techniques and by further refining the principles governing their use. Early in the project, we hit on the acronym DART, or 'directed activity related to text', to denote any of the activities recommended by the project, and not unnaturally, the term rapidly gained a certain currency among colleagues in schools, colleges and teacher centres. The ideas themselves must stand or fall by their own efficacy and do not depend on the word, so we have used it sparingly here. But there are certain principles that we have tried to build in to all DART lessons, and which we regard as essential, at least to begin with.

Main features of 'DARTs'

1. Text-based lessons are part of the curriculum

Several thousand lessons have been designed and conducted under the auspices of the project, and several hundred were developed by or in collaboration with members of the team. All of these lessons formed part of the curriculum in a recognised school subject. They did not constitute a separate reading or study skills course. With few exceptions the passages selected for study were taken because they were relevant to the particular topic being dealt with by the class concerned. Often, though not always, had the teacher not chosen to deal with the chosen area by means of a text-based lesson, that same same area would have been covered in some other way.

This is one of the most important and significant features of DART-based lessons as conceived by the project. But for that, we would hardly have been in a position to gain the insights that we did into the structure of texts, especially in science (see F. Davies and T. Greene, *Reading for Learning in the Sciences*, Oliver and Boyd, 1984) but in other areas of the curriculum too. These insights were the fruit of close collaboration with groups of subject teachers and local advisers. It should perhaps be added that all this was part of a deliberate policy, since the overall objective was to use reading as one way of learning alongside others.

This does not mean that English was left out. Not only was English included as a subject to which the DART method was very much appropriate, but English teachers, because of their special interest, played a considerable role throughout the work of the project. Thus in many schools we were able to encourage the formation of groups of teachers interested in language across the curriculum, or to capitalise on the interests of existing groups, and here members of the English departments were quite often prominent because of the special contributions they could make to language work in general.

2. The notion of text types

From the start of the new project we were determined to do two things. One was to develop ways of studying intact text as well as text that had been modified in some way. The other was to bring out those features of logical arrangement that were common to all well-written passages, and so far as possible to make these features central in our approach.

The first year was spent in developing methods of text analysis to use alongside the reconstruction of 'mutilated text', and in this way considerable headway was made with respect to the first objective. As to the second we continued to experiment with a wide variety of ideas until about the beginning of the second year. It was then that the notion of text type emerged, and it happened largely as a result of the actual work we had been engaged on.

We noticed that when we had asked a group of pupils to produce a table to bring out the essential information contained in a description of a suspension bridge and then went on to prepare a lesson around a passage dealing with the structure of a human tooth, the former experience was invaluable. Not only could we ask for the same kind of table to represent the essential ideas in the new passage, but the old headings could be transferred with little alteration: name of region or part, location, connection to other parts, appearance, composition, function. What this suggested was that all passages that were meant to convey the description of a *structure* carried similar classes of information, and because that information had to be arranged in an appropriate way, that organisation too was usually common to most such passages.

From here it was a short step to note that there were several other kinds of passage which kept recurring: texts that dealt with processes, some that formed a set of instructions, others that described some crisis situation in history and how it was dealt with, and so on. Each of these had its own characteristic generic headings and its own organisation, and each was fundamentally different from every other.

Maybe not everything that people write can be neatly packaged and docketed, but if a passage is going to be a useful stimulus to worthwhile learning, then it is particularly likely to run to type. In any case it soon became obvious that a teacher who wants to design a stimulating lesson programme around a selected extract must begin by deciding exactly what information lies in the passage and how it is set out. This was what we ourselves had been doing all along, but armed with this newly found insight, it could be done more quickly and more certainly by comparing every new passage with what we already knew of the relevant text type(s).

So the notion of text type is the second distinctive feature of lesson design incorporated in the work of the project. Techniques of analysis are used not only to prepare a set of analytical study tasks, but they are also an essential preliminary for designing what we have called text reconstruction lessons, ie completion (derived from cloze), sequencing and prediction. As will be apparent from Part II of this book, a thorough analysis of the passage enables one to decide what words or phrases to delete, or how and where to cut a passage into segments for a re-arrangement or for a prediction task.

Above all, what the notion of passage type (we have deliberately used the words 'passage' and 'text' interchangeably in most contexts) implies is that, properly designed, a text-based lesson serves three functions:

1. pupils are expected to learn the relevant topic;
2. they learn the kind of question to ask;
3. they learn how to learn in the relevant area, especially from reading.

3. Pupil discussion

The third distinctive feature of DART-based lessons is the central value we place on exchanges by pupils in small groups – often in pairs, sometimes in threes and fours, and only rarely in larger groups. There are several reasons for this emphasis.

First and most important is that such discussion enables pupils to test their own interpretations of the text and of the ideas contained in it against one another. The atmosphere is unthreatening. Nothing is written down, there is no teacher there to criticise them in public or even to say 'Yes, well . . . anyone got any other ideas?'

Then there is the fact that the text itself is there for everyone to refer to, and that means everyone is looking down and checking what it says. Interactions are therefore object-centred and not person-centred.

Next there is the opportunity for everybody to participate. In this connection it is worth recording that again and again one finds that a pupil who was doing the listening in the small group is keen to defend the group point of view later on against a challenge from someone in another group.

There is also the sheer pleasure of interaction in pursuit of a common goal.

Finally, there is the break from the routine of working as a class or as a set of isolated individuals, and this too leads to improved motivation.

For all these reasons the preferred pattern of working for all teachers associated with the project has been (1) class introduction, (2) work in small groups, (3) class discussion to exchange ideas, to bring out some key points, and generally to round off the lesson and perhaps set the scene for another. There can be variations on the pattern – for instance by bringing the groups together at more frequent intervals – and examples will be found scattered among the accounts that are given in the following pages. But very rarely would we omit intentionally the small group work and rely entirely on teacher-led discussion.

One by-product of this mode of working is that the tasks themselves need to be carefully prepared beforehand so that the pupil groups know what they are expected to do. Another is that the passage itself must be made available for study and for marking at least at the rate of one copy per pupil group, and preferably one per pupil. These are not difficult chores and although one should obtain publishers' permission to reproduce, that can be easily obtained. (See Appendix 3, page 241.)

Varieties of pupil tasks

This book is in two parts, the first being concerned with 'the analytic study of text' and the second with 'text reconstruction'. These are the two divisions of the tasks developed by the project team. When analytic study is used, pupils see the whole extract from the start, and the tasks are explicitly devised to assist them in penetrating beyond the outward form of words to the underlying ideas and the way they relate to one another. When text reconstruction is used the object is still to help the pupils to discuss the key ideas and relations, but now the method is indirect, since the problem is to find the missing words or the correct order of paragraphs.

Now it could be that because the latter methods are indirect, they are sometimes less comprehensive, more hit and miss, and the resulting understanding is less complete or less permanent. But there is almost no evidence for such shortcomings. And it should be recalled that text reconstruction tasks do compel the solver to go beyond local coherence (like text analysis), and that they are intrinsically motivating, because they are puzzles.

What is true is that analytic tasks are quite close to what well-trained readers do spontaneously when trying to come to terms with a difficult stretch of text. Text reconstruction is not like that, because most people rarely meet 'mutilated texts' unless they have been specially prepared. That is why we took trouble to design workable patterns for lessons using intact texts.

From a practical point of view, there is no need to choose. Both methods can and should be used, and they can even be used together in the same lesson (cf page 225). Nor are there any hard and fast rules for which technique to use in relation to each and every passage, although we can point to some considerations that are important. Also we can show how some types of text are ideally suited to one technique or another, and examples of these will be found throughout this book.

Nevertheless, it is one thing to say a particular technique will nearly always suit a given kind of passage and another to say that it must be chosen. The following extract is a good example of how passages can be studied in several different ways, all of them productive. A brief consideration of how this can be done will also help to provide a concrete referent for most of the ideas we have touched on in this introduction. We will therefore take 'Cattle' as a focus.

How would this be treated using deletion? What about sequencing and analytic study? The passage was in fact used as a basis for a text-based lesson with several classes, and so our discussion can draw on what was observed.

Figure 1 Cattle

<table>
<tr><td colspan="2">**Cattle**</td></tr>
<tr><td>*3 types of cattle for 2 uses*</td><td>Cattle are essential for our milk and meat supplies. Over the last hundred years there has been a great rise in population and so there   *6*
has been an increasing demand for more milk and more meat./Farmers have developed the best breeds of dairy cows for milk production   *II*
and the best breeds of cattle for beef. They have also bred 'dual purpose' cows to give a high milk yield as well as good beef./</td></tr>
</table>

Dairy cattle; needs, location	A cow eats about 150 pounds (68 kilograms) of grass and perhaps a few additional pounds of cattle food per day in summer/Rich meadow grass, about 4 or 5 inches (10 or 12 centimetres) high, in damp lowlands is best for dairy and dual-purpose cows, and so these are reared in the western areas where there is a good rainfall./But near the great centres of population even districts with low rainfall may have dairy farms. There are large dairy-farming areas near London.	9 4 2
Effect of rapid transport	Rapid transport by road and rail has helped in the expansion of dairy farming and milk now arrives fresh in towns and cities from farms and dairies often considerable distances away. This is a far cry from the days when cows were kept in the backyards and sheds of city streets!/	5
Dairy cattle; varieties	The Friesian cow gives the highest yield of milk – between 3 and 4 gallons (14 to 18 litres) a day on average. The creamier milk comes from the Jersey and Guernsey breeds/ Other dairy cows are the Shorthorn, South Devon, Red Poll, Ayrshire and Welsh Black. The Shorthorn, Red Poll and South Devon are also classed as dual-purpose cows./	3 7
Beef cattle; needs, location	Beef cattle are usually reared further away from the densely populated industrial districts. They can thrive on shorter grass and so can be kept on higher land./The upper limit for cattle rearing is about 1,500 feet (about 460 metres) above sea level. If there is not enough grass to fatten the cattle for slaughter, they are sold when they are about two years old to the lowland farmers for fattening. Unfattened cattle are called store cattle./	10 8
Beef cattle; varieties	The best meat comes from the Aberdeen Angus. Other good beef cattle are the very hardy Highland breed with the wide curving horns, the Hereford of the hill farms on the Welsh border, and the Beef Shorthorn./	1

From Haydn Evans, *The Young Geographer*

The side headings, obliques, boxed words and numbers in the margin do not figure on the original. They have been put in to facilitate the present discussion.

To begin with, the extract is one that does not resist 'type casting'. Overall, we have a sort of classification: several categories of animal farming are contrasted and each is treated successively in much the same way. But within this framework we have another form of organisation, not uncommon in geography text-books, which we might call 'siting of industry or agriculture'. The siting of an enterprise is determined by a number of familiar factors: where the raw materials are to begin with; other materials needed to process the output, including power; availability of labour; proximity to principal consumer. Each of these is modified by facility of transport, ie the chosen site can be a long way from, say, the consumer if the final product is easily transportable.

All this is very familiar ground to the geographer, and because these are the things that are always relevant they tend to dictate the form of the passage. Also, they are the ideas any teacher will probably wish to bring out in a text-based lesson. Certainly this was true of those teachers who did work on the passage.

How would a completion task be designed round the passage? One solution is to delete all the words that we have deliberately boxed. There are only thirteen of these in all, which is a great many fewer than one word in ten, but these words have been carefully selected because (a) they are central to the ideas just outlined and (b) there are enough left in the text to allow the pupils to make the necessary inferences. What this means is that one can be reasonably confident that these deletions, or a similar set, will provoke a lively, informed discussion and useful learning.

Now we turn to how the passage was used as a basis for an analysis lesson, as it has been on several occasions.

Because the chief considerations appeared to be those just outlined, pupils were first asked to find each of the following in turn:

1. types of animal mentioned and breed;
2. mention of animal products;
3. special needs for any group;
4. location.

These were to be underlined using a different colour code for each category. When this was done, each of the groups went on to complete a table with headings as shown in Table 1.

Table 1

Type of animal and breed	Product	Location	Special needs

The following is an extract from the taped proceedings of one such lesson, showing exchanges in a group of four 11-year-old pupils without immediate teacher involvement.

— Right, now, what are we looking for?

— Location, where it is.

— Yes . . . you don't have to put like where it says 'Jersey and Guernsey breeds'.

— Do 'western areas'?

— In the damp lowlands, third line down, near where it says about the centimetres.

— But you'd have to actually look at your map to see where the damp lowlands actually are.

— Yeh.

— No, wait a minute, what about the sentence before where it says 'districts with low rainfall'?

— '. . . many have dairy farms near great centres of population'.

— That's all about location, isn't it?

— What about 'towns and cities'?

— Yes, I thought that.

— Is that about the location of the cattle and sheep, though?

— Not really, no; that's where all the people are, isn't it?

— Yes, that's when the milk does arrive!

— But what about the 'higher land'?

— Yes, I was thinking about that, the next sentence. It tells you something else . . . where cattle can't be kept.

— Does that mean you've got to rear cattle 1500 feet above sea level? What does 'the upper limit' mean?

— The limit means the most . . .

— Yes . . . no . . . means can't be reared any higher than that, so that's really telling them they can't be, not where they can be. They can't be above 1500 feet. Really, no — that's when the sheep come in. That's why you get sheep on the mountains.

— Look, look. If you look there [draws attention to map supplied by teacher] the beef cattle, they're around the mountains in Scotland.

— Are they?

— Look where the beef cattle are.

— That part of Scotland's too high. It's too high!

Just as experience suggests that mastery of content can be as good following sequencing or completion as it can following analysis, so experience – typified by the above extract – shows that pupil involvement in text analysis can be at least as great as in the other kinds of lesson.

Still using the same extract, one can consider the possibilities of sequencing. Here we have no experience of class lessons to draw on, and it was suggested that the passage is probably ill-suited to sequencing since it was not a chronological sequence or a series of causes and effects. A number of student teachers were asked to have a go at re-ordering a set of slips of paper, each bearing one of the segments marked off by the oblique lines in our extract, each of these slips being numbered as shown on the right of the passage. (It should be noted in passing that each of these segments embodies a key package of information.) The sentences were retyped to remove typographical cues and linguistic cues are far from obvious.

The students concerned spent about 15 minutes on the task and refused to be interrupted till they had solved it to their satisfaction. In the event, the preferred solution was 6, 11, 9, 4, 2, 5, 3, 7, 10, 8, 1 which is of course the original order, and the second favourite was 6, 9, 4, 2, 5, 10, 8, 11, 3, 7, 1. This arrangement amounts to presenting all the information and arguments about location first, followed by the information about varieties of breed. Within each of these two broad sections, dairy cattle are dealt with before beef cattle. To all intents and purposes, the alternative ordering is as coherent and logical as the original. But unlike the original, there can be no cues in the sentence structure to point to an order which the author did not produce! One can safely infer that the groups concerned produced the order because they discovered for themselves just what information was in the extract and how it hangs together.

It was the sequencing task that provoked them (and their colleagues who got it 'right') to do this. Experience shows that what teachers can do in 15 minutes, pupils can do in half an hour. They are just as involved and, provided the passage is within their scope, they have similar insights. So the passage would, after all, produce a very worthwhile lesson using sequencing.

Implementation

It should be clear that the work of the project is very much in the flexible tradition of educational ideas in Britain. We have tried out many ideas and many suggestions are offered. Wherever possible we have sought to justify these suggestions both by example and by reference to accepted principles. But there are plenty from which to choose, and in the end the teacher, it is hoped, will have gained an added resource without being in any way constrained.

Text-based work is one form of learning. As we have shown, it has the advantage that pupils are encouraged to exercise a good deal of initiative in finding solutions to problems, and sometimes in asking questions themselves, and they learn from one another. Also, the lesson is designed in such a way that many will learn how to learn. Nevertheless, such work cannot replace all other forms of learning and in practice we have advocated its use on a fairly modest scale.

In general, teachers working with the project undertook to use DART material on a basis of two or three occasions per half term. A questionnaire returned to the evaluator, Roy Fawcett, shows that of 126 returns 28% used text-based lessons at least twice a month and 58% at least once a month, rising to 83% at least once every half term.

It should be added, however, that the method can be used with almost any subject, and, just as it calls for collaboration among pupils, so it will show best results when there is exchange and collaboration among teachers within a school. Reading for learning is one way of using the potential of language work across the curriculum in order to improve the quality of work in general. When three or four teachers in different subject areas elect to use a similar method even on a restricted scale, the total impact on the pupil can be considerable. Here, too, an extensive controlled study of the effectiveness of the project work showed that of nineteen paired comparisons between groups involved with the project and comparable controls, seven showed significant gains on reading comprehension over a period of less than a year, and wherever the level of the work had been at all intensive the advantage was clear.

It should also be added that of the 126 teachers who answered the questionnaire after having tried the ideas no less than 80% felt that they were 'worthwhile', and for the most part, those teachers had far less experience of the work than the group referred to in the previous paragraph.

Finally, a word about lesson duration. This can vary considerably and we have found that teachers of English will occasionally plan for a whole sequence of text-based lessons while teachers of science may include a 15 to 20 minute DART as part of a varied programme for a single period. For the most part, however, we and our collaborators have tried to plan for lessons of 35 to 70 minutes, ie single or double period length based on extracts of 1–3 pages in length, and the examples included in this book are all within these limits.

Detailed questions of lesson planning are best left for discussion in the main body of the book and the next section is therefore a guide to the book and its use.

Using the book as a guide

The book is in two parts, the first covering the analytical study of text including various forms of alternative representation, and the second dealing with text reconstruction. Part I begins with a full description of the method of analytical study and its rationale, including a description of text types, a preliminary discussion of all the relevant study techniques and suggestions for the planning and conduct of lessons. This is followed by a set of examples drawn from a wide range of subjects. In each case there are suggestions for preliminary study of the passage which served as the focus for the lesson(s) that are reported.

Part II follows a similar pattern, save that because it comprises several quite distinct techniques – completion, sequencing and prediction – each has its own introduction, followed by a small set of examples. Also, the introductions are shorter, since many of the considerations treated in Part I are equally applicable to Part II.

Finally, because the approach to text is new and central to the work of the project we have included an appendix containing a few examples of passages which were analysed to a level which slightly exceeds what might normally be expected either of the teacher preparing a lesson or of the pupil working his or her way through it. These are there for reference if desired.

It should be clear that the book was not designed to be read in the same way as a short novel, starting at the beginning and going through to the end. It is first and foremost a resource book and should be used as such. In particular, the introductory sections in Parts I and II need not be studied in detail until after the reader has worked through two or three of the relevant examples and perhaps tried out a lesson with a class. Similarly, we would not expect every user to study every example. Generally, it is recommended that the reader skims through the appropriate introductory sections as a preliminary to a detailed study of one relevant example, and this latter is best done in a group of two or more teachers working together. Further examples and closer study of introductory sections can safely be left to the individual reader's needs and discretion.

Wherever possible, however, working through the book should be a collaborative effort, either in a school or in a group of schools or in a region, and we therefore include notes of guidance for co-ordinators wishing to set up study groups. These will be found in Appendix 2 (page 238).

Note to page 14

The prevalence of children's failure to understand is well brought out in a recent experiment carried out by Ellen Markman at the University of Stanford, California. 'Essays' like the one on 'Ants' were read to children aged nine to twelve. These essays included deliberate contradictions. The majority of nine-year-olds failed to spot even one contradiction in four separate essays. Even the twelve-year-olds were successful only some of the time, and·then only when the contradictions were explicit. Yet adults had no difficulty whatsoever in spotting these contradictions.

Ants

Explicit condition There are some things that almost all ants have in common. For example, they are all amazingly strong and can carry objects many times their own weight. Sometimes they go very, very far from their nest to find food. They go so far away that they cannot remember how to go home. So, to help them find their way home, ants have a special way of leaving an invisible trail. Everywhere they go they put out a special chemical from their bodies. They cannot see this chemical, but it has a special odour. An ant must have a nose in order to smell this chemical odour. Ants cannot smell this odour. Ants can always find their way home by smelling this odour to follow the trail.

Implicit condition There are . . . invisible trail. (lines 1–0)
Everywhere they go they put out an invisible chemical from their bodies. This chemical has a special odour. Another thing about ants is they do not have a nose. Ants never get lost.

From E. M. Markman, 'Realising that you don't understand: elementary school children's awareness of inconsistencies' in
Child Development, 50, 1979

Part I
The Analytic Study of Text

SECTION A

General principles

The following outline contains a statement of the ideas on text analysis developed by the project team, together with an account of how these can be implemented in the form of text-based lessons. It is in four sections. The first is an introductory example: a text on the history of science, together with an explanation of how it can be analysed and how it was used in lessons. This is followed by a description of the variety of pupil tasks provided by the team or adapted from existing procedures to incorporate in lessons. The third section, which is in many ways the most central, is a statement of the theory of text types which was elaborated as part of the work of the project. It is a very informal sort of theory, but it is a useful one. Finally, the fourth section deals with the implementation of these ideas in lesson design, and this is in two parts – lesson preparation and lesson conduct.

It should perhaps be stressed from the outset that some of the ideas contained in the following pages may not be fully appreciated until the readers have also studied some of the examples in the following section and tried out some of the suggestions for themselves.

1. Introductory example

The passage chosen for this introductory example is one that has been used by several teachers with secondary age pupils and by groups of teachers as a part of their own introduction to text analysis.

Throughout this book we present before each extract a set of suggestions to the teacher or group of teachers who are working through the book. By following these suggestions it should be possible to see more easily what the problems were in designing an appropriate lesson based on the passage and thus arrive at a critical (but, we hope, sympathetic) appreciation of what the teacher actually did and of the further comments made by others (often but not always members of the project team).

Introductory Example

Subject Biology
Source From 'Man and Microbes' in *Introducing Living Things* (Nuffield Biology 1)
Passage Type Theory/Biography (interwoven)
Activities Labelling
Underlining
Grouping
Ranking
Tabulation

Suggestions for study

1. Read the extract through to the end.

2. It conveys two sorts of information. Decide what these are, and devise a suitable label for each. (If you can, discuss your choice with a colleague.)

3. Go through the text again, paragraph by paragraph, and show which of the two kinds of information it contains. (In some cases, you may have to split a paragraph if you think it moves from one emphasis to the other.)

4. Now re-read paragraph 1. Underline in this paragraph the clues given by the author about the two different kinds of information which are to be presented.

5. Now focus on paragraph 6. You will already have decided that this paragraph presents one general type of information, ie it fits one of the two broad categories you have identified. But the information in paragraph 6 can itself be broken down into smaller categories. Work out labels for the different kinds of information presented in this paragraph. Use oblique lines like this / to segment the text into the smaller information units and label them.

Life from nothing or life from life

Para 1   The experiments you have done in the course of this chapter will have told you a great deal in a short time about a question that puzzled men for many hundreds of years. The question is whether life can arise spontaneously (of its own accord) or whether life can only come from other living things. We understand the question better today because of the work of two men whose names have already been mentioned. They are Lazaro Spallanzani and Louis Pasteur. Here is some more about their lives and achievements.

Spallanzani

Para 2   The work of Leeuwenhoek and others had proved by the early eighteenth century that no large animals could be born by spontaneous generation. But those who supported the idea of spontaneous generation asked, 'What about the life that appears in rotting meat, sour milk, and other decaying substances?' One day food could appear fresh and good; the next it would be writhing with living organisms. Where did they come from? The microscopes of the time did not show any eggs or spores from which the living things could come. Surely here life appeared out of nothing.

Para 3   Lazaro Spallanzani was born in Italy near Modena in 1729. He studied at the University of Bologna where a woman cousin of his was professor of physics. He became a priest and eventually was placed in charge of the museum at Pavia by the Empress Maria Theresa who ruled that part of Italy. He travelled widely in the Mediterranean, even visiting Turkey to collect natural history specimens for the museum. He was fascinated by volcanoes and made surveys of Vesuvius and Mount Etna.

Para 4   In common with many scientists of his time, he studied a great number of subjects. He wanted to find out about the digestion of food and experimented first on a vomiting crow, studying what it brought up after various lengths of time, and second on himself, swallowing bags and tubes of food, in order to find out what happened to the food. In another series of experiments he showed for the first time that artificial insemination was possible in a frog, a tortoise, and a bitch – a discovery that was much later to have a profound effect on the breeding of farm animals.

Para 5   Spallanzani liked to try out experiments done by other people to see whether his findings fitted with theirs. In 1748 an English priest, John Needham, performed an experiment which he thought proved that organisms could be formed by spontaneous generation. Needham boiled some mutton broth and put it in a jar, taking especial pains to seal the jar, so that no one would be able to say that living organisms had been brought in by the air. When he opened the jar a few days later it was full of organisms. He tried the experiment again with other substances and always got the same result.

Para 6   Spallanzani, hearing of Needham's work, tried the experiments himself twenty years later. It struck him that as the organisms were so small and could barely be seen under the microscope, then their eggs or spores must be so small they must be invisible. First he boiled seeds in water, sealed them, and opened them after a few days. He found as Needham did that they were full of life. Next he tried excluding air altogether. He took two batches of jars, sealed one batch with a blow pipe and boiled it, and left the other batch (the control group) open to the air. This time the first batch had very few organisms in it while the other was full of them. Now he tried boiling the flasks for half an hour, instead of for a few minutes. The result showed no organisms when the flasks were opened. From these experiments Spallanzani decided that where organisms had appeared in Needham's and his own earlier investigations they had come from invisible eggs or spores on the walls of the flasks or, where the flasks were open, from the air. Some of these organisms could withstand being boiled for a short time but none could live through the prolonged boiling that Spallanzani subjected them to.

Para 7   Some were convinced by Spallanzani's arguments. Others said, no wonder nothing living appeared in the solutions boiled for a long time because this prolonged boiling killed off the delicate 'vital principle' in the air from which life came. It was left to Pasteur to settle that and many other arguments.

Para 8   Spallanzani's work did have one practical result. The Emperor Napoleon wanted to make his armies as efficient as possible and to make sure they were never held up for lack of food. When he was still a general in 1795, he offered a prize for the invention of a method of preserving food. In 1810 a chef called Francois Appert won the prize with a method of heating food and then sealing it from the air. This was an application of Spallanzani's work, depending on the fact that spontaneous generation does not take place and therefore food does not putrefy. From Appert's discovery stem the canning industry and all the changes that industry has brought to our habits of eating.

Figure 2 Preliminary analysis of 'Life from nothing or life from life'

Para 1 The experiments you have done in the course of this chapter will have told you a great deal in a short time about a question that puzzled men for many hundreds of years. The ques-

Scientific theory (ST) tion is whether life can arise spontaneously (of its own accord) or whether life can only come from other living things. We understand the question better today because of the work of two men whose names have already been mentioned.

biography (B) They are Lazaro Spallanzani and Louis Pasteur. Here is some more about their lives and achievements.

Para 2 ST
Para 3 B
Para 4 B
Para 5 sentence 1: B
         sentence 2: ST
Para 6 ST
Para 7 B
Para 8 B

Para 6 Spallanzani, hearing of Needham's work, tried the experi-

Introduction ST ments himself twenty years later./It struck him that as the

hypothesis organisms were so small and could barely be seen under the microscope, then their eggs or spores must be so small they

experiment 1 must be invisible./First he boiled seeds in water, sealed them, and opened them after a few days./He found as Needham

result 1 did that they were full of life./Next he tried excluding air altogether. He took two batches of jars, sealed one batch

experiment 2 with a blow pipe and boiled it, and left the other batch (the control group) open to the air./This time the first batch had

result 2 very few organisms in it while the other was full of them./

experiment 3 Now he tried boiling the flasks for half an hour, instead of for a few minutes./The result showed no organisms when the

result 3 flasks were opened./ From these experiments Spallanzani decided that where organisms had appeared in Needham's and his own earlier investigations they had come from invis-

Conclusion ible eggs or spores on the walls of the flasks or, where flasks were open, from the air. Some of these organisms could withstand being boiled for a short time but none could live through the prolonged boiling that Spallanzani subjected them to./

Getting things in focus

Figure 2 is a possible solution to the text markings called for on page 30.

How well does your analysis match with that shown in Figure 2? The match will probably be less than perfect, but that may mean only that different groups approach a text with different emphases and biases. These differences in bias can lead to differences in deciding what themes should carry most weight in categorising a particular paragraph. The categorisation of paragraphs 7 and 8 is especially controversial in our experience.

But consider what is not controversial. Most readers agree that, taken as a whole, the passage does present two sorts of information: there is an account of how a particular theory came to be evolved, with an emphasis on relevant observations and experiments, and there is background information about the lives of famous scientists. These two themes are interwoven, but not inextricably so.

Paragraph 3 is unambiguously biographical and paragraph 6 is unambiguously ST (scientific theory). Paragraph 2 sets out the state of evidence and the nature of the problem; although set in a particular context of time, it is more often classified as ST (the exact choice of label is of course unimportant). Paragraph 4 tells the reader about a lot of experiments, but it tells him or her very little about them, how they arose, how they were done, what they showed. We do know who performed them, however, and that is the leading thread. So if you choose to weight the fact that scientific experiments are cited, you will categorise the paragraph as ST; if you weight the fact that they are not very well related save that Spallanzani performed them, you will call it B (biography). Despite the divergence in conclusion, there is an underlying agreement about description.

Similarly, those who categorise paragraph 7 as ST are stressing the fact that here we have an alternative, albeit dated, interpretation of a series of experiments, and scientists need to be alive to these. Those who (like ourselves) categorise it as B are well aware of this, but see the response as so unrealistic for the present day reader that they regard it more as an account of how the ideas of Spallanzani were received by his contemporaries.

Finally, paragraph 8 is ST if it is interpreted as a convincing record of how a scientific theory may be applied, and B if the link between theory and application is seen as so tenuous that the facts are regarded as historical or even anecdotal.

Now we may turn to the more detailed analysis of paragraph 6. Here there is much less scope for controversy. The passage is one that has been used many times with teachers' groups and has quite often formed the basis for lessons with groups of pupils. Almost always it is this paragraph that is singled out as most important. Also there is rarely any argument about what sorts of information it contains.

Going back to the passage as a whole, it's worth stressing the thinking which it demanded. Agreement about the categorisation is not important. What is important is the analysis of the passage that leads one to fasten on to the fact that different items of information have different sorts of significance. The analysis leads one to an understanding of the structure of the information contained in the passage, as well as the structure of the passage itself – which is how the writer has chosen to put it over. Sometimes, of course, there won't be too much to say about the second, but this is one case where there is, and it is by no means atypical. The analysis of structure is essential for the teacher when preparing a text-based lesson. One way or another, it should also emerge from the pupils' activities when they come to grips with the passage, and that is what the teacher will try to ensure.

The teacher's own analysis

The job you have just completed on the Spallanzani passage is not unlike the work you might set as a lesson for your pupils. Before deciding on a suitable activity for children to undertake in relation to a passage, one has to study that passage oneself. In that sense, analysis is part of the teacher's preparation even when producing a reconstruction exercise like sequencing or completion.

The difference between the teacher's analysis and that of the pupils is partly that the pupils' work will be structured and guided by the tasks which are set by the teacher. The teacher of course will have to find his or her own way round the text. There is also a major difference in purpose: the pupil is asked to analyse the text to learn something about what it is saying; the teacher knows that already and his or her purpose is to exploit the potential of the text for securing specific learning objectives.

Going back to the analysis of the Spallanzani passage, we as authors were somewhat directive in our suggestions about the way the text should be tackled by new readers. But we would hope that, even while working through this book, teachers will be experimenting with the method on their own, using passages of their own choosing. When this happens, the teacher is asked to undertake his or her own analysis in order to work out an appropriate set of tasks to guide the pupils in theirs.

Here now is the way the Spallanzani text was used as the basis of a lesson with one class. (Others, of course, dealt with it rather differently.)

Lesson support for the Spallanzani passage

The teacher who first used the Spallanzani extracts wanted to achieve several objectives by using the text.

First, he wanted pupils to consolidate the experimental work they had been doing. Second, he wanted this work to be set within the broader perspective of the evolution of scientific theory and method. In addition, he wanted to train pupils in techniques for working independently at a text like the Spallanzani extract.

The class was a third-year, mixed-ability class in a Sheffield comprehensive, a group which included pupils of an ability level lower than that for which the text-book was originally designed. It was the only text-book available, and included a high proportion of background reading, using extracts like the Spallanzani text.

The teacher's view was that pupils reading the extract on their own, say for homework, would have been ill-equipped to sort out the different strands in the text and would not have dealt effectively with the important information. He believed, on the other hand, that pupils would be able to cope with the information given support and guidance in the classroom.

The question was, what sort of support?

The teacher and the project officers went through the text much along the lines that we have described as the teacher's analysis. On this basis they produced the ideas for the lesson. This involved several phases.

Introduction to the lesson Copies of the text were prepared for all pupils. The lesson was introduced with a discussion of the two purposes of the reading exercise, learning about science and learning how to use the text. There was also some discussion of difficulties which the pupils experienced when doing reading for homework.

Shared reading The text was then read aloud by the teacher with the pupils following.

Group work Pupils were then asked to work in twos or threes. They were asked to concentrate on the first paragraph and to underline one sentence which gave them a clear idea of what was to follow. This task was completed within a few minutes.

Teacher intervention Pupils pooled their ideas in a class discussion. Unlike the teacher groups which have analysed this text, the pupils were unanimous in selecting the sentence: 'The question is . . .'. This is not surprising since they approached the text in a scientific rather than a historical context.

It was then suggested to pupils that some of the sections that followed the first paragraph did not relate very directly to the question. They were asked to select the three paragraphs which related most directly to the basic question and then to order them in importance.

Second phase of group work This activity demanded all of their concentration for the next 20 minutes and involved vigorous argument and discussion.

Class discussion A class discussion followed. Groups of pupils and sometimes pairs of pupils put forward their ideas and justified their choices of paragraphs and the order in which they had rated them.

Paragraph 6 was included in the relevant section by all groups and paragraphs 2 and 5 were the next most popular choices. Of the others, paragraphs 7 and 8 were options chosen by some.

But pupils were not unanimous about the ordering of paragraphs. The criteria they used to defend their own selections or criticise those of others included:

> the priority of a hypothesis over an experiment in scientific thinking;
> the dependence of results on methodology;
> the necessity for caution in interpreting results;
> the possibility of alternative interpretations.

Alternative representation

The seriousness with which these scientific criteria were articulated and tested led the teacher to allow the discussion to continue and occupy time previously planned for a recording activity. However, both of the following ideas were considered by the teacher and the project officers as potentially suitable – had there been sufficient time.

There are two alternative representation activities appropriate for this text, and both are tabular representations. One focuses on a comparison of the two competing hypotheses and would thus involve pupils in completing a contrast table like the one shown in Table 2 on page 38. Before completing this table, pupils would be asked to locate the relevant information in the text using two different coloured pens to mark the references to the two different theories.

The alternative would focus on the methodology described in detail under 'class discussion'. Since this consists of a series of experiments, each consisting of certain steps, etc, the appropriate form of summary would be a table based on Table 3.

Table 2 Contrast table for Spallanzani passage

Observations and experiments which support life from nothing	Alternative interpretations if any	Observations and experiments which support life from life

Table 3 Alternative summary of Spallanzani passage

Experiment	Hypothesis	Test	Results	Interpretation

Comment

This account of a fairly typical lesson suggests that the teacher had every reason to be well satisfied with what had been achieved.

He started out with three objectives, one of which was to consolidate previous experimental work. We are assured that this objective was realised.

The second was to get the pupils to think about science methods in general. This provided the focus for the principal task of analysis: categorising the paragraphs as more or less relevant to the scientific theme and deciding which of the two theories stands the test of evidence. Pupils then went on to decide on the relative importance of each paragraph. When discussing this question they were able to talk intelligently about the relation between observation, theory and experiment. In other words, these pupils were beginning to think about some very important questions in a productive way.

The final objective was to improve the capacity for independent study. This must surely depend on an understanding of what cues to look for in deciding what is important and what isn't. Now of course we have no direct evidence that these pupils gained in their ability to interpret relevant cues as a result of this one lesson. But we do know how they were able to pick out such things as the difference between experimental evidence and incidental observation, or between the description of a scientist's interests and an account of what he actually did. Insofar as they had learned to look for these differences in the course of this lesson, one may reasonably expect that they will be more alive to them in the future.

Finally, we come to the question of motivation. Of course, this is an objective in every lesson for every teacher. Clearly that objective was attained, and one can see how it was achieved.

There was the support of an initial class reading which allowed the pupils to get a background and to overcome any problems of word identification. This enabled them to get to grips with the ideas embodied in the passage.

Then there was the opportunity to listen to a variety of ideas, and to try out their own in the unthreatening atmosphere of the small group of classmates. There was also the immediate feedback of peer comment as well as the chance of verifying what was said by reference to the text itself.

Finally, there was the paced intervention by the teacher who knew when to bring the groups' attention to a particular point and how to get them to draw the threads together at the end of the lesson.

Let us now turn to a consideration of the general principles underlying this sort of lesson.

2. Pupil tasks

We begin with a description of a range of pupil tasks upon which the teacher can draw. This is because the kind of text analysis we have evolved has a strong pedagogic basis: we have chosen this mode of analysis rather than any other because it is one that links up closely with the tasks that one can profitably set for pupils to complete.

There are three kinds of activities in which pupils can be asked to engage to arrive at a more thorough understanding of the issues raised in a passage. The first is *analysis* proper: defining just what it is the writer is saying and where. The second is to devise an *alternative representation* of the same ideas or of some of them; often the alternative representation will be more telling because it can be more graphic – a table or a diagram – than running text. The third is *extrapolation*, or going beyond what is actually said in the text, beginning with making decisions about the information that is missing and which one might want to look for elsewhere, but going on to such things as simulations or dramatic representations.

The following is a list of techniques that we have found most generally useful. We begin with four techniques for analysing a passage and then go on to consider alternative representation and extrapolation.

It is important to remember that each of these is an activity that can be used as a basis for part of a lesson. More often than not, the project team and the teachers with whom we have been associated have chosen to combine two or even three of these in a single lesson.

(a) Analysis

The four techniques to be described are underlining, segmenting, labelling, grouping and/ or ranking.

Underlining might be thought of as asking the pupils to underline the most important parts of a passage. And sometimes this can be useful. More often it implies picking out summary statements which can be rather empty and ignoring all the informative exemplification and detail. In this project underlining has been used more often in a selective way to alert the pupils to the categories of information contained in a text. For instance, in a passage describing the structure of a flower, they may be asked first to underline all the words and phrases that name different parts; then, using another colour, they will underline bits of the passage that describe the location of these parts; yet another colour can be used for the appearance and construction of these areas. When underlining such categories, they are, in effect, discovering what sort of information the text contains and how it is put together.

When selective underlining is used in this way, it is the teacher who decides on the target categories and this means that in a sense s/he has pre-digested the material. Whatever the reason, experience suggests that underlining is one of the easiest techniques to implement. The pupils enjoy it and they can cope with it from the start. So it is often a good way to introduce a new class to the close examination of text.

Segmenting was part of the second step undertaken in the study of the

Spallanzani passage, when it was suggested that the writer's paragraphing might not adequately reflect the ways in which the ideas had to be grouped in order to grasp them more fully. Later, you were asked to put in additional breaks in the long sixth paragraph. Segmenting can be used at a variety of levels (one could even group whole chapters) and in a number of ways. For instance, you could reproduce a passage without paragraph breaks and ask the pupils to indicate where they think the writer should have split it into paragraphs. Later, they could compare their solution with the writer's.

In practice, segmenting is quite challenging and rather more difficult than underlining. However, it can also be thought of as a crucial first step for the independent reader. It means asking oneself questions like what's this bit about and where does it end, what's that next bit about and how do they hang together? Only when you know the answers to these questions can you get down to detailed study. Whether or not it is done consciously, the teacher's own analysis often begins with segmenting (see 'Lesson planning'). Because the teacher has pre-digested the material, s/he can often start the class with an easier task like underlining or labelling.

Labelling is a useful alternative to underlining. When underlining is called for, the teacher provides the categories of information and the pupils establish where these are to be found in the text. When labelling is asked for, it is the locations that are given (either by the writer's paragraphing or by previous segmenting) and the category which the pupils must decide on.

It is important to note that there are many sorts of labels, ranging from the most generic type labels to the sub-heading that summarises a specific bit of content. The easiest sort of label for pupils to invent is the summary label. These are the labels featured on the left of the passage in the worked examples on page 33 and in the Appendix. They are shorthand statements of the ideas contained in the relevant section. At the other extreme, pupils can be asked to categorise the information in each section or paragraph. They will then be producing the kind of label shown on the right of the passage in the examples just referred to.

In our study of the Spallanzani text we relied exclusively on generic labels like 'experiment', 'result', 'conclusion', but we might have chosen to use more specific summary labels like 'digestion' and 'artificial insemination'.

As to the length of section for which labels are to be sought, a prior segmenting task can be used, eg 'How would you group this passage into just three sections, each containing one or more paragraphs?' or 'Can you find two important breaks in this paragraph?', etc. The easiest way, and one of the most popular, is to accept the writer's paragraphing, and label the paragraphs.

Grouping and ranking are natural outcomes of labelling or accompaniments to it. You are already familiar with the technique of grouping since this is the first task that was set for the Spallanzani passage. Pupils are asked to allocate each section or paragraph to one of two or three distinct categories. It is especially appropriate for the analysis of relatively long passages where the writer has elected to interweave two sorts of information, as when biographical material about the different persons involved in some historical development is given as background to the development itself. The Spallanzani passage is not atypical, and this type of organisation is especially frequent in history.

Ranking paragraphs in order of importance can be a way of helping pupils to sort out the essential from the superfluous. It is perhaps especially useful when dealing with texts that are a little long-winded or ill-organised. The task itself is easy to formulate: decide which is the most important section, then the next important, and so on down to the least significant (see example 9, page 202, for an instance of its use).

(b) Alternative representation

Here we will consider four techniques: listing, tabular representation, diagrammatic representation, and diagram completion.

We do not include a section on notemaking. This was a deliberate decision: we believe that useful notemaking is a difficult art and one which is best postponed until a solid foundation has been laid with more structured techniques. All too often notemaking at this level consists of copying significant extracts verbatim without bringing out their inter-relations. Paraphrasing the extracts (to avoid copying) can make matters worse!

Listing is a fairly natural extension to underlining: once the items in a category have been underlined it is easy to list them on a separate page. Why? Because putting them together brings out their essential relatedness. What is more, the bits that have not been underlined are omitted which is useful too, since generally these will be the incidental elements in the text. Just as underlining will often be successive, with different colours being used for different targets, so the listing will usually be multiple. The key features of listing, as of all forms of alternative representation are these:

representation should be selective;

presentation of information should be more memorable in some way than the original running text.

The items in the lists need not always be verbatim extracts from the original text. They can be paraphrases or even summary labels. So listing can be an outcome of labelling as well as underlining.

Finally, one is not bound to list the items in the order in which they are given in the text. Sometimes one will want to bring out the relative importance of these items and this can be done by re-ordering them. Alternatively, one will want the list to reflect a temporal sequence (or a spatial sequence). In Section B you will find a number of examples where teachers have used an ordered listing in this way.

Tabulation is the most generally usable technique for reproducing the key information in a convincing way. Most of the tables used by teachers and pupils in the project have been two-way entries, and more often than not the columns correspond to categories of information and the rows are sections of the material being presented. On page 38 we suggested two ways of tabulating selected material in the Spallanzani passage. Each of these tables represents a different selection from the content of the passage as a whole.

One of the most cogent reasons for producing this kind of table is that the column headings can often be general in character. For instance, 'Experiment', 'Hypothesis', 'Test', 'Results', and 'Interpretation' (Table 3) are not headings confined to the series of enquiries reported in the Spallanzani passage. They would apply to other passages dealing with a series of experiments relevant to a decision between opposing theories. The same sort of generality will be found to apply to many of the tables that appear in Section B.

Drawing up and completing tables of this sort is one way of becoming thoroughly familiar with the right questions to ask, at least when faced with a passage whose content is of a fairly standard type. (We have more to say about this restriction under the heading 'Types of passage', page 52.)

Diagrammatic representation Once again, there are all sorts of ways in which some or most of the key information in a passage can be shown in diagrammatic form. We have found the following to be most generally useful:

1. *A hierarchical table* or family tree diagram. This is illustrated in relation to the passage on Nottingham. This kind of diagram is especially suitable where the writer is introducing new material with a classification of content areas or topics. Additional comments can be added in boxes as shown in Figure 3.

Nottingham

Nottingham has much to offer in the form of entertainment and recreation. The Theatre Royal celebrated its centenary in 1965. Many shows are put on here prior to London production as Nottingham's theatre-goers are considered to be good judges of a successful show. The Nottingham Playhouse had its beginnings in Goldsmith Street, where it staged its last production in July 1963. With a small seating capacity and cramped conditions backstage, a move to new premises was inevitable. Their new building, which stands in East Circus Street, was designed by Peter Moro, Associate Architect of London's Festival Hall, and was opened on December 11, 1963 in the presence of Lord Snowdon. Its main feature is its cylindrical auditorium specially designed to accommodate two different forms of stage, the 'picture frame' type and the 'open stage'. It has a seating capacity of 750 with spacious foyers and a number of bars. Among the recreational facilities are the Ice Stadium, Lower Parliament Street, a Bowling Alley in Barker Gate, while the Harvey Hadden Stadium at Bilborough offers the athlete a fine running track, cycling track, and large arena for football pitch and field events. Nottingham is fortunate in having several fine parks. These include the Arboretum in Waverley Street, where band concerts are held during the summer months. There is a modern aviary here overlooking the duck-pond, and many beautiful trees and flower-beds. Within walking distance is the Forest Recreation Ground, which has many sporting facilities including cricket, football, and bowling and putting greens. On the first Thursday of October in each year Nottingham holds its annual Goose Fair on a site at the western end of the Forest. This fair, which had for many years been held in Nottingham's Market Place, was moved to its present site in 1928.

Thousands of city folk seek their recreation by the river, a most attractive place which may be taken as a model by many towns which waste their river banks. From time immemorial the crossing of the Trent at Nottingham has been an important link between north and south, but the first bridge of which we know was built of wood a thousand years ago. The mediaeval stone bridge had a chapel, and a shallow arch of it is preserved in the new traffic island.

From A. Mee, Nottinghamshire

Figure 3 Facilities in Nottingham

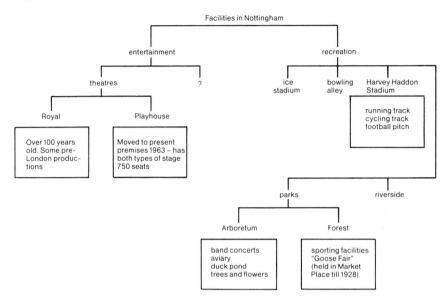

2. *A flow diagram.* This is illustrated by Figure 4 for the passage on aluminium manufacture. This type of diagram is especially appropriate as a representation of the principal features of a process. The central arrows show the states of the material as it passes through the process of extraction, while all the 'additives' (including electric current) are featured on the right and all the residuals are shown as 'lost' (or recycled?) on the left.

Aluminium-making process

The first stage in the production of aluminium is to make the pure oxide from the bauxite (which also contains oxides of iron and titanium).

This is done by treating the crushed bauxite with hot strongly alkaline sodium hydroxide solution. This dissolves the aluminium oxide, but not the other compounds present, so these are filtered off. When the remaining solution is cooled a few crystals of aluminium oxide are added and this causes aluminium oxide to come out of solution as a solid. This contains water and so is heated to produce pure aluminium oxide as a white powder.

This aluminium oxide is now dissolved in the molten 'cryolite' in a shallow steel box lined with carbon. The carbon, which is a good conductor of electricity, acts as the cathode (negative electrode) and the anodes (positive) consist of carbon blocks which are lowered into the liquid. When a heavy electrical current is passed, aluminium metal, which stays as a liquid at the temperature of the apparatus, collects at the bottom of the cell (or pot, as it is known) and can be tapped off from time to time. At the anode, oxygen from the aluminium oxide is given off and causes the carbon blocks to burn away as carbon monoxide and dioxide gases. Thus the anodes are gradually used up and so occasionally have to be lowered further into the pot and eventually need to be replaced completely. Aluminium oxide is periodically added to the molten cryolite to replace that used up in the electrolysis.

From M. W. Thomas, *Metals and Alloys*

Figure 4 Making Aluminium

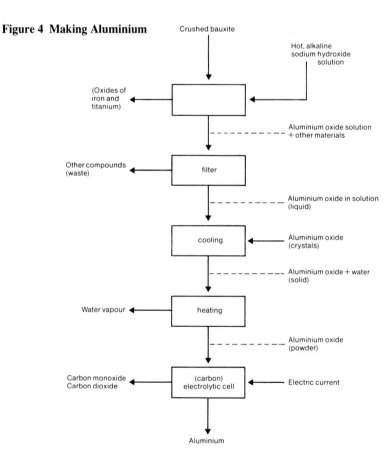

3. *An interaction diagram.* This type of diagram is especially suitable for pulling out the principal themes in a narrative. For instance, one might represent the actions and thoughts of each character by allotting them to separate columns. The vertical axis would be used to represent a time sequence and a series of arrows would show the flow of action and reaction. The short extract titled 'The day it all went wrong' was illustrated by a group of third-year pupils (mixed ability, secondary) and the accompanying sketch is typical of many (Figure 5).

The day it all went wrong

Craig and myself were getting bored of just riding about on our bikes. It was getting dark.

"Shall we go on a catwalk?" asked Craig.

"Yeah, but when it gets dark," I said.

By the time we got back to Craig's house, it was dark. We put our bikes in the garage, and went down to the bottom of the garden.

We climbed over the next door neighbour's fence, behind their greenhouse. We crawled on the grass up to the next hedge of thorns.

"Ouch!" yelled Craig as he put his hand on the hedge. Then we both started laughing. I had my gloves on so the thorns didn't hurt me. We just walked across the next garden and jumped over a low privet hedge.

"This is boring," said Craig.

"Yes it is, it's just too easy," I said.

"I know, let's go up this garden; the owner's out," said Craig.

"All right, sounds like a good idea to me," I said.

We set off up the garden, and then up the drive, when suddenly, the owner's car came down it.

"Run!" shouts Craig.

"Don't bother," says the man as he gets out of his car.

I felt scared and excited at the same time. None of us could move. I could see Craig turning white.

"And just what do you think you're doing?" asked the man.

A shiver went down my spine when he asked this.

"Er, we were taking a short cut from the woods," said Craig.

"Yes, that's right," I said.

"I could go to the police about this you know," said the man.

That really scared us.

"But I won't because I know you Craig and I know that you're sensible really. But, if I see you in my garden again, I will go straight to the police station," said the man.

"Can we go now?" asked Craig.

The man nodded.

> We set off up the drive and ran down to Craig's house as fast as we could. We went into the garage.
>
> "We better not go catwalking up the road again," I said.
>
> "No, better go down instead then," said Craig, then we both burst out laughing.
>
> Text written by a pupil, age 14

Figure 5 The day it all went wrong

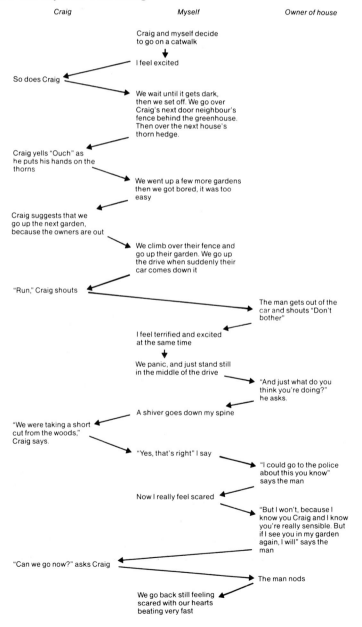

4. *A labelled and simplified line diagram.* This type of diagram is especially suitable for descriptions of structures and mechanisms, as in the illustration of an aneroid barometer on page 56. It should perhaps be added that more often than not teachers prefer to rely on artists' diagrams, as we will see shortly.

5. *Free diagrams by pupils.* The four types of diagram just listed are all well-recognised and useful for their purpose. They have been evolved because they answer specific needs. There is, therefore, much advantage in teaching pupils how to represent key ideas effectively with diagrams of this kind. Nevertheless, it has been no part of our intention to stifle the imagination of pupils (or of teachers) and we have seen many instances of less conventional forms of diagrammatic illustration used to considerable effect.

Figure 6 Three fingers are plenty

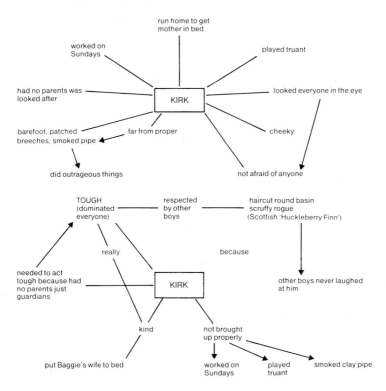

Despite the variations one finds, two categories are worth special mention. The first is a free network in which linked ideas are joined by lines or arrows. This is similar to a flow diagram, but the concepts and conventions are less constrained. It is often used to illustrate the interrelations between different aspects of the same character in fiction (see Figure 6 which shows the two pupil illustrations of the characterisation of the hero in a short story: *Three fingers are plenty*). Other uses are to indicate the relations between different sections of a book or play, or to bring out the interrelations between the different things that are said in introducing a new concept or theme.

Figure 7 Inshore breezes

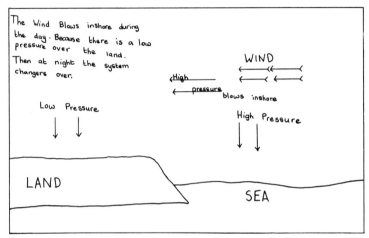

The second class of free drawing is illustrated in Figure 7 above. This is a fourth-year primary pupil's response to the task of illustrating the origin of inshore breezes after studying a passage about air taken from a geography text-book with prediction as the main lesson activity (see page 202 for the text and account of a relevant lesson). What this pupil is doing is to produce line drawings accompanied by arrows and captions. Typically, the drawing illustrates a simple process (unlike the complex sequence of extracting aluminium). So long as the required drawing is not too technical, pupils can safely be left to discover their own way of summarising whatever is wanted.

Diagram completion is really a cross between diagrammatic representation and the deletion type task described in Part II of this book. The pupils study the passage in front of them, and this has no gaps. But they use it to complete a diagram which does have omissions.

Good engineering and biological text-books abound with representational illustrations in the form of line diagrams, cut-aways, and so on. In geography and geology there are maps and charts. Historians use plans and reconstructions. Preparing such material demands high levels of knowledge and skill. Often the finished product is the outcome of interdisciplinary collaboration between a scientist with an artistic bent and an artist with a scientific interest. Only rarely would one recommend that teachers ask pupils to invent their own representational and semi-representational illustrations. The chances of error are far too great and when an illustration is erroneous, the result of making the drawing will probably be to perpetuate the error. Even if there is no obvious error in the illustration the learner cannot be expected to invent an image which can compare in memorability with the work of professionals. Sometimes, of course, these latter are so apt and so well-known that pupils are asked to copy and memorise the diagram itself.

However, while it is rarely worthwhile to require pupils to invent illustrative diagrams, something can be done to counter the tendency for such diagrams to be used as no more than intriguing ornaments to the text – a sort of resting place for the eye when reading grows tedious.

When illustration is essential to comprehension, the authors usually provide the drawings. If not, the teacher has little alternative but to find a suitable illustration from some other source. But the mere existence of diagrams does not ensure that the pupils will use them to follow the text. Even if they try to do so, they will often be satisfied with a very partial comprehension. The best way to improve matters is probably an adaptation of deletion technique.

Diagrams tend to be produced with every important part labelled. This helps the student who cares to compare the figure with the text. But paradoxically the best way to ensure that s/he will do so is to delete some or all of the labels and ask the pupils to supply them. Examples of this technique can be found on pages 119 and 220.

(c) Extrapolation

Only two activities need to be considered under this heading: pupil-generated questions and imaginative extension.

Pupil-generated questioning is a device used quite widely by teachers of all subjects, especially after they and their pupils have grown familiar with the aims and methods of the project.

It comes truly under the heading of extrapolation when the questions follow an analysis of the given passage and deliberately raise issues not dealt with at all or not dealt with adequately. Sometimes the questioning can serve as an orientation for future lessons or for homework. However, provoking questions is a flexible technique and you will not be surprised to find that it has been used immediately after a close study of a passage to serve as a focus for subsequent analysis (cf Part I Example 6, page 111) or even before the pupils are shown any text material, to achieve a better standard of learning by drawing out their ideas in advance (cf Part II, Example 11, page 210).

There are good psychological grounds for using pupil-generated questions in this way. Understanding what one reads or what one hears is a matter of comparing it with what one already knows about the matter. (One has to do this bit by bit as one goes along, and this means that what one knows already keeps changing.) Pupil-generated questions can facilitate these comparisons by bringing the relevant ideas to the forefront of one's mind.

Imaginative extension is often a substitute for alternative representation. It would be foolish for anyone to try to list all the activities that might come under this heading, since one can be certain that the collective imagination of teachers will go beyond the confines of such a list. The heading is intentionally biased, and will cover such activities as supposing (eg *how would we fare if* . . . (we had an exo-skeleton, etc) following a study in human biology; or, *what might have happened if* . . . following a study in history), simulation and various forms of drama.

However, while the possibilities are endless and exciting, we would suggest that imaginative extension should not be used as a sole staple method for all text-based lessons to the exclusion of the various techniques of analysis and representation dealt with earlier.

3. Types of Passage

(a) Topics and treatment

Quite early in the course of the project on Reading for Learning, we noticed that many of the passages teachers were selecting for study by their pupils were reminiscent of others we had encountered. What is more, the activities that seemed appropriate for promoting reflective reading and learning in the old passage were equally appropriate for the new one. Finally, we found that quite often some important variables which we had discussed when applying a technique were re-usable. These could include the targets that one might look to find when underlining, the labels that could usefully apply to the different sections of the passage, and the column headings that were found most suitable in a two-way tabulation.

There is, of course, a good reason why this should be so. Although there is no limit to the actual topics one might want to teach and to learn, there are some restrictions on the *kinds* of topic one can usefully discuss, perhaps especially within a particular subject and at a fairly elementary level.

Look at the six passages shown on pages 53–57. They all differ in content but they are not all different in form. To bring this out more clearly they are presented in pairs: 'Fossil fuels' with 'Mitosis', 'Medieval castles' with 'The aneroid barometer', and 'Making a compost heap' with 'Looking through a microscope'.

Take the first two passages. One deals with the origin of coal, oil and gas, the other with the formation of new cells. Both are processes, and the texts are *process* texts. What do they have in common? First, the kind of thing they deal with: how something changes or is changed into something else over time and under certain influences. Second, the way in which they are arranged: each process is described in a series of phases. The phases are represented by the numbers to the right of the text (five for 'Fossil fuels' and four for 'Mitosis', this being no more than a fragment of a much larger description of the whole process). Third, within each phase we find the same sorts of things being mentioned: the nature of the changes that take place, the agent or cause of the change, a description of the result of the change. Such texts are typical of many. Sometimes the descriptions of phases are much larger, and sometimes one will find other things being mentioned – such as by-products. But the three features we have indicated are common to all.

Fossil fuels

Have you ever had a close look at a piece of coal? Does it seem just like another piece of rock to you? Perhaps you already know something of the amazing history of coal.

phases

If we trace the path of some radiation from the sun arriving on earth millions of years ago, we shall begin to understand some of this history. The energy arrived at the earth and took part in the process of photosynthesis in a plant. The plants died and decayed on the floors of swampy land; later they were covered with layers of silt brought down by rivers and all this became compressed into what are called sedimentary rocks. High temperatures and pressures eventually changed the layer containing the plants into what we now know as coal, some of which lies near enough to the earth's surface to be mined. These changes occurred over many millions of years. Simple plant and animal life living in water has changed in a similar way, leaving us vast underground reservoirs of oil and natural gas. So from that original source, the sunlight falling on the green plant, we have, eventually, the sources of energy which led to the development of modern industrial societies – coal, oil and gas.

—1
—2
—3
—4

—5

From R. Stone and R. Dennien, *Longman Physics Topics: Energy*

Mitosis

Anaphase
The two chromatids now separate at the centromere and begin to migrate in opposite directions towards either end of the spindle. Experiments show that the spindle fibres play some part in separating the chromatids. The appearance is that of the chromatids first repelling each other at the centromere and then being pulled entirely apart by the shortening spindle fibres, although such a mechanism has not yet been verified.

phase

1

Teleophase
The chromatids, now chromosomes, collect together at the opposite ends of the spindle and become less distinct, probably by becoming uncoiled and therefore thinner. Then one or more nucleoli reappear, and a nuclear membrane forms around each group of daughter chromosomes so that there are now two nuclei present in the cell. At this point in animal cells, the cytoplasm between the two nuclei constricts, and two cells are formed.

2

3

4

From D. G. MacKean and P. J. Murray, *Introduction to Genetics*

Now consider 'Medieval castles' and 'The aneroid barometer'. These two passages could hardly be more different in subject matter, yet once again they have three things in common. First, they deal with the same kind of thing: both explain the *structure* of a class of objects. Second, like the process texts, they break up in a way that is characteristic of all such passages. Both consist of successive sections dealing with different parts of the object – three regions of the castle, two parts of the barometer (again, the extracts we have reproduced are incomplete). Notice that parts and/ or regions are not the same things as phases. Third, within each section, we find the same recurrent themes: what the part looks like and what it is called, how it is made and where it is situated, what its function and purpose is, and how it works. Actually, the last of these is true of the barometer but not the castle. There is a reason for this. Both describe structures but one of them is a static configuration while the other is a *mechanism*. A mechanism is a special kind of structure: it is a structure which has moving parts so arranged as to enable it to act on something else in a desired way. Understanding the structure of things is important in many areas of the curriculum. Once again, descriptions of structure differ in length, in detail and in other ways, too. But once again, the features we have indicated are common to them all. Incidentally, the section you are reading is a series of 'structures': each paragraph describes the composition of a different kind of object (class of text)!

Medieval castles

In order to rule a district, the Norman Lord was given permission to erect a stronghold, and he naturally did this in the way that was familiar to him in Normandy.

Having chosen a suitable site, the new lord ordered the local inhabitants to raise a huge mound of earth by digging a wide circular ditch and throwing the earth into the middle. This mound, called a motte, was flattened on the top and here, at the summit, a strong fence or palisade was erected. Inside the fence, a wooden tower was put up to serve as the lord's dwelling house and as the last point of defence. Even if stone was available it was not used, because the mound would not have taken the weight of a stone tower until the earth had settled for several years.

Beyond the mound was a good-sized yard or 'base-court', called the bailey, which was surrounded by another ditch joined to the ditch round the motte. The earth was thrown inwards to make a bank or rampart which was topped by a wooden palisade.

From R. J. Unstead, *Castles*

The aneroid barometer

Although the mercury barometer can be a comparatively accurate measuring instrument, it is rather bulky and 'spillable'.

Another instrument for measuring atmospheric pressure is the aneroid barometer ('aneroid' means 'without liquid'). In the aneroid barometer, air pressure is balanced against a powerful spring.

The vacuum box is made from thin corrugated metal. The two opposite sides are kept apart by the pull of the spring while air pressure tries to squash the box flat. The bottom of the box and the bottom of the spring are both fixed to a solid base-plate. Any increase in air pressure will move the top of the box and the spring downwards; any decrease in pressure will allow the spring to expand and move the top of the box upwards.

Because the amount of movement is very small indeed, it is increased by a lever, chain and pulley system which transfers the movement to a pointer on a dial.

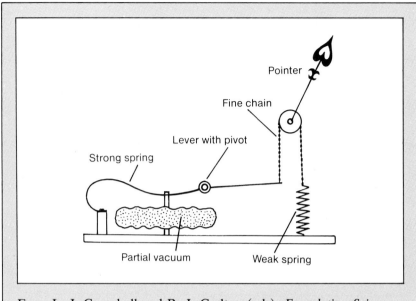

From L. J. Campbell and R. J. Carlton (eds), *Foundation Science*

Finally, we can turn to 'Looking through a microscope' and 'Making a compost heap'. Here the similarity of form is quite clear. Both texts are *instructions*. Both consist of a series of steps, sometimes numbered, which you, the reader, are asked to carry out in sequence if and when you wish to achieve a certain end. The successive segments of the text are the steps, and within each step we can look for certain specific categories of information: the action to be executed (what to do), materials needed, the end result – or when to stop (cf step 4 for the microscope and step 3 for the compost heap).

Looking through a microscope

When you use a microscope you must follow carefully the instructions given here to get good results.

Using the low power magnification

1. If there is a mirror, arrange it so as to reflect the light towards the stage. Light may be from a bench or from the sky (but not direct sunlight). Other microscopes may have a lamp built in below the stage.
2. Select the objective with the lowest power, that is, the one with the shortest mount and the widest lens.

3. Place your slide on the stage with the specimen you wish to examine near the centre of the hole. Hold it in position by the clips.

4. Look at the side of the microscope and turn the coarse focusing knob to bring the objective as close to the slide as you can without the two touching. (Remember that in some microscopes the focusing knob moves the tube and in others the stage.)

5. Look through the eyepiece and turn the focusing knob to move the lens away from the slide. NEVER FOCUS BY MOVING THE LENS TOWARDS THE SLIDE WHILE LOOKING THROUGH THE EYEPIECE.

From *Nuffield Biology Students' Text 1*: Introducing Living Things

Making a compost heap

This is a useful and warming exercise for an autumn day, if you have a garden.

Things you will need
All the garden rubbish you can find, except sticks and woody rubbish
A garden fork to collect it with
Some bricks or boards
Some sulphate of ammonia, or the special mixture you can buy to make compost

Gardeners like to make a compost heap for two reasons. One is that it is a good way to tidy the garden. But the second, and better reason is that it makes plant food.

How to make the heap:
1. First we have to clear a flat space about a yard square.
2. We build a wall of bricks or boards on three sides. If we use boards we may support them by pushing posts into the ground.
3. We spread a layer of dead plant rubbish, leaves, etc inside our space, about nine inches deep.
4. We sprinkle it with sulphate of ammonia, or compost maker.
5. We build up another layer, and go on till all the rubbish is used.
6. If the rubbish is very dry, we water it.
7. If it is very wet, we can keep rain out by putting a sheet of plastic over it. After a few weeks, the heap will have turned into nice brown compost, ready to use.

From V. E. Graham, *Activities for Young Naturalists*

(b) General comments

So far we have seen three distinct text types, each illustrated in two extracts of one to three or four paragraphs. Passages that belong to the same text type share a number of features: they deal with the same kind of content, even when the actual topic is very different; they tend to break up in the same way, yielding segments or sections that serve the same function (phases, parts, steps, for the three types discussed above); and the kind of information within these segments is more or less standard and predictable within each text type. An alternative way of talking about a particular text type is to think of it as a different *frame*. This is the term we have favoured in *Reading for Learning in the Sciences* (Oliver & Boyd, 1984).

Before proceeding to list the remaining text types we have found in the course of the 'Reading for Learning' project we should make a few general remarks.

1. Text types are only partial descriptions of text. It is a mistake to think of a notion like *process* or *structure* as some kind of metaphysical entity. Writers are free to choose what to say and how to say it. But unless what results is appropriate to the sorts of things users and readers (and in our context that means teachers and students) are looking for, the work may never get into print. So text types correspond to certain kinds of reader expectation. However, the correspondence is not always exact, nor need it be. What we have to say about text types is one way of describing text. It is certainly not the only way, nor would we claim that it is a definitive way to talk about everything that has ever been written.

2. Why text types are useful. Text types are useful for two reasons. For each type we have been able to identify, we have found that some activities are especially appropriate and knowing the type makes it a great deal easier to devise an effective lesson by designing suitable learning tasks in a telling way. The second reason is that the types recur and they recur within a subject. This means that in the long run, it is not just the teacher who learns to identify the type of passage but also the pupils. This implies that they learn to form the same kinds of expectation as writers of books and teachers of subjects. In other words, they learn the proper questions to ask in any area – *and that is the principal pay-off.*

3. How do instances of a text type occur in the context of a chapter or a book? Many novels and short stories include two sorts of things: those parts that belong to the narrative proper (including descriptions of people and places as well as actions and events, and including people's conversations and thoughts as well as their deeds), and the writer's reflections, where s/he seems to address the reader directly (a well-known device is to interpose an 'I' with a very distinctive standpoint, which is manifestly not that of the writer). Similarly, explanatory text-books include two sorts of things: those parts which carry the information and those parts that link them together, where the writer stops to address the reader to indicate what is coming next or to remind the reader of what went before.

So one way of isolating an instance of a given text type is to make use of the linking bits supplied by the writer. But writers do not always put in linking bits whenever they switch from one sort of information to another. So another way is simply to note how the writing breaks up. Needless to say, the author's use of sectioning and paragraphing and headings is immensely helpful. But so too is the reader's own intuition, the knowledge that s/he brings to bear on the text. It is probably a mistake to imagine that every meaningful text will always carry objective cues to every aspect of its structure. People do not write texts for computers or for Martians. They write them for people who already know something about the area and what to expect: for teachers and for pupils assisted by their teachers.

4. Beginnings, middles and ends. Despite these variations in style, there are some common features of texts that can be helpful when selecting a passage for use as the basis for a lesson. Such a passage will consist of a group of related ideas, and more often than not one will find that the writer begins a section of this kind by advertising the fact that the following few paragraphs will relate to the same topic. This can be done either by a linking passage in the text or by a sub-heading (cf the introductions to the six texts illustrated above – with the exception of the Mitosis text which is part of something much longer). One function of such 'announcements' (we are grateful to Mr S. Munslow for both the term and the insight) is to relate the new topic to what has gone before, and another is to delimit its content. This is followed by a central section, which is really the part which gives the text type its characteristic three features: type of theme, segmentation and recurrence of ideas that are similar in kind. Finally, the topic often concludes with a characteristic 'end'. This may take the form of a summary of a sentence or two which puts the account that went before in a wider context. So beginnings and ends are the kind of thing one looks for in isolating a stretch of text within a wider context that forms a unity and is likely to conform to a text type.

5. Parallel treatment, embedding, interweaving. Another way of looking at the same question is to consider the ways in which successive sections of text can be assembled when each deals with a distinct topic and conforms to a particular text type. It is not difficult to find four ways in which this can be done: parallel treatment of parallel topics, natural succession of one type following another, embedding, and interweaving.

Parallel treatments are probably the most common way of joining chapters and main sections in a book: they deal with different aspects of the subject in similar ways. The sections of text that are connected in this way are not always of chapter length. Parallel treatment is an obvious way of setting out information that is of a kind.

Natural succession is the next form to consider. This is an obvious complement to parallel topics. For instance, the writer uses one text type to introduce an area and another to follow up, as when a whole section of the subject is introduced in a *classification* (see page 66) and then the various topics can be treated in parallel – alternative *processes*, different *principles*, etc. Or again, the several types may be represented once only in accordance with a natural (or conventional) succession. Perhaps the most familiar case is this is the way in which scientific articles are organised: introduction, method, results, discussion.

Embedding is what we find whenever a writer interrupts one coherent text type or frame by putting in another. For instance, a *process* consists of a sequence of phases, each of which describes a transformation together with some indication of how that change is effected. If the description is brief, the process text is virtually uninterrupted. But if the explanation is substantial, it will usually take the form of another recognisable text type: *mechanism*. This can be perfectly acceptable for some topics and some combinations. But it can also make 'dense' and awkward text, and one of the things one tries to do when rewriting is to 'disembed', eg by deferring any protracted explanation of the mechanism until after the description of the process is complete.

We use the term 'embedding' to denote a single interruption to the natural flow of a passage, as dictated by its text type or frame. When there are several interruptions and these are all of the same kind, the effect is more one of *interweaving* one frame with another. The Spallanzani passage is a good example and typical of many, since interweaving will often be met with in discussions of the history of things, eg the development of printing or transport, or the history of London Bridge.

6. Homogeneous and heterogeneous sectioning within passage types. Just as one can have parallel and successive types in a longer run of text, so the different text types themselves fall into two categories, depending on the structure of the main or central part of the text. Structures, processes and instructions are all homogeneous in the sense that one expects to find the same kinds of information reappearing in the successive segments (apart from the beginning and end).

But not all text types are of this kind. Some are heterogeneous, in the sense that one expects the middle section to break down into a predictable succession of related segments, each presenting different kinds of information. Nevertheless, the information and ideas tend to be grouped in predictable ways, especially within the main segments. Consequently, these passages lend themselves to quite similar lesson techniques to those that feature homogeneous segments.

Among the text types featuring examples of heterogeneous segments, one that we have encountered frequently is the description of a 'situation'. This is a fairly specific text type or frame, usually found in history or in discussions of current affairs. 'Hard times for the farmer' is a good example. We have therefore chosen this passage to illustrate how one can mark a text in such a way as to point out those features which it shares with others of the same type.

(c) Text marking

The passage shown in Figure 8 is one which has been used many times in lessons inspired by the work of the project (see example 4, page 94). It has also been used with several teacher groups as an introduction to the principles underlying the notion of text types. As presented in Figure 8, the passage has been marked in three ways. We have used obliques to mark off the main segments, and these have been labelled in two different ways. The labels shown on the left are specific to the passage, similar to the sub-headings one finds in newspapers. Those on the right are generic.

Figure 8 Illustration of a text type: historical situation

Summary labels	Hard times for the farmer	Generic labels	
Farmers faced problems	The widespread intolerance and prejudice of the 1920s made it an unhappy time for Americans who wanted to change and improve their country. Another and more numerous dissatisfied group was the farmers./During the war years, while	Introduction	Beginning
They fared well in wartime	opposing armies had trampled the crops of European farmers into the ground, American farmers had obtained high prices for their wheat and other food crops./By	Antecedent conditions	
After the war, exports declined	1921, however, this had changed. The world was at peace and the countries of Europe no longer needed to buy such great quantities of food from the United States./ At home, too, the farmer was finding it more difficult to sell his products. For one	First set of problem circumstances	

Home
demand
fell too

thing, the country's population was no
longer increasing as quickly as before,
partly because of the passing of a law in
1921 which limited the number of
immigrants allowed to enter the United
States. The boom in motor vehicles also hit
the farmer, for as people stopped using
horse-drawn vehicles the demand for
animal feeding stuff declined./

Second set
of problem
circumstances

Main
Section

Farmers
lost money

For these and other reasons more and
more American farmers found themselves
in difficulties in the 1920s. Large numbers
of them lost money steadily, and by 1924
six hundred thousand of them were
bankrupt/Members of Congress from
farming areas persuaded the Government
to try to help. It was made easier for
farmers to borrow money to help them over
their difficulties. A Farm Board was set up
which bought crops like wheat and cotton,
which the farmers could not otherwise have
sold, with money from the Government./
But despite these efforts to help the
farmers, they found it more and more
difficult to make ends meet. As American
industry climbed steadily to ever higher
peaks of prosperity, American farming slid
with increasing speed into a deep state of
depression.

Effects of
problem

Measures
were taken
by
Government

Event (action
to overcome
problem)

These
measures
failed.

Outcome

End

From D. B. O'Callaghan, *Roosevelt and the United States*

Both kinds of label are useful and both have been used by pupils in lessons. However, it is the generic label that signals the passage type. In effect, the plight of the American farmers was unique to that situation and so, too, were the measures taken by the US Government. But history abounds with instances in which a particular group seems to 'take centre stage' for a period because its situation has changed. Whenever this happens, an account of that incident will usually include: background, account of antecedent conditions, statement of the problem and its effects, what was done to overcome the problem, and outcome. This, then, is the generic type.

Although the segments are not homogeneous, with problems being different from antecedents and so on, they do follow in a natural sequence. Also, within several segments one finds that there are repeated items like the listing of problems and of actions. As in the homogeneous types discussed earlier, these distinctive repeated constituents are characteristic of the text type, and it is these that one will rely on in interpreting its essential content.

Moreover, the teacher will focus on these constituent elements when designing a lesson.

It is perhaps worth adding that, again and again, when groups of teachers are asked to mark off seven segments in the passage, they tend to agree on those shown in Figure 8, albeit with two reservations. Not having been warned to look out for 'beginnings', they often put the first break after the first sentence instead of the second; and not everybody agrees about just how the list of problems should be divided. For the rest, there is usually total agreement. Yet none of these groups has been indoctrinated to begin with. The segmentation and the type answer to the character of what is being discussed and the way it can best be communicated. They therefore correspond to the expectations of knowledgeable persons even if they are untutored in these methods of analysing text coherence as such.

Marking texts in this fashion is an exceptionally useful exercise for teachers as a first step in planning a lesson. Even if you do not dot every 'i' or cross every 't', it is always advisable to gain a good working knowledge of the structure of the passage, the generic labels which will be most appropriate to its parts, and how these correspond to the specific summary labels.

(d) Some useful text types

Here now are ten text types that we have found it useful to distinguish. Each of these has been found to recur again and again in the passages set for study by pupils in secondary schools.

1. Narrative This includes biography as well as fiction material. Narrative passages deal with the feelings and doings of individual people, real or imaginary. The following 'generic' labels would cover most of the significant segments one encounters in passages of this sort:

setting	*description* (of individual)
goal	*character* (of individual)
obstacle or *problem*	*options*
event or *action*	*outcome*
interpretation	

This sort of text often lends itself to flow diagrams or interaction diagrams.

2. Structure or mechanism The difference between these is that a structure is conceived of – or is described as having – a static configuration adapted to a function but is itself unmoved, like a bridge or a flower, while a mechanism interacts with the outside world in the course of its operation. So a mechanism is a 'structure plus'. Thus a tooth will often be described as a simple structure, but an organ like the stomach will more often be thought of as a mechanism.

Useful generic labels for such passages are:

part	*function*
location	*mode of action* (of mechanism)
appearance	*effect* (of mechanism)
composition	

Passages of this nature usually require the support of an illustration. Suitable techniques therefore include diagram completion. However, tabulation may also be found useful, or even (for mechanisms) a flow diagram.

3. Process Reference has already been made to the phases in the production of something. Suitable generic labels are:

phase .	*action*
place	*mechanism*
initial state (of product)	*by-product*
final state	

Representation will usually take the form of a flow diagram or a table (with phases as rows and some of the remaining labels being used for column headings).

4. Principle A general explanatory rule, often in science, with examples of its applications and implications. Passages of this sort considered in the course of the project include texts dealing with the principle of gravitation, the expansion of metals, and heat capture. Suitable generic labels include:

statement	*application*
example(s)	*advantage(s)*
evidence	*disadvantage(s)*
	how these are overcome

Two-way tabulations and hierarchical diagrams have been used to bring out the essential information in this type of passage.

5. *Theory* The Spallanzani passage (page 30) was a good illustration of the sort of text we have in mind. Essentially, it consists in the statement of a theoretical problem and the consideration of alternative solutions.

Generic labels therefore include:

statement of problem	*example*
solution (number . . .)	*evidence*
objection	

Evidence may consist of real or imaginary experiments. Usually, the writer will consider alternative wrong solutions before the right one, and positive evidence is generally cited before objections. The final section of a theory passage may be a brief mention of applications, as it is in the Spallanzani passage. Although this sort of passage does not lend itself readily to diagrammatic representation it is ideally suited to tabular representation.

6. *Problem-solutions* This is similar to theory, save that the problem is an appplied one, and the solutions are alternative forms of action. Such texts can occur in scientific contexts but are at least equally liable to be found in subjects like history or geography. Appropriate labels for the segments are similar, save that 'advantage(s)' and 'disadvantage(s)' will probably be more appropriate than 'evidence'. Problem-solutions can refer to a class of situations, like how to plan crop rotation, or to individual problems, like the building of a Channel tunnel or bridge.

7. *Historical situation* We chose this type of passage to illustrate the general approach in Figure 8. The relevant labels include:

antecedent conditions	*circumstance(s)*
cause(s) of change	*problems*
effects	*action(s)*
outcome	

We note that the main difference between this type of passage and the last is that problem-solution stresses the action(s) to overcome a problem while situation is more concerned with the origin of the problem. It follows that these two types of text will sometimes follow one another in a natural order: situation – (eventual) solution. But this is far from universal among writers and unless a chosen extract deals with an issue at a minimal level of depth (2–3 paragraphs) it is hardly suitable material for an analysis activity.

Unlike problem-solution, accounts of historical situations lend themselves well to reconstruction by a flow diagram.

8. Classification This type of passage will be found most frequently in the opening chapter of a book or in the opening section of a chapter where the writer is trying to map out a field of study by drawing the reader's attention to the more important variations, how these can be recognised, and what their effects are. Usually, there will be an element of contrast between neighbouring categories.

Any classification will result in a number of classes which differ by one or more criteria. For instance, one passage used in the project distinguished between the three states of matter (solids, liquids and gases) in terms of their molecular structure: how tight is the packing of molecules and how mobile? Another distinguished between beef cattle, dairy cattle and dual-purpose cattle, going on to list the varieties of each, where they were kept, and why. Yet another was concerned with the classification of plants into simple plants, mosses, ferns, and seed-bearing plants, with further sub-classifications.

So it looks as if the most useful labels for categorising the information in this type of text would be words like 'class', 'sub-class', and 'criterion'. And it is true that such labels would be very general. Unfortunately, however, they have very limited usefulness (because they are too abstract) and in practice it has been found that it is better to use specific labels for each classification (eg beef cattle, dairy cattle, Friesian, Jersey, rather than class and sub-class, etc). So although it is useful to recognise a common structure in classificatory texts, there is less profit in using generic labels.

As to the most appropriate techniques for reconstructing the material in a memorable way, hierarchical tree diagrams are often an obvious solution, but no less useful are a variety of two-entry tabulations – using specific headings rather than generic ones.

9. Instructions We began by calling this form of organisation a 'recipe' and recipes are the most obvious examples of text organised as a list of instructions for achieving some end. However, there are plenty of other examples, including instructions for setting up an experiment. Instructions are often recognisable by the use of the imperative; this is relatively rare in other sorts of passage.

Almost by definition, instructions take the form of a series of ordered *steps* each consisting of an *action* that ends in a *result*. Other useful categories are *caution* and (*additional*) *requirements*.

Either flow diagram or tabulation can be used as alternative ways of representing the text. In addition, many teachers have found it useful to cut up the text itself and present it as a sequencing task (see Part II of this book, 'Text reconstruction').

10. Theme Every classification needs a let-out class to act as a catch-all or sweeper, and this is ours. If a writer has something worthwhile to say, then what s/he writes will hang together. It will be coherent in some way, and we have seen a number of different ways of achieving coherence. Each features particular kinds of information, often arranged according to a characteristic structure. There may be others we have missed. But there is still the case where the coherence of what is said derives only from the fact that the writer has elected to tell us several things about some common *theme*.

The theme may be anything from blank verse to California. The important thing is that several points are made about that theme, each of them appropriate, and all of them disparate.

Since each such piece of writing differs from most others, we cannot say anything useful about themes in general. But listing is often useful and some kinds of diagram can also be helpful.

4. Lesson design

The aim of this section is to communicate the project's experience for the benefit of teachers who are interested in implementing our ideas as part of their own work. It would be useful to think of lesson design as comprising two phases: preparation and lesson conduct.

This section follows directly from the last inasmuch as the teacher's study of text and text type is an important preliminary to lesson design. We make this claim for text reconstruction no less than for the analytical study of text. In general, the problems and principles of lesson design are similar for all text-based lessons. However, when discussing the choice of specific techniques within the present section, we have restricted ourselves to those that are based on analysis of texts that have not been altered either by deletions or by scrambling.

(a) Lesson preparation
Selecting a text

The first step in preparing a text-based lesson is to select an appropriate passage. It was one of our basic tenets that reading should be a part of learning and the lesson must arise naturally out of the teacher's curricular objectives. This means that throughout the project it was the individual subject teacher who selected the passage for study. Experience seems to suggest that, over and above the need for curricular relevance, the following considerations may be generally useful.

First, the passage must be informative and should not be peripheral: it should contain ideas that you would want pupils to study in some detail. Second, it should not be too long. Studying a text takes time, not least because so often pupils themselves get the bit between their teeth and want to resolve the issues which you have raised for them, or which they have raised for themselves. As may be seen from the examples included in this book, three or four average paragraphs are usually adequate. The third point worth noting is that because of the guidance that is built in through reading for learning techniques, the level of text difficulty can be greater than that which you would normally set for any given group.

Teacher's analysis

Once the text has been selected, the most essential step is to make your own analysis. We hope that the last section will have provided a useful background for doing this. Very probably, when you have built up a reserve of experience you will be in a position to build up your own methods which may differ from those of others. But if only as a starter, here are seven steps which you will find helpful:

1. Read through the whole passage quite rapidly. Depending on the familiarity of the material, the rate of reading here will vary between a straightforward 'receptive' style (ie not skipping but not pausing very often to sort out any questions that may arise) and a 'skim' (skipping a great deal, because you are simply verifying a structure which you anticipated).

2. Make a decision about the kind of passage you think it is. You can do this by comparing it to other passages with which you are familiar or by considering not just the theme of the passage but the type of theme, as outlined in the last section.

3. Go through the passage and mark it off in segments corresponding to the major transitions in content. This can be simply a matter of following the breaks between paragraphs. But the author's paragraphing can be individualistic or even downright misleading and you may want to break some paragraphs and group others together.

4. Put in some kind of side labels to bring out the nature of the segments you have just identified and their role in the treatment as a whole. You may wish to use generic labels, as shown on the right side of Figure 8 and as was done for the Spallanzani passage. However, you may find it more helpful to use the familiar summary label, the side heading or side label which tells you in brief what this bit is about. Both kinds can be useful.

Although it will rarely be necessary to use both at once, it is a good thing to put in one or the other so as to end up with a written framework for thinking about the passage.

5. If the passage is a long one, decide on the key segments or paragraphs in the light of the information they convey and repeat the process of steps 3 and 4, at a higher degree of magnification as it were. This, essentially, is what we did for paragraph 6 in Spallanzani.

6. By now you will be very aware of the structure of the passage as well as its content. You will know its strengths and weaknesses. And of course you will know the points you want your pupils to get to grips with.

But before you are ready to prepare the lesson, we would recommend you to go over steps 2–5 in your head. This time consider just what were the cues (the words and phrases) in the text which led you to make your decisions about the major breaks, what was being said where, what was important, and so on. You may find it useful to underline these words and phrases – because they are the ones you will want your pupils to fasten on, since the pupils will also be required to work out exactly what the text tells them and how.

7. Finally, we would urge you to discuss your own analysis with a colleague before launching it on the class. This will not always be essential but it is surprising how often the same text can lend itself to different interpretations, and your pupils are quite likely to discover them if you do not.

Designing the tasks

The techniques described earlier fall into three categories: analysis, representation and extrapolation. The first category can be omitted, but only at considerable risk. The second or third will be included if there is time, which also means if you think that the material is sufficiently important to warrant it. Usually it is.

Analysis, you will remember, is a matter of identifying the key elements of information contained in each section of the passage together with the actual phrases and sentences in which they are expressed.

There are two basic ways of helping pupils to identify these key elements. One is to start with a category and look for all the relevant examples, which is what one does when underlining for selected targets. The other is to go through the passage section by section and decide what each bit is about. This corresponds to segmenting and labelling.

Of course you are not committed to using one to the exclusion of the other. An ingenious teacher with an experienced class can combine them in many ways: for instance, by getting the pupils to make guesses about how to categorise the rest of the passage after labelling the information in the first paragraph.

Just as underlining and labelling are alternative ways of helping readers to discover the key elements in a passage and how they fall into different categories, so tabulation and diagrammatic representation are ideal for helping them to see the relevant structure by trying successfully to produce an alternative representation, one which makes that structure more salient. We can say 'trying successfully' because if the teacher has chosen the passage appropriately and has given the right introduction and provides proper support, the effort will be successful.

A third group of procedures is extrapolation. This too is best seen as a follow-up to the initial analysis procedures. Examples will be found on pages 79 and 105. Because there is a limit to the amount of time they may wish to spend on a specific topic, teachers usually choose between representation and extrapolation. The former offers the advantage that at the end of the lesson the pupils retain a graphic representation of the gist of the passage – one to which they themselves have contributed. On the other hand, extrapolation can be highly motivating, especially when introduced on an occasional basis.

Preparation of material

To achieve successful text-based activities, it is important to provide each pupil with a copy of the text and any relevant diagram, preferably on a separate sheet of paper, so that s/he can mark the text without defacing the book from which it was taken. Teachers are advised that they should write to the publishers to obtain permission to copy material in this way, and the information required by publishers is provided in the appendix.

In addition to copies of the text, you may wish to provide supportive material, eg diagrams or an outline paper, and these too will need to be made available at a rate of one per pupil or pair of pupils.

(b) Conduct of the lesson
Sources of feedback

There are two important points to remember about conducting a text-based lesson. The first is that the lesson has been deliberately devised to provide for a variety of sources of feedback of which the teacher is only one. *Text-based lessons are open-ended. They have to be if they are to achieve their end as lessons in how to study.* The second point is that the teacher cannot step aside. The teacher planned the lesson to start with and is there to monitor it as it proceeds — to put things right if they go wrong, and to capitalise on them when they go right.

Each lesson consists of a set of tasks that relate to a chosen text. There is not usually just one right solution and indeed there may well be an almost infinite number, but more often than not all these right (or acceptable) solutions will have a great deal in common. However, although there may be many right solutions, there are certainly as many wrong solutions. How do the pupils find out whether their solutions are right or wrong? How do they know when they're on the right lines?

There are three ways: from the text itself, from other pupils, and from the teacher.

We have already seen how the text itself provides feedback. If you think a particular category of information occurs more than once in a passage then you should be able to point to these occurrences. So too, we would argue, there is always some evidence in the text about the structure of relations between elements; sometimes directly, as in connectives, and sometimes by the arrangement of ideas. True, the evidence isn't always perfect (few texts are perfectly written) but such as it is it is worth exploring and must be used.

The second source of feedback is the group. Within the project, text-based lessons are meant to be group activities. The pupils are expected to exchange ideas and learn from one another. Have I missed a cue? Have I put the right interpretation on a particular sentence? If not, I've probably drawn a wrong conclusion, but someone is very likely to tell me so. Because the work goes on in small groups – often in twos and threes, sometimes in fours and fives – and each group is working towards a common solution, such telling can be done without any feeling of irritation.

The final source of feedback is the teacher who can move about the class, see if there are difficulties, offer extra prompts, sometimes be the devil's advocate (to make sure that the pupils can defend their judgements) and so on. At the end of the lesson, there will always be a full discussion, in the course of which the teacher can reinforce the main points if necessary, or bring in extra information, or suggest further lines of enquiry. But what is important is that the teacher is just one source of information, not the only one. The teacher is still there as a fall back and as a coach, but the pupil is being helped towards independence.

Teacher intervention and remediation

Suppose things are not going well. Let us consider some possible reasons:

1. The material is too difficult

It may be too late to do much about that now, but perhaps something can be salvaged by lowering your sights and setting an easier task. Anyhow, it is worth recalling for the future that the difficulty could be due to insufficient preparation, and more time may be needed to give more background information.

2. Presentation in the chosen text is too difficult

Too many off-putting new words? Too many rambling sentences? Too many assumptions and short-cuts? 'Shared reading' could help. If it wasn't thought necessary to start with (and the teacher doing the Spallanzani passage did think it necessary), you might think of interrupting the group work to go through the passage (or a part of it) with the class as a whole.

Or there may be just a few points of difficulty you find as you move from one group to another, and some may be so important you want to tell everyone about them.

3. The task is too difficult

Every one of the techniques we have described — underlining, labelling, making a table or a diagram, etc — is difficult if the passage and the ideas are new to the group, and easy if they are familiar.

But that is only half the story. The task is also more difficult (and potentially more rewarding) if it is left open for the groups to complete as best they can, and easier if part of it is done for them.

For instance, if the teacher has supplied all the headings for the rows and columns of a table, completing it is easier; if only some of them are given, it is harder. If none of them is given it is harder still, and it's hardest of all if even the number of rows and columns is left open. At the other extreme, if several of the actual cells have been filled in, the pupils' task is made easiest of all the possibilities.

The same principle applies to diagrammatic representations, when the form of a suitable diagram may be given as a prompt or deliberately withheld, and where once again even some of the labelling may be supplied for greater support.

Even in the initial analysis tasks – underlining, labelling, segmenting – the degree of support can be varied by the number of targets given by the teacher versus those which are left for the pupils to discover. Some headings or none can be supplied, and hints may be offered about how a passage can be segmented.

From all this it follows that the amount of support will have been gauged by the teacher when planning the lesson, having regard to the experience of the pupils and the difficulty of the passage. Just the same, if it turns out that the work is more difficult than you had anticipated, you may be able to make it easier by offering additional cues.

4. *The task is too easy*

Paradoxically, this is more difficult! You can't take away cues once they've been given. However, you may be able to improve the quality of discussion and of learning by suggesting additional tasks.

In this connection it is worth mentioning that in our experience:

tabulation is more demanding than listing;
diagrammatic representation is more demanding than tabulation;
representation is more demanding than analysis;
extrapolation is more demanding than analysis.

5. *Not enough discussion*

This of course may be a variant of point 4. Maybe the discussion is missing because the pupils do not experience – or do not spot – the difficulties. However, they may also be inexpert in discussion – too wary of each other, or of the teacher, etc. Or they may be insufficiently motivated.

Here again, the experienced teacher will be able to find a way round the problem. One can stimulate discussion by taking the part of devil's advocate. Or that part may be delegated to appointed pupils. This in turn leads to the possibilities of role-taking generally, on the principle that pupils (and people generally) who will not let their hair down in their own character are often quite happy to do so when enacting a part.

Role-taking leads to simulation, and simulation is a form of extrapolation, so the possibilities are endless.

But it would be stupid to pretend that every lesson held under the auspices of the project was an unqualified success, or that every situation is remediable on the spot. In the end, you may have to settle for less, and build up your lesson strength for the next occasion.

PART 1

SECTION B

Examples

Each of the nine examples is based on an extract from published material and is identified by subject, type of passage, and techniques used in one or more lessons based on the extract. Readers are urged to study some and to skim others.

Table 4 List of examples in Part I

Example No.	Topic	Subject	Passage Type
Introductory Example	Life from nothing	Biology	Theory/ Biography (interwoven)
1	The Pearl	English Literature	Narrative
2	The Hindenburg	Chemistry	Structure/ Narrative (interwoven)
3	Paper Making	Geography	Process
4	Hard Times for the Farmer	History	Historical situation
5	The Domesday Book	History	Classification
6	Sir Thomas More	History	Narrative (biography)
7	Exploring Electricity	Physics	Theme (natural force)
8	The Kidneys	Biology	Mechanism
9	River Basins	Geography	Classification

The examples are not arranged in any strict sequence, but later examples are apt to be more complex than those occurring earlier.

Particular attention is drawn to example 2, which includes an extensive and not atypical lesson transcript.

The list (Table 4) should prove helpful in enabling you to decide which examples to study and which to omit. It has already been said that at least some of the examples should be studied by two or more teachers working in collaboration with one another, and so far as possible we have tried to include suggestions for joint study in relation to every example both in this section and in the corresponding sections of Part II.

Activities	*Comment*
Labelling. Underlining. Grouping. Ranking. Tabulation.	–
Underlining. Labelling. Diagram. Prediction. Extrapolation.	–
Underlining. Simulation.	Useful hints on selective underlining
Segmenting. Tabulation.	Transcript of pupil discussion
Diagram completion. Underlining. Listing.	Some discussion of diagram conventions
Underlining. Segmenting. Labelling. Simulation.	Good use of simulation
Underlining. Listing. Pupil questions.	Comparison of DARTs and traditional comprehension questions
Underlining. Tabulation.	Discussion of ordering of tasks in selective underlining
Underlining. Diagram completion. Ordered Listing. Flow chart.	Discussion of diagrams and relation to text
Labelling. Ordering. Diagram.	How to help pupils tackle less than perfect text

Example 1

Subject English Literature

Source From John Steinbeck, *The Pearl*

Passage Type Narrative

Activities Underlining
          Labelling
          Diagram
          Continuation of text in manner of writer

Introduction

The following extract was presented for close study as a preliminary to reading the novel in its entirety. The object was to involve the pupils in the characters, their attitudes and their problems, and how these were portrayed by the author.

1. Underline 10–20 phrases selecting those that best bring out the attitudes of the two characters and their changing inter-relationships.

2. The passage may be divided into five segments of unequal length. Where would you put the four main breaks?

'I hear you,' he said dully.

'Kino, this pearl is evil. Let us destroy it before it destroys us. Let us crush it between two stones. Let us – let us throw it back in the sea where it belongs. Kino, it is evil, it is evil!'

And as she spoke the light came back in Kino's eyes so that they glowed fiercely and his muscles hardened and his will hardened.

'No,' he said. 'I will fight this thing. I will win over it. We will have our chance.' His fist pounded the sleeping-mat. 'No one shall take our good fortune from us,' he said. His eyes softened then and he raised a gentle hand to Juana's shoulder. 'Believe me,' he said. 'I am a man.' And his face grew crafty.

'In the morning we will take our canoe and we will go over the sea and over the mountains to the capital, you and I. We will not be cheated. I am a man.'

'Kino,' she said huskily, 'I am afraid. A man can be killed. Let us throw the pearl back into the sea.'

'Hush,' he said fiercely. 'I am a man. Hush.' And she was silent, for his voice was command. 'Let us sleep a little,' he said. 'In the first light we will start. You are not afraid to go with me?'

'No, my husband.'

His eyes were soft and warm on her then, his hand touched her cheek. 'Let us sleep a little,' he said.

Example 1   77

The late moon arose before the first rooster crowed. Kino opened his eyes in the darkness, for he sensed movement near him, but he did not move. Only his eyes searched the darkness, and in the pale light of the moon that crept through the holes in the brush house Kino saw Juana arise silently from beside him. He saw her move towards the fireplace. So carefully did she work that he heard only the lightest sound when she moved the fireplace stone. And then like a shadow she glided towards the door. She paused for a moment beside the hanging box where Coyotito lay, then for a second she was black in the doorway, and then she was gone.

And rage surged in Kino. He rolled up to his feet and followed her as silently as she had gone, and he could hear her quick footsteps going towards the shore. Quietly he tracked her, and his brain was red with anger. She burst clear out of the brush line and stumbled over the little boulders towards the water, and then she heard him coming and she broke into a run. Her arm was up to throw when he leaped at her and caught her arm and wrenched the pearl from her. He struck her in the face with his clenched fist and she fell among the boulders, and he kicked her in the side. In the pale light he could see the little waves break over her, and her skirt floated about and clung to her legs as the water receded.

Kino looked down at her and his teeth were bared. He hissed at her like a snake, and Juana stared at him with wide unfrightened eyes, like a sheep before the butcher. She knew there was murder in him, and it was all right; she had accepted it, and she would not resist or even protest. And then the rage left him and a sick disgust took its place. He turned away from her and walked up the beach and through the brush line. His senses were dulled by his emotion.

He heard the rush, got his knife out and lunged at one dark figure and felt his knife go home, and then he was swept to his knees and swept again to the ground. Greedy fingers went through his clothes, frantic fingers searched him, and the pearl, knocked from his hand, lay winking behind a little stone in the pathway. It glinted in the soft moonlight.

Juana dragged herself up from the rocks on the edge of the water. Her face was a dull pain and her side ached. She steadied herself on her knees for a while and her wet skirt clung to her. There was no anger in her for Kino. He had said: 'I am a man,' and that meant certain things to Juana. It meant that he was half insane and half god. It meant that Kino would drive his strength against a mountain and plunge his strength against the sea. Juana, in her woman's soul, knew that the mountain would stand while the man broke himself; that the sea would surge while the man drowned in it. And yet it was this thing that made him a man, half insane and half god, and Juana had need of a man; she could not live without a man. Although she might be puzzled by these differences between man and woman, she knew them and accepted them and needed them. Of course she would follow him, there was no question of that. Sometimes the quality of woman, the reason, the caution, the sense of preservation, could cut through Kino's manness and save them all. She climbed painfully to her feet, and she dipped her cupped palms in the little waves and washed her bruised face with the stinging salt water, and then she went creeping up the beach after Kino.

A flight of herring clouds had moved over the sky from the south. The pale moon dipped in and out of the strands of clouds so that Juana walked in darkness for a moment and in light the next. Her back was bent with pain and her head was low. She went through the line of brush when the moon was covered, and when it looked through she saw the glimmer of the great pearl in the path behind the rock. She sank to her knees and picked it up, and the moon went into the darkness of the clouds again. Juana remained on her knees while she considered whether to go back to the sea and finish her job, and as she considered, the light came again, and she saw two dark figures lying in the path ahead of her. She leaped forward and saw that one was Kino and the other a stranger with dark shiny fluid leaking from his throat.

Kino moved sluggishly, arms and legs stirred like those of a crushed bug, and a thick muttering came from his mouth. Now, in an instant, Juana knew that the old life was gone forever. A dead man in the path and Kino's knife, dark-bladed beside him, convinced her. All of the time Juana had been trying to rescue something of the old peace, of the time before the pearl. But now it was gone, and there was no retrieving it. And knowing this, she abandoned the past instantly. There was nothing to do but to save themselves.

Her pain was gone now, her slowness. Quickly she dragged the dead man from the pathway into the shelter of the brush. She went to Kino and sponged his face with her wet skirt. His senses were coming back and he moaned.

'They have taken the pearl. I have lost it. Now it is over,' he said. 'The pearl is gone.'

Juana quieted him as she would quiet a sick child. 'Hush,' she said. 'Here is your pearl. I found it in the path. Can you hear me now? Here is your pearl. Can you understand? You have killed a man. We must go.'

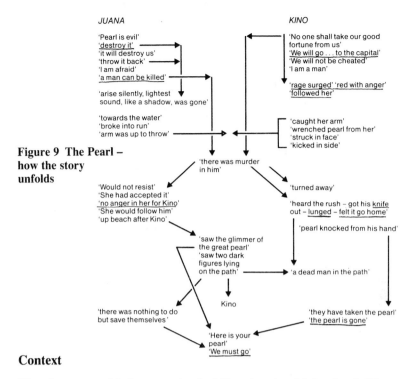

JUANA

'Pearl is evil'
'destroy it'
'it will destroy us'
'throw it back'
'I am afraid'
'a man can be killed'

'arise silently, lightest
sound, like a shadow, was gone'

'towards the water'
'broke into run'
'arm was up to throw'

KINO

'No one shall take our good
fortune from us'
'We will go . . . to the capital'
'We will not be cheated'
'I am a man'

'rage surged' 'red with anger'
'followed her'

'caught her arm'
'wrenched pearl from her'
'struck in face'
'kicked in side'

**Figure 9 The Pearl –
how the story
unfolds**

'there was murder
in him'

'Would not resist'
'She had accepted it'
'no anger in her for Kino'
'She would follow him'
'up beach after Kino'

'turned away'

'heard the rush – got his knife
out – lunged – felt it go home'

'pearl knocked from his hand'

'saw the glimmer of
the great pearl'
'saw two dark
figures lying
on the path'

'a dead man in the path'

Kino

'there was nothing to do
but save themselves'

'they have taken the pearl'
'the pearl is gone'

'Here is your
pearl'
'We must go'

Context

The class was a third-year, mixed-ability class in a high school. The passage
was chosen for two reasons. It fitted into a series of lessons on plot structure and character interaction, while also serving as a first introduction to
the novel from which it was taken. The class was occupied with the work
described below for one 35-minute lesson and one 70-minute lesson. Prior
to looking at *The Pearl* they had studied two other extracts, in the course
of which they had gained some initial practice of underlining as well as
constructing a diagram to represent the interplay of persons in a narrative.
They had also had the experience of working together in small groups of
two or three.

Course of two lessons

Pupils in their usual groups were given copies of the text. The passage was
read aloud by the teachers to some dramatic effect. Pupils were then asked
to go back over the passage in their groups, underlining a few key phrases
and sentences, these being selected because they highlighted the two main
characters and their changing inter-relationships. In addition, they were
invited to devise a few labels for what they thought were key paragraphs,
to indicate their content.

When this part of the work was completed, the pupils were asked to
join together in larger groups (five to eight) to compare notes about the
phrases they had selected and to begin to think of ways of producing a
diagram to represent the unfolding of the story, still centring on the two

characters. In this way, initial ideas for the diagram were elicited from the group to serve as a basis for the class work which formed the next phase. The class discussion which followed was centred on a diagram constructed on the blackboard on the basis of suggestions from the pupils (Figure 9). The discussion was chaired by the teacher, but she was careful not to impose her own ideas. However, she did bring out the fact that this was a story in which things happened and relations underwent change. Whenever appropriate, she invited suggestions about what might have preceded the extract and what would ensue. Thus she prepared the ground for the final part of the exercise, which was to produce either a next instalment to the story or a possible ending. This was an individual assignment, begun at the end of the second lesson and completed for homework.

Comment

The success of the lesson is well brought out by the diagram. This is reproduced in the form in which pupils were asked to copy it into their notebooks. The diagram includes all the phrases offered by the class as a whole, while those underlined represent the ones chosen by a particular group. The significance of the arrows is self-evident, though not always consistent.

Perhaps the least successful part of the exercise was the labelling, which was sporadic, generally limited to three or four labels per group, eg 'The careful work of Juana', 'The rage of Kino'.

On the other hand, the continuations were generally at a very high level, the one reproduced on page 81 being especially remarkable. The exchange between the two villains sounds out of place and period, but one is struck not only by the felicity of the style but by the sense that feeling and thought can be no less significant than action and that, in the end, the central thread of the book is likely to be neither Juana nor Kino, but the pearl itself.

It may be added that the second suggestion made in the introduction might have served to highlight the way in which the story is constructed: with successive episodes marked by changes in the pace and the perspective of the narrator as well as by changes in the story itself. It is possible, but not certain, that such an exercise would have brought about some extra insights and more successful labelling.

The boy who produced the ending shown here, however, could hardly have got more out of the work, and it is appropriate to record that this class went on to read the novel with more enthusiasm than any previous group in the teacher's experience. As to the reason, opinions may differ, but one of the elements stressed by many teachers of English is the potential offered by a detailed study of a small section of a work which yet concentrates on what is central and significant to the young reader.

Example 1   *81*

The Pearl (Pupil's ending)

So they went. Juana, her calm almost returned, took Coyotito from the hanging box, and went to join her husband on the beach. He sat, stunned, on a rock rolling the pearl in his palm, aware of the throbbing pains in his head and leg. He had been wrong, he realised dully. The pearl had just destroyed their happy life. Juana had been right. But now it was too late: that man was dead and murderers are not put to trial: they are hunted down and killed themselves. They had to get away and quickly. Juana penetrated his misery and set him to walking, stumbling, trudging. As they passed other huts, Juana prayed that their child stay silent, for in the silence of the night the crying of a baby carries far and stirs people from sleep as, say, the hoot of an owl or the night noises might not. For in the senseless discordant wailing lies a tone which switches on the maternal and paternal instincts: until the child stops they are attentive in the knowledge that the baby needs help. But Coyotito stayed mercifully silent and despite the rough passage he was having, remained oblivious of all in the cushioned shell of his dreams.

Juana thought to the future, of how they would survive and where they would go. She could visualise a nomadic life's style, belonging nowhere and being no-one, strangers wherever they went. She could see no way out, but that which the pearl suggested. How she loathed it, and yet was at its complete mercy. Her husband's mind was set, she was sure: the pearl was evil she knew he must realise and yet she still felt that in the pearl, Kino could see a way it could help them. And maybe it could.

Kino was barely conscious all this time. His legs walked by themselves, his eyes saw but his mind did not register the picture. His thoughts were confused, worthless and negative. For him the future held nothing in store, save suffering and hardship. He, the man, was being led by this woman, this instrument of *his*, and he was following. Something like anger stirred behind his glassy pupils. He knew it was wrong, following his woman, like a dog. But he did not feel like complaining. He was happy, just for once, to be a subordinate, because he did not in the least feel like working, picking their way through the scrub. Juana was doing that for him now. She was somewhere ahead now, waiting for him to catch up. Patient, if stupid, he thought. All because of the pearl. He stopped a moment and took the pearl from the pouch he wore round his neck. He admired its beauty in the moonlight. Like women, he thought – the more beautiful the more sinister and evil. Even he was beginning to feel a kind of vibration pulsating from it, an evil tide, like its luminescent glow in the moonlight. He thought he heard Juana call him softly and went forward once more. . . .

The long blade entered Kino's body at the point between the sixth and seventh ribs where access to the heart is most easily attained. He jerked once, twice and then collapsed. Two figures hovered around him.

"Found it?"

"Nah – 's not here."

"Must be – woman not got it."

"Not here."

"Sure this is the one?"

"This man killed our friend! I've tracked them for miles."

"Must be deaf, not hearing you kill the woman."

"Nah. Just stupid."

"Found it?"

"Nah."

"Ah, mucking hell!"

"Maybe swallowed it."

"Ah?" The other indicated where it would come out. The other dismissed the idea with a curt shake of his shaggy head. Then they kicked and urinated on Kino's dead body out of sheer contempt and left.

As the moon dipped lower in the sky, its paling light shone down the narrow, deep cleft between two great boulders. The pearl glinted in reply. There was something more tangibly sinister about it now, but yet it still eluded precise definition. Maybe responsibility for four deaths veiled it, maybe its past was more turbulent than ever supposed.

The moon sank behind the mountains and the cliff was as dark as a moonless night. Not even an evil glow to betray what it held.

Example 2

Subject Science/Chemistry

Source Adapted from Richard Hart, *Chemistry Matters*

Passage Type Narrative interwoven with structure

Activities Underlining
         Simulation

Introduction

The extract describes both a structure and an event.

1. Read it through to the end and mark the text with oblique lines.

Example 2   83

2. Label each segment you have marked off.

3. Now concentrate on the 'structure' part. Work with a colleague and underline those parts of the text which describe the materials used in the construction of the airship.

The Hindenburg

The Hindenburg was a huge German airship that was built in 1936 by the Zeppelin Company. The airship was a vast framework of rings and girders to make a rigid structure nearly 50 metres high and 250 metres long. The framework was made of a light alloy of aluminium and copper. The outside of the structure was covered with cotton fabric and then coated with silver paint to protect it from the sun and rain.

The ship was hollow inside, save for the skeleton of metal girders. The hydrogen used to make the ship float was contained in 16 gas bags. These were made of specially treated cotton fabric and between them held 200,000 cubic metres of hydrogen.

When fully laden the ship's total mass was 236 tonnes. Four powerful diesel engines attached to the outside of the ship could propel it along at a cruising speed of 140 kilometres per hour. The ship could stay in the air without stopping for fuel or supplies for 5 days, with a range of almost 20,000 kilometres.

The crew consisted of 15 stewards and cooks who cared for the 50 passengers. The ship was manned and piloted by about 40 engineers, navigators, riggers and officers. Passengers on the Hindenburg spent their journey in hotel luxury. Also the airship, unlike an aeroplane, did not pitch and roll in bad weather. It was a very safe way to travel except that it contained hydrogen and hydrogen, when mixed with air and ignited, exploded violently.

Rigorous safety precautions were taken on the Hindenburg to prevent the hydrogen being set on fire. The gas bags were isolated from the engines and kitchens. The area around them was ventilated so that any leaking gas would be carried out of the ship immediately. People were only allowed to smoke in designated safe areas. Crew members who visited the hydrogen storage area had to wear special shoes with no metal parts in them so that there was no chance of a spark being made.

On Monday, May 3rd, 1937, the Hindenburg left Frankfurt in Germany for the U.S.A. A saboteur, angered by the German government's part in the Spanish Civil War, had planted a phosphorus incendiary bomb in one of the gas bags. The bomb exploded as the airship was about to land at Chicago.

> The fire, slow at first, quickly expanded as the gas bags burned open and the hydrogen mixed with the air. As the ship lost its buoyancy and sank to the ground, the passengers and crew made desperate attempts to escape. Some jumped while they were still 30 metres above the ground. Some waited until the framework had fallen and then fought their way through the white hot metal. Many were trapped and burned before they could get away.

Choice of activity in relation to text

The passage illustrates how different kinds of information may be interwoven in the same short passage. In one sense, the structure of the airship is the setting and background for the disaster that occurred. In another sense, the structure is central because it is an application of a scientific principle which makes the event a tragic, but secondary, consequence.

The context of the lesson and the teacher's purpose will determine which aspect of the text is focused on. This text could be used either as the starting point for a study of the properties of hydrogen in chemistry or as the starting point for a historical study in which the emphasis would be socio-scientific. Alternatively, it could be used in the context of a study of safety at work.

The focus on structure in your own analysis was intended to show how underlining can be used to locate detailed information, to give you the feel of the task undertaken by pupils, and to bring out some important implications.

In marking those parts of the text which describe materials you will certainly have included *alloy of alluminium and copper* and *cotton fabric*, and you may have underlined *metal* and the second occurrence of *cotton fabric*. Alternatively, you may have thought these redundant. Again, there was probably uncertainty about *silver paint* and, in another category altogether, about *hydrogen* and *diesel*. On the one hand, hydrogen and diesel may not count literally as materials of construction; on the other hand they must be considered substances essential for the functioning of the airship.

The example illustrates the problem of defining the boundaries of categories. This issue arises in most underlining tasks. It takes the form: 'What is to be included; what to be left out?' As such it illustrates a strength, rather than a weakness of directed reading activities. Deciding where the boundaries lie is an important part of the analysis because it forces one to examine the criteria for membership of a class or category. It frequently results in a recognition of the need for a further category: in the case of our example, a category for 'sources of power' or 'fuel'.

Example 2   85

A text-based lesson in science

This text was used in the context of a study of hydrogen in chemistry. The pupils working on it were a lower-band second year in a comprehensive school.

Pupils were provided with copies of the text. The background to the lesson was discussed and the text was read aloud by the teacher with pupils following.

Pupils were then instructed to group themselves in pairs or threes. Final adjustments in grouping were made by the teacher. The instructions below were then given out and read over, and pupils were asked to work through each task in turn. They were told that help would be available, if required, from the teacher and two observers.

1. Underline in the passage the names of the materials that were used to make the airship.

2. Underline in the passage in a different colour the parts of the passage which describe the advantages of an airship.

3. Underline in the passage in a third colour the parts of the passage which describe the disadvantages of an airship.

4. Make an advertising poster showing the advantages of visiting the USA from Germany on the Hindenburg. Remember that it is 1937 and at this time an airliner meant a 21-seater Douglas DC-3 which had to refuel every 2000 kilometres.

5. Write out a list of safety rules that you would issue for a factory where a lot of hydrogen is going to be used. Remember that the employees may well be smokers, have steel-tipped shoes and wear nylon jumpers. They will switch on lights and work electrically-operated machines.

6. If you were to design an airship, what gas would you use other than hydrogen?

Pupils made their greatest demands on teachers when engaged on the first task. All pupils agreed about the alloys of aluminium and copper but some wanted to include hydrogen and diesel. Nevertheless, in discussion it became apparent to them that these did not belong in quite the same category. For most, the problem was resolved by the creation of two categories, one for structural materials and one for fuel. Pupils responded very positively to the suggestion of using a separate code (two different colours) to show the distinction.

A class discussion in the early stages of the lesson served to reinforce the idea that one can create new categories or labels to deal with awkward facts and that having to decide where things fitted was an important part of the task, not an indication that the answer was wrong.

Pupil confidence was thus restored and increased with tasks 3 and 4. No-one in the class managed to complete all six tasks during the 50-minute lesson, but motivation to go on working was so high that the pupils volunteered to complete it for homework.

The teacher rated the lesson very highly. He felt that it served the purpose of consolidating previous work in chemistry as well as showing its application. Even more significant, he felt, was the fact that in the group situation these pupils were sufficiently motivated to read the passage and make sense of it, even though they would probably have been unable to do so on their own, and certainly unwilling. Also, the reading was judged to be effective: everybody made sense of the passage, and 80% managed to find the targets in the first three tasks. Task 4 was the least successful. It was agreed that this task should constitute a separate activity to be undertaken with more support, since it requires detailed research into the history of airliners and airships.

Example 3

Subject Geography
Source From J. G. Rushby, J. Bell and M. W. Dybeck, *Study Geography*
Passage Type Process
Activities Segmenting
            Tabulation

Introduction

The following passage describes a number of stages in paper making. The teacher will find it useful to carry out the following steps which are essentially the same as those that were devised for a group of 10- and 11-year-olds.

1. Mark off each stage by an oblique line (/). If possible, check your decisions concerning these boundaries by discussing them with a colleague.
2. Decide on a suitable label for each stage or phase.
3. Prepare a table in the form of a matrix, using one row for each of the phases you have identified. Row labels will be those you have selected in 2. Can you decide on appropriate headings for the columns? Here is a clue: one of the columns could be headed 'Machinery', since in each phase whatever is done is achieved by suitable machinery, and this is mentioned in the text. What about the remaining columns?

Example 3   87

Paper making

At the pulp mill the logs first go into the barking plant. Here any remaining bark is stripped off the wood and the pieces of bark are washed away by water. The wood is then chipped up by machines and the wood chips are cooked with chemicals in large tanks, known as digesters, of which Mantta has 6. This reduces the wood chips to wood pulp, which consists largely of cellulose.

In the paper mill the pulp is boiled with more chemicals and bleached, the bleach being removed by further washing with fresh water. Next, the cellulose fibres in the pulp are separated out by a process known as beating, which is carried out in large tanks, and the result looks like rather thick cream. This 'cream' is thinned by adding water, and the liquid, which consists now of about 99 parts water and 1 part cellulose, is fed by a machine on to a moving belt or apron made of very fine-meshed wire. The machine is designed to spread an even layer over the apron, which may be as much as 10 or 12 ft wide. As the apron moves on, an even sheet of something looking like thick, wet paper begins to form. Much of the water drips through the wire mesh, and more is removed by suction as the apron passes over suction boxes, but the paper still contains a large amount of moisture and further steps are taken to dry it. It leaves the wire apron and is fed on to a conveyor belt made of felt. This carries the paper slowly through sets of rollers. Some of these just squeeze the water out; others are gently heated to help with the drying. When this process is complete the paper is reeled off on to large wooden bobbins.

Choice of activity in relation to text

1. 'Process' passages lend themselves well to segmenting. Deciding on the segments immediately points the pupil in the direction of what is done at each phase, how and why. There are verbal cues like 'next' and 'then' as well as content cues to help those decisions.

Table 5
Skeleton
table for
Example 3

Phase		Machinery	
1 Barking			→
			→
↓	↓	↓	

2. The tabulation helps the pupil to know what to look for at each stage. It will serve as an aid to revision as well as assisting comprehension.

Hopefully, your table will have included 'State of material' or 'Transformation' as one of the column headings. Actually, this is the central heading for a process. Putting in a single column for 'Transformation' as in Table 6 is one solution. An alternative would be to put in two: one for 'Initial state' and one for 'Final state'. This last would allow an easy transition from a tabulation to a flow diagram, since the 'action' transforms the initial state into the final state.

Table 6 Phases in paper-making

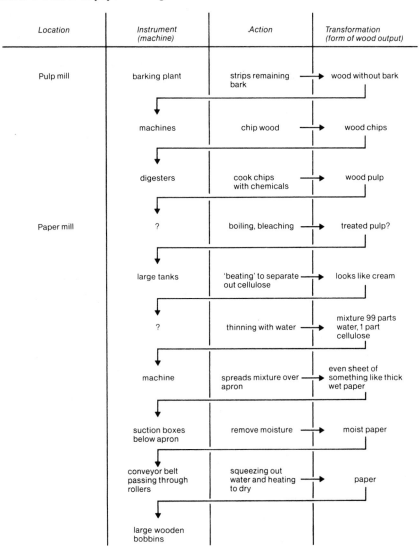

Location	Instrument (machine)	Action	Transformation (form of wood output)
Pulp mill	barking plant	strips remaining bark	wood without bark
	machines	chip wood	wood chips
	digesters	cook chips with chemicals	wood pulp
Paper mill	?	boiling, bleaching	treated pulp?
	large tanks	'beating' to separate out cellulose	looks like cream
	?	thinning with water	mixture 99 parts water, 1 part cellulose
	machine	spreads mixture over apron	even sheet of something like thick wet paper
	suction boxes below apron	remove moisture	moist paper
	conveyor belt passing through rollers	squeezing out water and heating to dry	paper
	large wooden bobbins		

Example 3   89

Lesson and transcript

The first part of the activity was designed for use with a group of 10- and 11-year-old pupils who had some previous experience of text analysis. This experience had included the analysis of another text describing a process. The project officer who was working with these pupils wanted to see if they would transfer what they had learned about one type of text to a text of the same type, ie another 'process' text.

He prepared copies of the text for a group of eight pupils of mixed abilities. He then started work with the group.

The transcript shown on pages 89–93 is a record of the discussion which took place as pupils worked on the text with the teacher present.

You will find the transcript more informative if you mark it as you read it.

Mark in one colour or code evidence which indicates that there may have been transfer from an earlier study of a process text. Mark in another the parts of the text which show pupils deliberating about where a step begins and ends. In a third colour, mark parts of the text which show pupils differentiating between 'effects' of an operation and the operation itself.

Lesson transcript
(12 minutes)
Several (more than 1): Sev
Individuals: J, R, B, A, G, S, V, D.
Teacher: T
Time sequence shown in minutes

00.30	*T*	I want you to read through this one to yourself. Read it yourself. Now you should have finished that pretty well. This, it's about . . .
	R	Making paper.
02.00	*T*	Can you give a kind of general name to what's being described here?
	V	The main things . . .
	D	Process?
	T	Process.
	G	That's a process, paper making.
	T	Now what kind of information are you being given in the process?
	V	The main parts.
	S	What the paper goes through.

	B	What the wood goes through.
	Sev	What the wood goes through, the main parts of the paper, the main parts that happens, and it does say the detail.
02.30	*T*	Can we give a name to (what we would call) the 'main part that happens'?
	Sev	The details, briefly, the general information, main parts.
03.00	*T*	What's the first main part?
	Sev	The logs go into . . . the logs are breaking . . . barking plant.
	T	Let's number these!
	Sev	The logs go into the barking plant.
	T	So that's number 1.
03.30	*R*	Whereabouts do you put it?
	B	You can put 1 up there as well after 'plant' – to show where it stops.
	T	Just put a line through if you like where you think it stops.
	A	Just the first sentence?
	S	'The wood' . . . 'the wood is then chipped up by machines.'
	G	The bark is stripped?
04.00	*J*	The bark is stripped off the wood.
	D	That's the first operation.
	T	What about number 3?
	Sev	Wood is chipped — chipped by machines.
	B	So you're counting them — pieces of bark are washed away by water is the same as remaining bark is stripped off? That's all one.
	V	I don't think it is.
	Sev	They are the same, because the wood is chipped off, the bark is off the wood, the wood is washed and then chipped by machines. No, it's washed away by water, the bark is.
	R/G/A	It's all part of the same thing, isn't it?
04.30	*Sev*	Yes.

Example 3   91

	D	Number 3 then is chipped by machines.
	T	What about number 4?
	Sev	Cooked, cooked, the wood chips are cooked.
05.00	*S*	We don't need 'digesters' do we?
	Sev	(reading to themselves) Wood to . . . wood pulp . . . wood chips are cooked.
	T	What about number 5?
	Sev	(reading on) wood chips to wood pulp – wood pulp.
	A	That's the cooking, isn't it?
	B	Yes, that's what happens when it's cooking.
	T	So, what's the next thing?
05.30	*A/J*	It is boiled with chemicals, the pulp is boiled with the chemicals and bleached.
	Sev	Yes, number 5. Yes.
	D	Where are you going to end that? At bleached?
	Sev	Yes.
	T	So what's number 6?
	V	Pulp is separated by a . . . no, pulp is just separated.
06.00	*B/D*	Yes, pulp is separated.
	G	What about that second sentence, the second line.
	A	Oh, the bleach being removed by . . . by washing.
	S	That's different, isn't it?
	Sev	Yes.
	T	You boil it and bleach it, then wash the bleach out.
	Sev	Yes. So that's number 6 then.
06.30	*R*	Where do you go from there?
	J	The bleach being removed by further washing with fresh water.
	D	Then it's separated.
	Sev	Fibres in the pulp are separated.
	T	That's 7, what about 8?
07.00	*B*	Er, that's what the result, it . . .
	A	The cream is thinned by adding water.
	B/G	That's what the result is.

	D	Yes, we need that, so we can go on to the . . . the cream is thinned.
	Sev	The cream . . . this cream is thinned by adding water. That's 8.
	D	No, we've got to have . . . er . . . it's got to be . . . er . . . what cream?
	V	Yes, because we don't know, what cream . . .
07.30	J	And the result looks like rather thick cream. This cream is thinned.
	R	We can go back and find the beginning and end of each operation and then that cream will come in then, won't it?
	Sev	Yes, thinned by water.
	T	How far do you want to go on?
	Sev	Just thinned by water.
	A	What about the next bit?
	B	Yes, this bit, 99 parts of water and 1 part cellulose.
08.00	D	We could just miss that, we don't need those for the moment do we?
	G	Where do we go to then?
	J	It is fed onto a moving belt.
	R	Where's number 8 going to?
	J	Made of fine meshed wire.
	R	Where's number 8 going to?
	Sev	We've already said that . . . water . . . this cream is thinned by adding water is number 8.
	T	And then number 9?
08.30	B	Which consists now of about 99 parts water.
	G	That's just a definition of the liquid, isn't it?
	D	Shall we do that for now?
	A	We haven't worked it out yet. What about 9?
	B	We could put that if we wanted. That which consists of 99 parts water but we can leave that out.
	R	We can leave that till we get the beginning and end bits, can't we?
	J	Where are we going to then?

Example 3   93

09.00	*A*	Is fed by machines onto a moving belt made of fine meshed wire.
	T	That's 9, is it?
	Sev	Is fed by machine onto a moving belt or apron.
	B	We don't need what the moving belt is made of do we?
	J	Is fed by a machine, where to?
09.30	*B*	Apron.
	D/G	The machine is designed to spread an even layer over the apron.
	Sev	Yes, the machine.
	R	But, what's the next thing that happens to the er . . .?
	D	Er, the water drips.
	V	Wet paper begins to form.
10.00	*Sev*	Yes, that's 10.
	A	Water drips through the wire mesh and more is removed by suction.
	D	Well, we don't need that yet . . . as the apron passes . . . the paper still contains a large amount of moisture.
	A	But the paper still . . .
	R	That's an ending part. We've done all of it now.
10.30	*B*	What about these last four lines?
	J	Is fed onto a conveyor belt made of felt.
	D	It's squeezed out . . . er, no . . . slowly. It is carried through.
	Sev	It leaves the wire apron.
11.00	*V*	Number 12 it leaves the . . . to the end.
	A	It leaves to the end?
11.30	*B/R*	It leaves right to the end, number 12 then.
	Sev	Yes, right to the end, that's just the finishing.
	A	What, five lines?
12.00	*Sev*	Yes.

Comment

'Process' is one of the text types that was briefly described on page 64. It is found quite frequently in science and geography text-books, and is very different from, say, 'structure' or 'theory'. The segmenting exercise as well as the tabulation was specifically designed to help in the recognition of this type of passage. Quite early in their secondary schooling, pupils can be taught to anticipate what kind of information will be found in a variety of different passage types. Later, they can approach the demands of examination and non-examination reading with a powerful tool.

The recognition of a text type also has immediate practical spin-offs. It is a signal to the learner to look for certain kinds of information. In the case of a process text these are steps or stages along with locations, instrument, action and transformation. These elements, or some combination of them, are always given in a description of a process. Having experience of focusing on one of these elements at a time will give pupils confidence in analysing such texts and an understanding of the different elements. This is the first step in training.

This lesson is also interesting as an example of segmenting with first-year pupils. Segmenting is a valuable technique and one that can be used for any type of passage. But it is also quite difficult and we therefore recommend that, at least to begin with, it should be restricted to texts in which the appropriate segments can be isolated with some confidence. The present passage is a good example, as is clear from the transcript which shows that even very young pupils can work effectively at segmenting a process text when they are given enough guidance to start them off.

The transcript also shows the way in which small group discussion allows pupils to ask and answer their own questions, to put forward and revise their own ideas, and to give and receive feedback. This feature of small group discussion must be compared with solitary silent reading and the answering of written questions for its full potential to be recognised. In the latter case, the only feedback available to pupils is the delayed and non-informative feedback of a cross or a tick beside a written answer.

Example 4

Subject History
Source From D. B. O'Callaghan, *Roosevelt and the United States*
Passage Type Historical situation
Activities Diagram completion
        Underlining
        Listing

Introduction

You will recognise the following passage as the one we have used to illustrate the general notion of passage type (page 61).

You will find it helpful to begin by analysing the passage for yourself

Example 4 95

and if possible comparing your solutions with someone else's. This can be done by identifying what you consider to be the main segments of information.

1. Mark these off from one another by putting in oblique lines (/) as separators (ie marking off fairly large units of information as opposed to separate clauses).

2. Compare your solution with that offered on page 61. It is well to remember that since we have not produced a rigorous set of rules for doing this kind of thing, you should not expect more than approximate agreement.

3. Consider how you would present these in the form of a flow diagram.

Hard times for the farmer

The widespread intolerance and prejudice of the 1920s made it an unhappy time for Americans who wanted to change and improve their country. Another and more numerous dissatisfied group was the farmers. During the war years, while opposing armies had trampled the crops of European farmers into the ground, American farmers had obtained high prices for their wheat and other food crops. By 1921, however, this had changed. The world was at peace and the countries of Europe no longer needed to buy such great quantities of food from the United States. At home, too, the farmer was finding it more difficult to sell his products. For one thing, the country's population was no longer increasing as quickly as before, partly because of the passing of a law in 1921 which limited the number of immigrants allowed to enter the United States. The boom in motor vehicles also hit the farmer, for as people stopped using horse-drawn vehicles the demand for animal feedings stuffs declined.

For these and other reasons more and more American farmers found themselves in difficulties in the 1920s. Large numbers of them lost money steadily, and by 1924 six hundred thousand of them were bankrupt. Members of Congress from farming areas persuaded the Government to try to help. It was made easier for farmers to borrow money to help them over their difficulties. A Farm Board was set up which bought crops like wheat and cotton, which the farmers could not otherwise have sold, with money from the Government. But despite these efforts to help the farmers, they found it more and more difficult to make ends meet. As American industry climbed steadily to ever higher peaks of prosperity, American farming slid with increasing speed into a deep state of depression.

Classroom support

The segmenting exercise is far from easy, since it requires one to analyse the passage sentence by sentence and decide (a) just what information is being conveyed and (b) how far this is a new item rather than a natural expansion of the information that went before.

The passage and the chapter from which it was taken have been used as the basis for historical study by a teacher working with third-year CSE students. (This same series of lessons has been drawn on for Example 11 in Part II of this book.) Many of these pupils were slow readers and segmenting without support would have been out of the question. In fact the passage was used with more than one group, and we are therefore in a position to present two alternative approaches.

Figure 10 Hard times for the farmer – captions and flow diagrams

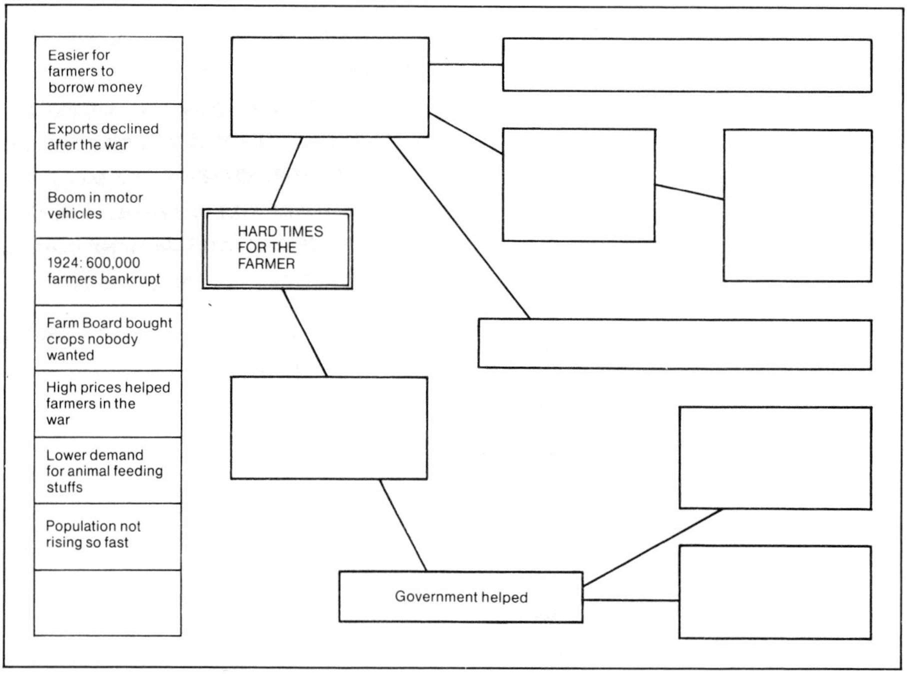

First solution: Figure 10 is a handout given to pupils by the teacher the first time he decided to use this passage as the basis for a text-based lesson. The task was to compare the text with the diagram and the captions on the left, then decide where these should be inserted within the flow diagram to represent the sense of the original passage.

Example 4   97

Comment

When considering the course of this lesson and its outcome, the teacher was not altogether satisfied. Certainly, judged in terms of outcome, the lesson was successful. The pupils could do what they were asked to do. But were they being sufficiently stretched, was there enough scope for using their own initiative? Was it indeed essential for the teacher to pre-select the key items and for the teacher to reformulate these and for the teacher to draw up the outline of the diagrammatic representation?

Second solution: On the next occasion, the teacher devised an entirely different method. This time it was the pupils who were to do the work, but once again, because of the difficulty of conducting the analysis from scratch, they were given a good deal of guidance, as shown in the following set of instructions:

Instructions given to pupils: second session

Stage one
Begin by talking. Do *not* write anything down yet.
Sort out with your partner what you see as:

1. the *problem* here. Who had it? What was it?

2. the suggested *causes*. How many are there? What were they? How and why did they make things difficult?

3. the attempted *solutions*. How many are there? What were they? Who made them? How were they supposed to help?

4. The eventual *result*. How well did things work out?

Stage two
Move on to underlining. Use a different kind of underlining for each task here if you can.

1. Underline some words which together make a useful statement of the problem (say about 10 words in all).

2. Underline some words which together give an explanation of the three suggested causes (say about 40 words in all).

3. Underline some words which together make a statement about the two solutions which were tried in an attempt to solve the problem (try to be really economical here and underline fewer than 10 words – seven might well be enough).

4. Underline some words which together make a statement of how well the problem had been solved (try for a six-word version).

NB You can underline odd words here and there: they don't all have to be in a running line (but it's nice if afterwards the underlined words make something of a sensible sentence). You don't have to match your ration of words exactly but if you're going way over the top, call in a teacher for advice.

Stage three
End with a little bit of writing. It's important to use your own words, and try to keep within a strict ration of 40 altogether. See if you can manage with less and still do a proper job.

   Work together with a partner. There are to be two versions: a first draft and an improved final copy. Arrange for one of you to 'push the pen' for each attempt but be sure you both decide equally what words are to go down at every stage.

First draft. Write four headings, nicely spaced:
1. problem   *2.* causes   *3.* solutions   *4.* result

Cover the text – so you *can't* see it – and 'talk up' a statement for each heading. If you can't remember things well enough for this, cheat (by peeping at the text) until you can.

Then, *keeping the text covered*, 'write in' your first draft version of suitable statements to go under the headings. Check to see you haven't used too many words. Change your mind and alter things where you wish. Consult with a teacher.

Final version Compare your first version *both* with the text and with what other pairs have done. When you feel you are ready, write up a final version.

Comment

Once again, the lesson was successful in terms of outcomes. The pupils did end up with succinct sets of notes featuring problem, causes, remedies and result. What is more, they were active and involved, and of course the teacher was ever present to help when needed.

   It is interesting to compare the form of this lesson with the previous one and also with the analysis suggested for teachers at the beginning of this example. In the first lesson, the short captions were devised by the teacher; in the second, the pupils were asked to work these out for themselves. However, they were given a great deal of direction both for finding them and for grouping them under the right headings. All this our own teacher readers were asked to do without guidance beyond what was needed to achieve some sort of agreement on the scale of analysis (coarse versus fine grained).

   Taken together, the three tasks in this second lesson make up a very carefully thought out underlining task, including a great deal of help for finding the ideas and also for using the underlining as a first step in devising captions or labels to summarise each unit of information.

Example 4   99

Better diagrams?

Compared with the first lesson, there is one possible loss: diagrammatic representation at its best can be used as a visual resource when revising. While constructing the four lists may involve a similar amount of work to completion of the diagram (less than its construction), these lists fail to bring out the causal structure of the ideas contained in the passage as effectively as one could do using a diagram.

Clearly the main consideration was how best to apportion a certain amount of time which was limited. Perhaps another was dissatisfaction with the actual diagram used in the first lesson: how much more does it convey than the lists of the second version?

The central problem is to find a way of separating out causal and temporal relations. One possible solution to this is shown in Figure 12. Note that this uses certain simple conventions. They are not the only possible conventions, but it is worth stressing that in the long run if children are to gain the maximum benefit from making their own diagrams they will need to have some conventions, and these will need to be taught.

Figure 11 Hard times for the farmer – visual revision aid

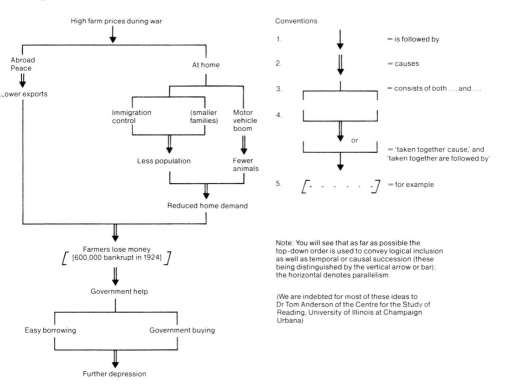

Example 5

Subject History

Source From I. M. Tennen, *This England from the Earliest Times to 1485*

Passage Type Classification

Activities Underlining
        Segmenting
        Labelling
        Simulation

Introduction

The passage is a relatively long one which makes it all the more important to study it very carefully before designing a suitable lesson round it. After reading it through quickly, you should first of all segment the text and decide on an appropriate label for each segment. If possible, discuss these with a colleague. The following suggestions should prove useful.

1. The passage as a whole breaks up into three broad sections, with the central section being the longest and the most important. Find the breaks between these sections.

2. Look for small segments. To save time, confine your analysis to the central section. See if you can find five subsections within the main central portion.

The Domesday Book

We have a splendid source of information about life in England at the end of the Conqueror's reign. It came to be known later as Domesday Book (because it was the book of 'final judgment'). No such thorough survey of a whole land, its people and its livestock was ever made anywhere at any time till recent years. It was undertaken partly because of another threat of a great Danish invasion. William meant to exercise the old right of the Saxon kings to levy a special tax to meet the expenses of dealing with such an invasion. Most of the money would have to come from profits of every kind derived from the ownership of land. He also wanted precise information to help his judges to decide the endless disputes about the ownership of land. Lastly, he wanted all the information he could get about the realm of which he was proud to be king – 'how it was peopled and with what sort of men'.

He sent officials out to groups of counties where they visited the chief towns and interviewed small committees of local men, English and French, from groups of villages and asked them certain questions, recording the answers only when they had reason to be satisfied their information was correct.

Example 5   *101*

Later other officials went round, checking the first reports and any serious differences between the first and the second set of figures meant a summons to the earlier officials to explain the difference before the King or his chief ministers.

The information was finally recorded, partly under the headings of tenants-in-chief and other large landowners, partly under place headings. We still possess the two volumes in which the completed survey was later written down. It remained the basis of land taxation for centuries and it is one of the greatest historical treasures in the world.

As regards the information required from each village or manor, the commissioners asked first of all what the village was called, and for most of our villages that is their first record in history. They wanted to know 'how many "hides" are there?' We are not certain exactly what that means, but it looks as if it meant the entire area of the village from a tax-paying point of view. The next item states that there is land for so many (ox-) teams. This seems to mean the amount of land which was cultivated in the time of Edward the Confessor (the reign of Harold being ignored). The next two items are the amount of land cultivated as demesne and the amount cultivated by peasants, both reckoned in terms of work for so many teams of eight oxen. (In those days horses were not used for ploughing.) The number of peasants of each grade was given.

The areas of meadow and pasture land were recorded as two quite separate items. Meadow land was reserved for growing hay and it always had a stream flowing down one side for irrigation to produce richer grass. Pasture land was the rougher ground on the coarse grass and weeds of which the livestock could try to browse most of the year. They were recorded under the headings of plough-ox teams, horses (mainly riding), cattle, pigs, sheep and goats.

You might have guessed that most of the above information would be required and you might think it was quite enough as a basis for claiming land-taxes. But remember that just as income-tax officials nowadays want to know the tax-payer's income from every source, so the commissioners wanted information about every sort of profit that could be made from the ownership of land.

They were very inquisitive about the woods, especially how many pigs fed there. If there were oaks and beeches the pigs would get a little fatter in the autumn, before they were slaughtered, grunting happily amid the masses of acorns and beech mast. The lord could charge his villeins as much as one pig in ten for 'pannage', permission to graze their swine in the woodland. "Is there an eyrie in the woods?" the commissioners wanted to know, because if so the lord would make something out of selling the young hawks to his friends for training.

"Are there (wild bee) hives there?" for that meant honey, mead and wax for church candles.

Last, but not least, "were there any deer-hays in the wood?" These were enclosures where hunted deer could be shot. Deer carcases meant profit as well as good sport. All this was in addition to the woodland's value as a source of timber and fuel.

Land can be valuable for industry as well as farming. Most villages had a water-mill for grinding corn and malt. The stream that enriched the hay meadow and provided eels and other fish, turned the great creaking wheel. (There were no wind-mills in England yet.) The villeins were compelled to have their corn ground at the lord's mill, paying him 'the 16th grain', and in some cases he could compel them to transport his new set of mill-stones. This profitable monopoly of grinding has sometimes lasted till recent times and large sums have been paid to modern lords of the manor to end it.

Sources of fish were carefully noted. They were specially valuable in an age when the Church forbade the eating of meat on many days of the year. The fish most commonly mentioned in Domesday are eels, but we also hear of lampreys, salmon, and, off the south-east coast, herrings. There was no question of rod-and-line sport in those days. They were after food and used traps and various forms of nets.

Salt works are frequently mentioned, for great quantities of salt were necessary. They could not afford to feed all their cattle and pigs in winter, when the outdoor grazing was no longer available, so many of these were slaughtered in November and the carcases were cut up and kept in barrels of salt.

Quarries were a source of great profit when there was so much building of stone castles and monasteries going on, and the ownership of lead and iron mines had to be noted too. Vineyards were not uncommon in this country in those days, for the Frenchmen did not share the Saxon's passion for ale.

We get some information about the royal castles from Domesday Book because each castle had an estate attached to it for its upkeep. The warden of a royal castle was called the 'castellan' or 'constable' and it was a post of great honour.

It is mostly a picture of the countryside that Domesday Book gives us, but there are glimpses of the town, because the land on which it was built usually belonged to a lord who could exercise some of the manorial rights over its citizens and claim rents and market fees, if not work rights.

When the corporations of some of our northern cities were being formed, roughly about 100 years ago, it came as an unpleasant surprise to the citizens to find out that there was still a local lord of the

Example 5   *103*

manor who held all sorts of rights in their town.

It was only after a long dispute that Manchester, for instance, was able to cancel all rights of the lord of the manor for a payment of £200,000.

In one of our Channel Islands, the lord of the manor (for many years it has been 'the Dame') still has ruling powers and many feudal rights. Corn must be ground only at the Dame's mill, for which she is paid the 10th grain. She is entitled to a tithe of the fowl and a tithe of the sheep's wool.

This case of a Dame of the manor instead of the usual Seigneur is a reminder that women could hold any rank under the 'feudal system', from tenant-in-chief to villein. We find married women holding large estates without any sort of control by their husbands. At the other end of the scale we find records of women having to do ploughing for the lord of the manor as well as other heavy farm work in return for their holding of land. Women are often described as carters or waggoners. When women labourers are paid they often received the same pay as men.

Churches and monasteries are registered in Domesday not merely because the Normans were pious but because of the estates that paid for their upkeep. The number of parish priests, too, was noted, because they were usually appointed by the lord of the manor and even that could be a source of profit.

The owners and the money values of the manor in 1066 had to be recorded as well as those of 1086. The King's officials had also to note whether more could be got out of the manor, ie, whether the lord by better management or harsher treatment of his tenants could make more and so be taxed more.

Domesday Book, in its own way, is just as much a proof of the power and energy of the Normans as are the great cathedrals. The English did not like it, not so much because it placed heavier burdens on them (many of them were not much worse off than before 1066), but because to them it seemed to call for too much undignified 'snooping'.

Choice of activity in relation to text

Here, to begin with, is our own analysis of the passage. There are three main sections. The first, which might be called *historical context*, consists of the first four paragraphs. The second is essentially a *categorisation* of the *information* collected by the officials and subsequently recorded. This is made up of nine paragraphs and ends at 'the Saxon's passion for ale'.

The remainder of the passage is concerned with what might be called the *historical significance* of the Domesday Book.

Within the central section, we would identify the following categories of information: *name and size of manor*, ending half way down the first paragraph in the section with the words 'being ignored'; *land cultivation*, ending at the end of the next paragraph 'sheep and goats'; then the next paragraph on its own, being a commentary on the *comprehensiveness* of the list; next follow two paragraphs dealing with *wealth from woodland*; then a further four paragraphs devoted to *other sources*. Needless to say, this last blocking is a little arbitrary, and so too perhaps is the decision to treat the paragraph commencing 'You might have guessed' as a sub-section on its own.

Because the central section is a categorisation of the information contained in the book together with comments on why this was sought, and because that detail was seen as significant by teachers, the decision to focus on that section was hard to resist. However, this study was preceded by a brief look at the first paragraph, designed to set the scene. As to the actual tasks, the first job was clearly to highlight the structure of the categorisation contained in the text, since it is a useful way of grasping the information. So pupils were asked to segment and to label.

Now it would have been possible to go on to a tabulation, using one row for each source of wealth and perhaps four columns headed, say: 'Source', 'How exploited', 'Typical questions', 'Comment'. If necessary such a task could be made easier by getting the pupils to begin by underlining the relevant phrases and sentences, using a different colour for each of these headings. Another alternative would be to produce a sort of family-tree diagram to bring out the categorisation structure in the text. In fact, the teachers involved did neither of these things. Instead they opted for a simulation exercise which achieved exactly the same effects and was at least as enjoyable and memorable an experience.

Class work

The passage has been studied by a number of groups ranging in age from 10 to 13. The form of lesson was agreed by members of the project team and the teachers concerned. Essentially this fell into three parts.

To begin with, pupils studied the first section of the text, concentrating on the first paragraph. Here they were asked:

1. to underline three sentences which tell you why the Domesday survey was ordered;

2. to underline one or more sentences which tell you what the questions of the survey are likely to be about.

Example 6   105

The search for these targets was followed by a class discussion in order to reach a concensus about the general nature of the survey.

After this, pupil attention was directed to the more specific nature of the survey. They were asked to locate those paragraphs which gave details about the information recorded in the Domesday Book. Having found these, they were to concentrate on them. In some cases children actually did the segmenting and labelling of the second section more or less exactly as outlined above. Others discussed the successive sections of the text less formally before proceeding to the next exercise which was a simulation. Working in pairs, children used the clues in the text in order to design questions which might have been used by members of the Domesday Commission.

Not surprisingly, this exercise provided material for two stimulating lessons. It shows that analysing a text is not incompatible with imaginative exploitation of its potential. The simulation exercise was more motivating than a written record would have been and it achieved the same ends: the pupils had to concentrate on the sorts of questions and supplementaries that would produce the information the king wanted.

Example 6

Subject History
Source From M. Macefield, 'Sir Thomas More' in *The House of History*
Passage Type Narrative
Activities Underlining
        Listing
        Pupil questions

Introduction

Read the passage through. Then, working with a colleague, mark the text as follows:

  1. underline no more than three sentences (they need not be consecutive) which show most clearly the central or critical event in the story;
  2. mark any words, phrase, or sentence which provide information about Thomas More and his character.

Sir Thomas More

The best loved name that has come down to us from the England of the Renaissance and the Reformation is that of Sir Thomas More. Even in his boyhood his lively mind and sunny nature won high praise from Cardinal Morton, Archbishop of Canterbury and trusted counsellor of Henry VII, in whose household he was page. One day, when the boy was waiting upon the archbishop and his guests at dinner, Cardinal Morton said: "This child here waiting at table, whoever shall live to see it, will prove a marvellous rare man."

A few years later the young Thomas More won the hearts of Colet and Erasmus, and Erasmus wrote to one of his friends that nature never made a sweeter and happier character than More's.

Yet this young man with his great talents, his many friends, and his love of fun, longed to give his life to the service of God, and thought of becoming a Carthusian monk. It was Dean Colet who persuaded him that he could also serve God in the world of men of learning and affairs; but More always wore a hair-shirt next to his skin, and spent part of every day alone in prayer.

At the wish of his father, who was a judge, he became a lawyer, and soon made an honourable name in his profession. Later, when he was Lord Chancellor, the highest lawyer in the kingdom, he went every morning to the court where his father was judge, and kneeled down to receive his blessing before he began his own day's work.

More's marriage was very characteristic of him. He fell in love with the second of a family of pretty sisters, but he knew that in those days it was a disgrace to an elder sister if a younger one married first, and so he "framed his fancy" to the eldest instead. The marriage was very happy, and More taught his wife, a country girl who had not learned very much, to love literature and practise music. Their happiness only lasted six years, when the wife died, leaving him with a son and three daughters.

He married again, and it was the second wife who was mistress of the charming house at Chelsea, of which Erasmus wrote (to a friend in Holland) that "his whole house breathes happiness, and no one enters it who is not the better for the visit".

His son-in-law describes it as a fair house by the riverside, with a garden and orchard, and in the garden a building known as the gallery, to which More could withdraw when he wished to be alone for prayer.

This same son-in-law reports that in sixteen years spent in his house he "never perceived him so much as once to fume". More himself wrote gaily to his children: "I have given you kisses enough, but stripes hardly ever." He taught them that they must "take virtue and learning for their meat and play but for their sauce."

Erasmus tells us that even the birds of Chelsea loved him and flocked about him to be fed, and in his garden he kept a tame fox, a monkey, a ferret, and a weasel.

Every day, after morning prayer together, his children went with

Example 6   *107*

him to the riverside to give him a last kiss as he stepped into the boat which carried him down London's great highway, the Thames, to his work.

Love of books and fun did not prevent More from being a most capable lawyer, and his strict justice won him great honour in days when judges and statesmen were not always ashamed to take bribes. When he was Lord Chancellor a lady whose case he had to try sent him a glove filled with gold coins. More poured out the gold and told her messenger to take it back to her, but added that he would keep the glove, as it would be rude to refuse a lady's present.

Such a rare man could not long escape the notice of young Henry VIII, with his keen love for scholars of the New Learning. Soon the king insisted upon More becoming one of his Privy Council, and also made him Lord Chancellor. Erasmus says that no man ever struggled harder for a high place in the king's service than More struggled to escape. When the king found his talk so delightful that he would scarcely let him leave him to go home, More pretended to have grown dull and stupid, until the king was willing to part with him for a time.

But Henry followed More home; he, too, felt the charm of the house at Chelsea, and he would walk in the garden with his arm round More's neck, and insisted on staying to dine with him.

When his son-in-law congratulated him on the king's friendship More replied wisely: "Son Roper, I may tell you I have no cause to be proud thereof, for if my head would win him a castle in France it should not fail to go off".

At last a time came when More felt it his duty to cross the king's will. He did not think it right for Henry to divorce Queen Catherine, and because of the disagreement he gave up the office of Lord Chancellor. Then he was summoned to attend the king's wedding with Anne Boleyn, and he would not go, and so fell into great disfavour.

Now Henry determined that he would make all the leading men in the kingdom bow to his will and accept him as head of the Church. Accordingly a number of bishops and others were summoned to Lambeth, More amongst them, and ordered to take an oath declaring the king to be Supreme Head of the Church of England.

More refused; he did not believe that any man who was not a priest could be head of the Church.

Very soon he was sent as a prisoner to the Tower of London; as he entered he had to take off his coat and put on a coarse (and not very clean) one provided at the gate. After a while even his beloved books were taken from him, and the Lieutenant of the Tower told him, with tears in his eyes, that he dare not give him anything better than the rough food of ordinary prisoners.

From his wife poor More had little comfort. "Son Roper" describes how she sent to scold him, beginning briskly, "Tillyvally, Mr More!" And she asked him how he, who had always been thought so wise a man, could "now so play the fool as to lie here in this close, filthy prison, and be content to be shut up amongst the mice and rats," when he might so easily take the oath and be set free.

To this More quietly replied: "I pray thee, good Mrs Alice, tell me one thing."

"What is that?" quoth she.

"Is not this house as nigh Heaven as mine own?"

His daughter Margaret, the wife of "Son Roper" was his greatest comfort. On hearing from her how Anne Boleyn kept the court merry with dancing and sporting, he said that she might dance until she spurned off men's heads like footballs, but he feared her own head would dance the same dance some day. "Alas, Meg, alas!" he exclaimed, "for it pittieth me to remember to what misery she, poor soul, shortly shall come."

The day came when More was condemned to be executed for treason. The night before his death he wrote a last letter to his daughter Margaret, although all he had to write with was a piece of coal, and also sent to her the hair-shirt he had worn, as he did not wish to make a show in public of his private penance.

At the last his sense of fun was uppermost. He found the steps to the block shaky, and said to the Lieutenant of the Tower: "Assist me up, and in coming down I will shift for myself."

At the news of his death a shock ran all through Europe, and the Emperor Charles V, who had finer feelings than Henry VIII, declared that if he had possessed such a servant he would rather have lost the best city in his empire than him.

More's chief memorial is his book *Utopia*, a name formed from Greek, and meaning "nowhere", in which he tells the story of an imaginary land whose people ordered their lives far better than in the old countries of Europe.

There was a king in Utopia, but his crown was taken from him if he tried to "enslave his people"; the children all went to school, no one who could work need be poor, men were not hanged for stealing (as they were in England in More's time, so that they were tempted to murder as well if it would save them from discovery); and all were free to worship God in the way they thought best.

More's book was read in many countries, and set men thinking. To this day we speak of ideas which are almost too good to be carried out in this world as "Utopian".

Example 6   *109*

Choice of activity in relation to text

Biographical and fictional texts abound with passages in which character description is interwoven with narrative. In history at least, one is entitled to assume that the narrative is factually correct. By contrast, the description of character involves interpretation. So sorting out narrative from character is essential to separate two distinct strands in the argument. It also serves to distinguish between fact and opinion. Searching for 'the critical event' forces the reader to decide which sections carry the narrative and which do not. An alternative would have been to underline *all* the narrative sections in one colour.

The second task, underlining, is of particular interest because it may well have presented you, as a sophisticated adult reader, with some difficulty. Very probably, you will have found that many sections offer evidence of character even though they are also records of events. What is more, some passages like the incident with the glove are deliberately presented as evidence of character, while others provide indirect evidence.

Underlining pre-selected categories of information is often the easiest of exercises one can set for pupils because here the teacher offers most support. The close interweaving and even overlap between story and evaluation make it more difficult here, but also eminently worthwhile.

Pupils were asked to do the two tasks suggested for teacher readers on page 105. In addition, they were invited to divide the observations on character into two categories in any way they could. (It was hoped that they would discover either the division into gentle and tough aspects of character, or the division into statement and evidence.)

Classroom support

This lesson was designed for a second-year, mixed-ability class in a Nottinghamshire comprehensive school.

The teacher felt that the Thomas More extract was highly readable for most pupils, but required reflective, critical reading, to be properly used.

Table 7 shows most of the phrases and sentences which were selected in answer to the two questions (each group having made only three choices for each question).

Table 7 Pupil answers to questions 1 and 2 on Sir Thomas More

Question 1	*Central events in More's life*
para 1	In Cardinal Morton's household he was a page
para 4	he became a lawyer
	then he was Lord Chancellor, the highest lawyer in the kingdom

para 12	Henry VIII insisted upon More becoming one of his Privy Council
para 15	because of the disagreement he gave up the office of Lord Chancellor. Then he was summoned to attend the king's wedding with Anne Boleyn, and he would not go, and so fell into great disfavour.
para 17	More refused
	he was sent as a prisoner to the Tower of London
para 22	More was condemned to be executed for treason
para 24	at the news of his death a shock ran all through Europe
para 25	More's chief memorial is his book *Utopia*
Question 2	Clues to More's character
para 1	lively mind, sunny nature
para 2	won the hearts of Colet and Erasmus
	sweeter and happier character
para 3	great talents, love of fun
	More always wore a hair shirt next to his skin, and spent part of every day alone in prayer
para 5	The marriage was very happy
	happiness only lasted six years
para 6	married again, his whole house breathes happiness
para 8	sixteen years
	so much as once to fume
para 9	even the birds loved him
	he kept a tame fox, a monkey, a ferret and a weasel
para 11	love of books and fun
	his strict justice won him great honour
para 12	no man ever struggled harder for a high place in the king's service than More struggled to escape
	king found his talk so delightful
para 15	at last a time came when More felt it his duty to cross the king's will
para 16	now Henry determined that he would make all the leading men in the kingdom bow to his will and accept him as head of the Church
para 17	he did not believe that any man who was not a priest could be head of the Church
para 23	At the last his sense of fun was uppermost

Pupil marking of the central events in the story shows that the support of a familiar framework, the narrative, enabled them to identify critical events with a degree of confidence. They are helped by the familiar story framework and also by verbal cues like "at last a time came when . . ." and "he would not go and *so* fell into great disfavour".

By contrast, the portrayal of More's character is harder to read. On the one hand, his obvious virtues are clearly spelt out by the writer: 'his lively

Example 6   *111*

mind', and 'sunny nature'. Evidence in support of this portrayal is provided by quotes from Erasmus.

On the other hand, the sterner and more singular qualities of the man can only be inferred from his actions – his challenging of the king, his refusal to take the oath, his resistance to persuasion – or from his own observations and forebodings which show a shrewd assessment of the situation. That pupils were less sensitive to More's political sophistication than to his human qualities is indeed suggested by the fact that his observation to Son Roper was not underlined at all.

It should be stressed that these pupils were relatively inexperienced and this was the first lesson of its kind that year. Later on, they became more thoughtful, especially as their teacher was able to draw out many of the missing insights in the course of classroom discussion which followed the group exercise.

This discussion was very lively, and in the course of it all of the following questions were raised by the pupils themselves:

1. The nature of the evidence used: from what sources did Erasmus obtain his observations? What about the other commentators on More?

2. From what sources were other episodes drawn?

3. What is the bias of the writer?

4. How accessible is More's own writing?

5. What can we say about the nature of historical evidence in general?

Among the topics judged to be relevant for further study were the sources of Erasmus' observations and More's *Utopia*.

Comment

Once again, the lesson shows that it is not always necessary to follow up an underlining or labelling activity with a tabulation or diagram. Not every lesson based on a text must end up with an alternative visual presentation of the information. Often this will be the case, and there is no doubt that it can be worth while. But here at any rate the discussion and the questions that it raised furthered the pupils' learning both of this passage and of others like it.

There is another important issue to consider. This example is a good illustration of the kind of question that fits in with our emphasis on the underlying structure. Both the first question (picking out the key events in the story) and the second (finding clues to character) are standard sorts of questions, in the sense that you can often find similar questions inserted by text-book writers. In the absence of such provision, teachers are quite happy to set them for themselves.

On the other hand, what we have deliberately avoided are questions like: 'What was More's attitude to Henry's divorce?' or 'How do we know that More liked animals?' These would be specific questions that simply invite the reader to scan the passage for a particular target sentence.

Let us say at once that finding such sentences is an intelligent and purposeful activity and one that we would want pupils to be good at. It involves scanning for key words like names of animals or 'divorce', 'marry', etc, and scanning for half-remembered places as when one recalls that a certain bit of the passage dealt with More's love of animals. Effective readers have to be able to scan passages in this way, both at first reading and on re-reading, depending on the context and purpose of their study. Then why avoid such questions?

There are three reasons for doing so. One is that the same ends are achieved by asking the more general questions. For instance, both love of animals and disapproval of unprincipled behaviour on the part of kings were a part of More's character. So, by asking the pupils to find how his character is described in the passage, we can get them to decide what sorts of descriptions and incidents might be relevant, then look for them. (To begin with, they are more likely to go about it the opposite way: skim each paragraph quickly and then decide whether or not it is relevant. But this is nearly as good, and it is certainly a necessary step along the way.) This means they will be practising the scanning, but they will also know why they are scanning, because they will have discovered how the target sentences fit in with the structure of the passage as a whole.

The second reason is that by putting the general questions, we stimulate thinking and discussion. The pupils get involved in what they are doing. This is obvious from the kinds of questions that came up in discussion and especially from the liveliness of that discussion. (Answering specific teachers' questions can only be made exciting by turning a lesson into a competition or panel game, and it is difficult to see how that could carry over into such things as effective study at home.)

The last reason is one that we have tried to insist on throughout this book. By asking general questions, we are seeking to alert the pupils to the kind of passage they are dealing with: one that tells a story about people and the part they played in historic events, but at the same time (a) conveys information about the people's character and their motives and (b) gives us some hints (not always deliberate) about the kind of evidence that the historian has been using. In other words, the activity as a whole is designed not only to enhance their appreciation of this bit of history, but also to equip them with a number of general insights. These

Example 7   *113*

in turn should enable them to approach other similar passages with more confidence and a sense of purpose.

Example 7

Subject Science/Physics

Source T. Duncan, *Exploring Physics*, Book 2

Passage Type Theme (natural force)

Activities Underlining
            Tabulation

Introduction

Read the text through to the end. Then, with a colleague, mark and label those parts of the text which discuss:

1. three effects of current;

2. different measures of current;

3. the applications of the effects of current;

4. the requirements of a circuit.

Exploring electricity

Electrical appliances such as lamps, heaters, irons, cookers, vacuum cleaners, washing machines, refrigerators, etc play an important part in our daily lives, whilst radio and television sets are familiar objects in our homes. These are but a few of the inventions of electrical science and if we are curious we will want to know at least the principles on which they operate. This is one reason for exploring electricity, but there is another ...

The study of atoms has shown that electricity requires circuits. Some circuits are tiny like those in computers, whilst those forming the Grid System stretch great distances all over the country to distribute electricity from power stations.

Simple circuits

Circuits must have wires or metallic connectors all the way round from the battery to the lamp (or any other electrical appliance) and back to the battery again. Two connections are therefore made to every battery and every lamp.

You will now have realised that for full normal brightness one lamp requires one battery, and (in this type of circuit) two lamps require two batteries correctly connected, three lamps need three batteries and so on.

Scientists say, for a reason we will discover later, that there is a current in an electric circuit. For the present we will take the brightness of one of our lamps as a measure of current and 'one lamp's-worth' of current as the current which lights one lamp to its full, normal brightness.

Conductors and switches

A circuit only works if there is a complete metal path all the way round. Metals can carry currents and are called electrical conductors. We will now investigate various other materials to see whether they are conductors or insulators (non-conductors).

A switch gives us control over a circuit and is just something which completes the metallic path when we put it on and forms a gap in the circuit when it is off. Here, we must 'bridge that gap' with a switch!

Effects of a current

We cannot see, hear or smell an electric current and in our experiments so far we have relied on a lamp to show when current is present. The lamp emits light because the current makes the small coil of very thin wire (called the lamp filament) extremely hot, white hot in fact. This heating of things is one of the effects of an electric current and you can now check for yourself that it does happen.

Many electrical appliances use the heating effect of a current. The 'elements' of electric irons, fires and cookers are made from wire of an alloy known as 'Nichrome'. This alloy contains nickel, chromium and iron and does not oxidise when heated.

An electric current has another effect by which it can be detected.

A lighted lamp, a wire that gets hot, or a coil that magnetises iron are all clues given by electric currents.

A current balance

Judging the size of a current from the brightness of a lamp is not a very satisfactory procedure. What objections are there to it? Using the magnetic effect it is possible to construct a simple instrument which enables more reliable current measurements to be made.

Ammeters

As a unit of current the 'lamp's-worth' is not very satisfactory since even lamps that are supposed to be the same can differ quite a lot.

Example 7   *115*

Electrical engineers and physicists use the ampere (shortened to A) as their unit and they measure current by using an instrument called an ammeter. You will learn later how this works, but briefly it does the same job as the current balance you made and has a pointer which moves over a scale marked in amperes. Like the current balance it also depends on the magnetic effect.

An ammeter is an expensive instrument and should be treated with care. One of its terminals is marked with a plus or positive sign (+) and the other with a minus or negative sign (–). The signs tell you how to connect the ammeter into a circuit. The + terminal (sometimes coloured red) should be connected either directly, or through lamps, switches, etc, to the positive terminal of the battery. The positive terminal of the battery is the small metal stud in the centre of one end. Damage may be caused if you connect an ammeter the wrong way round and so you should always ask your teacher to check the circuit before you complete it.

Classroom activity in relation to text

The activity was designed to direct attention to the important elements of information in the text and to emphasise the relations amongst these elements. This is why the order in which the targets were given did not correspond to the sequence in which they were discussed in the text.

'Effects of current' is the basic element of information – that from which everything else follows. This is why it was the first target. As the conceptual core of the information it gives rise to certain principles and applications. An analysis which focuses on a basic concept first is designed to structure the processing of information so as to bring out the underlying conceptual structure.

The text is discursive, seeking to emphasise the practical content for a study of electricity and inviting the the reader to reflect. A number of important questions are left unanswered. This is to be expected in a text in which advanced concepts are being introduced to pupils perhaps for the first time. It is interesting to compare this introduction to electric current and circuits with the highly structured chapter on electric current in *Physics for Today and Tomorrow* by the same author (John Murray, 1977).

Because this introductory text is rather loosely structured, the context and way in which it is used are all important.

The teacher who originally used it in the project was working with a third-year, mixed-ability class. Pupils had already done the relevant experimental work on circuits.

In this context the re-reading of the chapter from which the extract was taken was intended to be a revision lesson. The objective was to get pupils to revise the principles on which the use and measurement of electricity are based and to relate these to applications.

Pupils worked in twos to underline the following targets:

1. the facts (or principles) we make use of when building circuits along which electricity can travel;

2. the fact we make use of when building in switches to stop and start the movement of an electric current;

3. the effects which enable us to detect when an electric current is present;

4. the facts about electricity which enable us to make irons, fires and cookers.

Comment

1. The pupils found the task too demanding and teacher support was required throughout the lesson. Nevertheless, interest and concentration were maintained and it was agreed by all that the activity had been extremely rewarding. Indeed, the teacher rated the level of learning to be very high.

2. Nevertheless, the project team (who had planned the original lesson) felt in retrospect that the lesson as given would have been more appropriate as an introduction than as a revision lesson. Ideally, a revision lesson should incorporate a summarising or restructuring of important information. For this example, the summary should show the relationship between the principles of electricity, the effect of an electric current, and the application of these effects. Also, it should be clear and helpful for later revision.

We therefore devised an alternative lesson plan for the same passage. This consists of the underlining and labelling with which you began this study to be followed by a table completion activity using the outline table shown in Figure 12.

Further comment on the table and its uses

The task of constructing a table or completing one is ideally suited for showing relationships which link different elements of information. At the same time, your own analysis will have shown you that if the activity is to be successful it should be preceded by underlining and labelling.

Example 7   *117*

Figure 12 Table for completion on Electricity passage

Effects of a current 1. 2. 3.
How to set up an electric current and make it do work
Two ways of measuring current 1. 2.
Application of electricity 1. 2. 3. 4.

Notice that the table is not a two-way table like Table 5. Instead, there are four separate sections, all but one of which is a listing. This is because there is nothing here to correspond with the phases of the process where we could find parallel bits of information in each phase. It is true that one could devise a presentation of the topic which would make a close link between effects and applications, but that would be a little artificial as well as unjustified by the text which was chosen.

On the other hand, the key elements are not peculiar to this text but are very definitely brought out in it. The key elements are:

1. the effects of a force;
2. the set up needed to produce those effects;
3. how to measure the force by its effects;
4. applications.

These key elements can always be identified in any discussion of electricity, as well as in texts describing other forces such as gravity or mechanical energy.

The recurrence of the same categories of information in different contexts eases the teacher's analysis. It means that s/he can draw on experience in analysing passages instead of having to treat each new text as if it were unique.

Example 8

Subject Biology

Source From E. J. Ewington and D. F. Moore, *Human Biology and Hygiene*

Passage Type Mechanisms

Activities Underlining
          Diagram completion
          Ordered listing
          Flow chart

Introduction

The following passage deals with the fine structure of the kidney and its action. We are a assuming that you already know that:

1. the kidneys are two bean-shaped organs situated on the dorsal wall of the abdominal cavity, hard against the lower ribs – which offer them some protection;

2. the function of the kidneys is to get rid of waste matter in the blood;

3. blood from the aorta flows to the kidney through the renal artery and most of it returns to the bloodstream through the renal vein;

4. 'most of it' means all the red and white corpuscles, all useful nutrients, and most of the water content;

5. excess water and waste matter will have been taken off by the kidney; these are collected into the ureter from which they pass to the bladder in the form of urine;

6. if you cut a vertical section through the kidney you would find it is made up of three regions – a paler outer region called the cortex, a darker region called the medulla, and a fibrous inner region called the pelvis;

7. all the vessels that connect the kidney with the rest of the system enter or leave via the pelvis.

Many of you will have most of this information as part of your general knowledge. It forms an essential preliminary to the passage and will presumably have been covered in an earlier lesson.

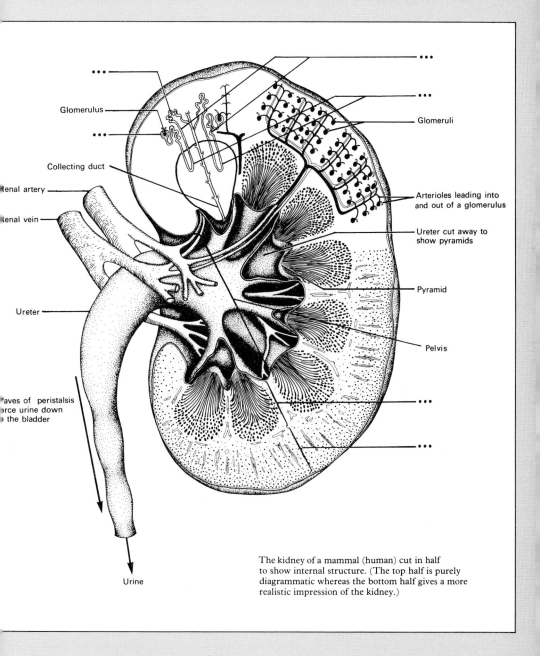

Glomerulus

Collecting duct

Renal artery

Renal vein

Ureter

Waves of peristalsis force urine down to the bladder

Urine

Glomeruli

Arterioles leading into and out of a glomerulus

Ureter cut away to show pyramids

Pyramid

Pelvis

The kidney of a mammal (human) cut in half to show internal structure. (The top half is purely diagrammatic whereas the bottom half gives a more realistic impression of the kidney.)

1. Read the first paragraph carefully and compare it with the diagram. Some of the labels have been deliberately removed from the diagram. Complete the labelling by marking:

  (a) the cortex, the medulla, the pelvis, the renal vein, the ureter (all these have been mentioned in the introduction);

  (b) the Bowman's capsule, the first convoluted tubule, the loop of Henle, the second convoluted tubule, the collecting duct (some of these are shown twice).

2. Now read the second paragraph.

  (a) Underline those parts of the text that describe the changing composition of the solution as it passes through the kidney.

  (b) Underline in a different colour the several fine structures of the kidney which are involved in these changes.

  (c) Draw up two parallel ordered lists, one column showing parts of the kidney, the other what happens in each of these parts. The order should be a sequence from input to output.

3. Optional: use your own work and the passage (and the diagram too, if you wish) to produce a flow diagram illustrating the several stages whereby the blood separates out (filtration), some of it recombines (re-absorption), then what's left is 'led off' and the purified blood is returned to the bloodstream.

The fine structure of the kidneys

The kidney is composed of a vast number of tiny tubules held together by connective tissue. Each tubule has a cup called **Bowman's capsule**, whose wall is one cell thick. The capsule opens into a coiled tubule known as the **first convoluted tubule**. This lies in the cortex of the kidney. The tubule continues as the **loop of Henle** which occupies the medulla, returning to the cortex to become the **second convoluted tubule**. This second convoluted tubule connects with one of the collecting ducts which opens into the pelvis of the kidney. The Bowman's capsule surrounds a knot of blood capillaries called the **glomerulus**.

The functioning of the kidneys

The diameter of the branch of the renal artery entering the glomerulus is considerably greater than that of the branch leaving it. This imposes a considerable pressure on the contents of the capillaries of the glomerulus and results in the blood being filtered under pressure. Sugars,

Example 8   *121*

salts, urea and even quite large molecules like proteins pass through the semi-permeable wall in solution into the cavity of the Bowman's capsule. The solution then passes through the first convoluted tubule into the loop of Henle, where much of the water and all of the glucose and other useful substances are re-absorbed. In this way, the composition of the blood is regulated. The urine then passes through the second convoluted tubule and the collecting duct into the pelvis of the kidney. Day and night, urine drips down the ureter into the bladder where it collects. The wall of the bladder is composed of muscular and elastic tissues. The urethra is kept closed by the contraction of the sphincter muscle at the neck. As urine accumulates in the bladder, the elastic walls are stretched until it contains about half a litre. Eventually, the sphincter muscle, which is a semi-voluntary muscle, relaxes and the muscle fibres in the bladder wall contract, expelling the urine through the urethra.

Comment

If your biology is at all rusty, you may well have found this analysis tough going. The passage is a demanding one – even though it was deliberately chosen as an easy description of kidney function.

Needless to say, the set of tasks you have worked through is one that could be given only to abler pupils. Later we will see how the work can be adapted and note the kind of additional support the teacher can provide for the less able.

Why is the work difficult? There are two reasons. One is that the structure and function of the kidneys bristles with problems for the uninitiate: the notion of filtration and re-absorption, the opposition between fine structure and gross appearance, and the contrast between physical arrangement and order of function. Yet it is surely an important part of the biology syllabus and one would like pupils to have some understanding of how it works.

However, it is the second reason that concerns us more particularly. The passage describes a *mechanism* and all such descriptions are demanding. A mechanism is a *structure* which is adapted to perform a *function*. Usually the function involves the processing of a *substance* which is not itself part of the structure. The connections between the different parts of the structure must be such as to facilitate the function, but their actual arrangement need not be a sort of linear representation of the process. Most mechanisms fold back on themselves for greater compactness (like a human appendix or even a modern trumpet!) and there may be quite complex interconnections. All this means that descriptions of any mechanism will tend to be difficult.

A good directed analysis is one that helps the reader to sort out these aspects and come to terms with them. The tasks you were asked to do were designed with this end in view.

1. Because a mechanism is a structure, the arrangement of its parts is important. One has to know what the parts are and where they are. So a diagram is essential. But will it be used for coming to grips with the construction of the mechanism or will the diagram be scanned superficially and independently of the text? *Deleting the labels is one way of ensuring that the pupils will master the relevant information in the text and in the diagram.*

Blocking out labels is not difficult, but do make sure you leave enough labels in to allow the reader to make the inferences that are needed. That can usually be done by studying the text to find obvious points of contact in the form of labels that have not been erased.

Incidentally, sorting the missing labels into two blocks was quite deliberate, as the two blocks correspond to the gross and the fine structure. Obviously, it pays to begin with the former. Separating the labelling task is one way of overcoming one of the problems we've just noted, that the arrangement of parts doesn't always mirror the sequence of function.

2. Just as the first task focused on structure so the second focused on function, ie how the various sectors of the kidney help the process of filtering out impurities in the blood. Once again the task can be demanding, not least because one has to infer that there are two streams of fluid, one in the capillaries and one in the named tissues, with matter passing between them through semi-permeable walls. Also you have to infer that what is eventually excreted does not become 'urine' until the end of the process, when re-absorption is complete.

However, once you've worked your way through the task, you end up with a neat and easily remembered representation of the essential elements that mediate the process, together with their function – albeit in gross terms because the presentation is elementary.

3. The final task is one that arises naturally from the ordered listing. Flow diagrams can be difficult to construct and an ordered listing is often a helpful step on the way. Nevertheless, such a representation is probably the best prompt for understanding and recall, especially if you've made the diagram yourself.

Whether or not you've produced your own you can look at Figure 13 which is one possible representation of this information about the kidney.

Example 8   123

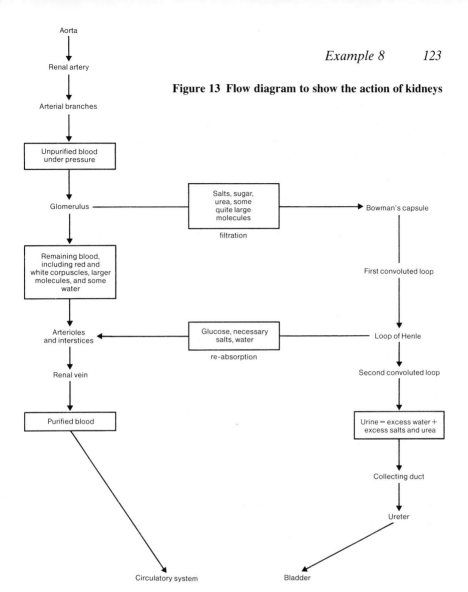

Figure 13 Flow diagram to show the action of kidneys

Classroom support

The text and the diagram were chosen by a biology teacher in consultation with a teacher of English who had a special responsibility for language across the curriculum in the school. The class concerned was a fourth-year CSE group who were by no means enthusiastic learners. Together, these two teachers undertook the daunting task of designing a text-based lesson for this very difficult topic.

Because of the ability level of the group, this text was selected as being rather easier than some. The supporting diagram, however, was taken from *Biology* by P. S. Beckett, which was judged to be more informative than the one that goes with the chosen text.

Although the teacher's introduction dealt with some of the problems referred to, even the list given in our own introduction is quite a daunting one, and it looks as if an extra lesson might be needed to deal with it. If the learner doesn't know what's happening (in the kidneys) and why, the task can be somewhat meaningless.

In this connection one wonders whether a magazine article on kidney machines and kidney transplants might not prove a useful additional resource for bringing home to pupils the excitement that this topic might arouse.

Figure 14 The Kidney – instructions given to pupils

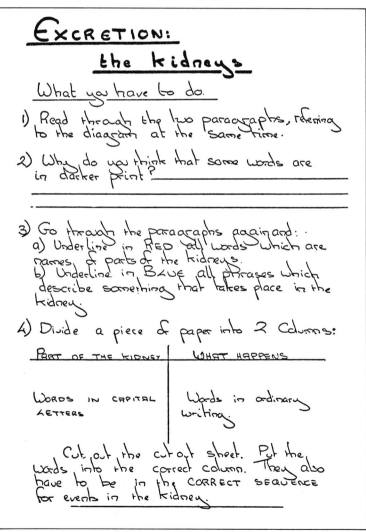

Example 8   125

The central portion of the lesson was devoted to the production of two ordered lists, with pupils working in twos and threes. Figure 14 (pages 124 and 125) shows the written instructions prepared for each group and the scrambled lists they were given to work on – these had to be cut up with scissors for rearranging.

The first part of the lesson was a class-taught introduction, with the teacher going over the parts set out at the beginning of this report and using the diagram for support. Needless to say, both diagram and text were available as resources for the re-arrangement, and the ordering could not be done without a close study of the passage.

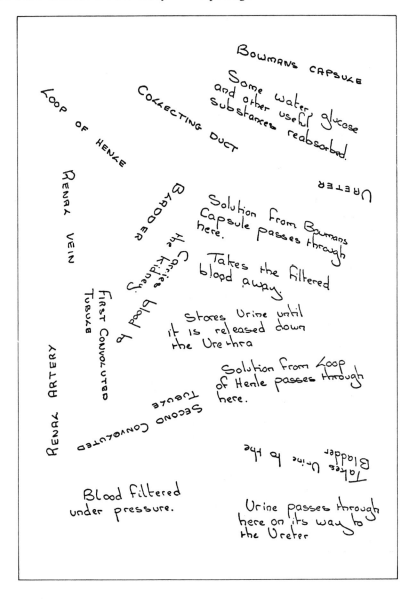

Comment

Although the teacher was present and available for help to all of the groups, the activity was only partly successful. Some of the groups solved the problem but a few were unable to complete the work in the time. Motivation was quite good, but there was no genuine enthusiasm.

The task given to these pupils was essentially the same as the one you've completed, but the cut-out sheet acted as an additional – and much needed – prop.

The fact that the diagram was only there to be looked at if the pupils wanted to was certainly a weakness, since it meant the names of the structures didn't mean too much to many of the pupils. Time taken to supply missing labels would have been time well spent.

Nevertheless, given the size of the problem, this might be called a qualified success. Certainly, the two teachers have planned a repeat, but with improvements. Notably, a different text may well be used, one which puts the mechanism over more clearly. Also, some of the labels will be deleted along the lines of the figure on page 119.

Figure 15 Solution to task shown on Figure 14

Renal artery	Carries blood to the kidney
Bowman's capsule	Blood filtered under pressure
First convoluted tubule	Solution from Bowman's capsule passes through here
Loop of Henle	Some water, glucose and other useful substances reabsorbed
Second convoluted tubule	Solution from loop of Henle passes through here
Collecting duct	Urine passes through here on its way to the ureter
Ureter	Takes urine to the bladder
Bladder	Stores urine until it is released down the urethra
Renal vein	Takes filtered blood away

Example 9   127

Example 9

Subject Geography
Source River Basins
Passage Type Classification
Activities Labelling
        Ordering
        Diagram

Introduction

The passage is one that we encountered quite early in the work of the project. It was awkward in some ways, and this meant that it was not easy to devise a good lesson round it. But we persevered, and in the end produced a lesson plan which pupils found enjoyable and constructive. What is more, some of us thought we learned more from the work put in on this extract than we did from any other. In order to appreciate the problems, you are invited to go through each of the following steps.

1. Read the complete extract. Then, working with a partner, decide on a short heading or label for each paragraph. You may find it helpful to start with those paragraphs which are easiest to label instead of taking the seven paragraphs in order.

2. Decide on a title for the extract which best summarises what it is all about.

3. Order the paragraphs with respect to that theme in terms of their relative importance.

4. Some of the information in the passage can be shown graphically by completing the labelling of the tree diagram shown in Figure 16. Do so.

Figure 16 Uses of river water

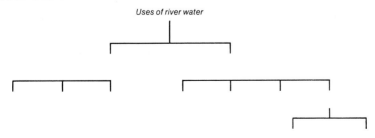

Uses of river water

5. Consider ways of representing the rest of the ideas in the passage.

6. If you think the passage is not well written, try to articulate your reasons.

River basins

Because Great Britain is small, its river basins too are small. In parts of the world where there are vast stretches of plains, there are river basins covering a million square miles or more.

Sooner or later the waters of most rivers reach the oceans. Many pass through lakes on their way. But some rivers end in lakes or inland seas that have no outlets. The best known of these is the River Jordan in Palestine. It flows into the Dead Sea, and there its waters come to rest. Because the Dead Sea has no outlet, it loses water only by evaporation, and that makes it a salt sea.

Rivers are nature's way of draining the land and carrying away the surplus water. As they move on their way from source to mouth, they serve the needs of men in many ways.

Domestic water supply is the water used by people in their homes and public buildings. In countries like Great Britain, most domestic water is carried in pipes to buildings where it is used. Water from wells is used chiefly on farms too far from towns to have pipes laid on.

You can easily guess what is meant by industrial water supply. It is the water used by mills and factories, and you would be surprised to know how much they need. In any large manufacturing city, the industrial use of water is much greater than the domestic use.

Nothing is manufactured without some water, and many industries need huge quantities of it. Among the 'thirstiest' industries are textile manufacturing, paper making, and certain kinds of food processing, such as canning and jam-making. It may surprise you to know that seven or eight gallons of water are used in refining every pound of sugar sold in the shops. Even metal industries use great quantities of water. For example, in order to produce a single pound of aluminium, about 160 gallons of water are needed.

In some places, ground water from wells or springs supplies the domestic and industrial needs of the people. But in the world as a whole, rivers are the greatest source of supply. In countries or regions where large supplies are needed, rivers are dammed to hold back part of the water in reservoirs. This is a way of storing water for use as it is needed.

Classroom activity in relation to text

To begin with, there is the question of deciding the principal theme of the extract. Although the text is a little confusing, the only solid and detailed information is a categorised listing of the uses of river water, and that is

Example 9   *129*

why we have taken the passage to be an instance of a classificatory text. Unless a teacher wanted the group to concentrate on this part of the passage it would hardly have been chosen for study.

But the main information is buried, the first paragraph is in some ways misleading, and the final paragraph too is perhaps confusing. So the first job is to establish just what the passage says. Accordingly, the first three tasks suggested above were also set for the pupils. Segmenting and/or labelling is always a useful preliminary task although sometimes it can be difficult, and in that case we recommend selective underlining either as a preliminary or an alternative. But this passage is not difficult in terms of content, and underlining would not have been too helpful since for the most part the things that are of the same kind are grouped together anyway.

Getting pupils to rank ideas in importance is an excellent way of helping them to sort out the inessential from the central information, so that was the next task. Finally, since the main information is a classification of information, the work of producing a family tree diagram serves to bring out its structure. The table itself can then be available as a permanent record for revision.

Classroom support

This passage has been used as the basis for text-based lessons by a number of teachers with classes ranging from the first to the third year of secondary schooling. In addition, it has been a focus for discussion with many groups of teachers. Instructions have varied from one group to another, although usually they are along the lines of the first four questions on page 127.

Just as the instructions varied, so too did the responses. Nevertheless, there are certain features which emerge with some consistency.

First, the labelling of paragraphs is fairly straightforward. Among the most popular labels are:

para 1	river basins
para 2	river outlets
para 3	purpose of rivers
para 4	domestic water supply
para 5	industrial water supply
para 6	thirsty industries
para 7	sources and storage of water.

Second, very few groups of pupils or teachers accept that the order of paragraphs in the text is the one that makes the best sense or that it reflects their relative importance to the theme as a whole. Instead the preferred order is often 7, 3, 4, 5, 6, 1, 2 or 7, 4, 5, 6, 3, 1, 2. Many pupils (and teachers) want to delete paragraphs 1 and 2 altogether, and some would prefer to dispense with paragraph 3.

In fact, as we've argued in an appendix, paragraph 7 is probably a better introduction than paragraph 3, and if you do promote this paragraph, then paragraph 3 does become redundant. It is significant that youngsters aged 11–14 seem to understand this so readily. They also recognise that the information in paragraphs 1 and 2 is not of a piece with the rest of the passage.

So far, none of these groups had been given the extra support for diagrammatic representation contained in Figure 16. Instead, they were asked to produce their own diagram and encouraged to include all the information in the one figure. Perhaps because of this, several found their task a difficult one and needed a fair amount of help from the teacher.

Figure 17 River Basins – diagrammatic representation

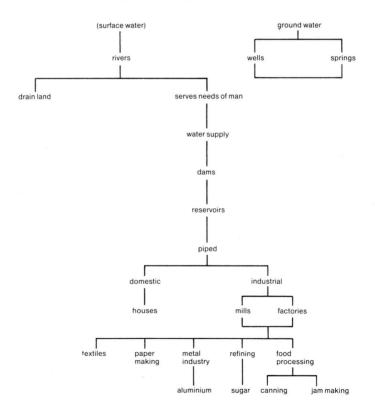

Figure 17 is an interesting example of a comprehensive representation arrived at with substantial teacher support. In effect, it is both a hierarchy (like Figure 18) and a flow diagram. However, some groups who were

Example 9   *131*

content to present only part of the information in the paragraph found ways of doing so with rather less teacher support.

Additional comments

1. A good representation is both a graphic summary and a precis of the passage. (The word 'graphic' should be taken to imply that some of the most important relations can be shown by their spatial arrangement and don't have to be said in words, although they may be.) In this sense, Figure 18 is perhaps preferable to Figure 17, despite the fact that it carries less information – or rather because of that fact.

Figure 18 Uses of river water – key points

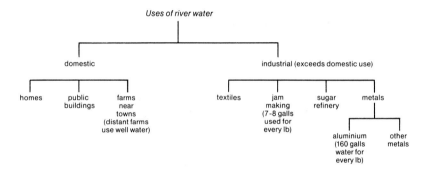

2. Most of the groups who studied this passage were able to sort out the wheat from the chaff. What is more, they were able to arrive at their own mode of presenting the key points in an effective way. The fact that they had to overcome the handicap of a less than perfect input means that they had to put in more of an effort, and this, as we know, promotes more effective learning.

A less than perfect text need not always be a handicap to study. We prefer to stick to this rather conservative double negative, since we cannot always show that a bad text is better than a good one, and indeed this would not very often be true.

3. Those pupils who produced the order 7, 4, 5, 6 . . . arrived at an insight into the best way of presenting this kind of classificatory information. It is an insight which is very likely to stand them in good stead when dealing with analogous extracts.

Readers who have the stamina and the leisure may like to study the analysis on page 229 which shows how the passage is typical and also why it is anomalous.

Part II
Reconstruction
of Text

INTRODUCTION

In text analysis lessons, the pupils are given an extract to work on in its original form, with a minimum of editing by the teacher. Then it is the tasks which will spur them on to analyse the passage, to find out how it is put together and how effectively it conveys the information and ideas.

But in text reconstruction lessons the teacher deliberately alters the form of the text beforehand so as to present it in the form of a puzzle. There are three main ways of setting such puzzles: deletion, rearrangement and partial concealment.

For the first of these, the teacher removes a number of words or phrases or sentences from the passage and replaces them with a gap or a line; the puzzle is to decide how to fill the gaps, using the rest of the passage as the main source of clues. We have called these lessons *Completion DARTs*.

For the second activity, the teacher reproduces all the phrases and sentences and paragraphs of the original passage, but the order of these elements is deliberately jumbled. Depending on the nature of the passage, one can decide on the size of the unit to be jumbled: jumble the order of phrases but preserve the paragraphs in their original order, or keep the paragraphs intact but jumble their arrangement, or you may even jumble both if the result is not too difficult to handle. Whatever has been jumbled, the puzzle for the pupils is to restore the material to a proper order, to impose coherence on chaos. We have used the term *sequencing* as a convenient label for this kind of task.

The third series of activities involves the pupils in making *predictions* ahead of their reading. This can be achieved in several ways. One of the best known is to study the beginning of a passage and make some plausible inferences about the outcome. Another is for the teacher to present a passage one paragraph at a time and ask the pupils to revise their predictions in the light of the new evidence. A third method is to present a part of a text which need not be the beginning and ask the pupils to guess the nature of the whole and the place of the given section within it. Again, this technique can be extended by introducing a second section, then a third, these too being taken out of sequence. Finally, one can ask the pupils to make predictions about the contents of a chapter before reading. Knowing the title, they will be making predictions on the basis of their existing knowledge of the matter.

Techniques such as these have a long tradition in the teaching of literature but they have been little used in connection with expository material.

Finally, it will be recalled that text-based lessons were never designed to be over-prescriptive and still less would we wish them to be restrictive. Members of the team have therefore encouraged teachers to combine a variety of text-based activities within a single lesson, especially when different parts of a passage seemed to call for different kinds of clarification. So this part will conclude with a few examples of such 'multi-DARTs'.

Altogether, then, Part II falls into four sections: text completion, sequencing, prediction and mixed activities, the last being quite short.

Several of the features of reconstruction lessons are common with text analysis. Thus we continue to stress the need for curricular relevance, the need for a careful study of the chosen passage by the teacher, and the importance of pupil discussion in small groups. However, while a well-designed text analysis lesson usually involves the pupils in a variety of complementary activities, text reconstruction is more likely to involve just one form of activity in any given lesson. This is partly because the passage needs to be presented in a way which suits the chosen activity, be it completion, sequencing or prediction.

It should be added that apart from the general considerations which we have already dealt with in Part I, each of these reconstruction techniques presents its own sort of challenge both to the pupil and to the teacher. So instead of preceding all the examples by an introductory section which deals with the whole range of techniques, we have preferred to present this in four distinct sections, each dealing with a different method.

Each of the first three sections is introduced by a brief statement setting out the rationale of the method, the main points to watch for, and the problems one might need to overcome. This introduction is always woven around a first example, and it is followed by a set of example lessons. These have been carefully chosen to represent a variety of subject areas and to bring out as much as possible of the experience gained in the course of the project. In some cases, we have been able to include part of a lesson transcript to illustrate the degree of pupil involvement and to chart the course of their learning. As in Part I, all of the examples cited represent actual lessons used with one or more groups of pupils, and in all cases the passages chosen by teachers in schools were part of the curriculum being studied. A complete list of examples in Part II appears in Table 8 overleaf.

Table 8 List of Examples in Part II

Example No.	Title	Subject	Passage Type	Activities	Comment
Introductory Example (Section 1)	Expansion of Solids	Physics	Principle	Completion	General discussion of method of deletion
1	My Grandmother	English	Poem	Completion	Includes lesson transcript
2	Jumping Waterfalls	Humanities or Biology	Behaviour mechanism	Completion	
3	After the Black Death	History	Historical situation	Completion Underlining	Compares single word deletion with phrase deletion and analysis
4	Shardik	English	Narrative	Completion	Sentence completion following author's style
5	Coniferous Trees	Geography	Biological adaptation	Completion	Comparison of phrase completion and selective underlining
Introductory Example (Section 2)	The First Revolution and the Second	History	Evolutionary process	Sequencing	General discussion of sequencing
6	A Constellation Viewer	Physics	Instructions	Sequencing	Use of DART as a prelude to practical
7	During Wind and Rain	English	Poem	Sequencing	Notable for classroom support

			Process	Sequencing	
8	Transmission of Sound	Physics	Process	Sequencing	Single prediction
Introductory Example 1 (Section 3)	The Hound of the Baskervilles	English Literature	Narrative	Prediction	Section by section prediction: narrative
Introductory Example 2 (Section 3)	The Fun They Had	English	Narrative	Prediction	Section by section prediction: expository passage
9	The Air	Geography	Process	Prediction	Combination of prediction and sequencing
10	Stonehenge	History	Structure	Prediction Sequencing	
11	The Roaring Twenties	History	Historical	Prediction	Use of pupils' existing knowledge
12	The Ear	General Science	Mechanism	Diagram Labelling Comparison of Text and Diagram	Planning a series of lessons, cf. Ex. 14
13	Building a Polder	Geography	Process	Matching text and diagram Questions	Use of DART with remedial group
14	How the National Theatre Silenced its Critics	Physics	Problem solution	Completion Prediction Diagram Construction	

PART II

I. COMPLETION

Introduction

Of all the activities that have been tried and tested in the course of the project, completion is the one which has the greatest initial appeal, especially for pupils who have had little experience of small group discussion as a way of learning. The idea of filling in the missing words or phrases is one with which everyone is familiar. If the passage and the gaps are well chosen, the task can be engrossing, and when it is undertaken as a group activity it can be exciting as pupils vie with one another to find a reasonable solution or a telling clue.

Once the passage has been chosen, the teacher's main initial consideration will be how and when to make deletions in such a way as to maximise its potential as a stimulus for learning. Thereafter, the task is mainly one of introducing the lesson and providing the conditions for vigorous and effective discussion. Both issues can best be dealt with in relation to an illustrative passage, and the one we have chosen is taken from an introduction to general science by C. Windridge.

Focus of deletions

There are several recipes one might use for making deletions in a passage. For instance, one could delete every *n*th word, say every seventh or every fifth. This technique can be very useful when deletion is used to test the readability of a book for a particular class by sampling their ability to tackle the language and ideas in two or three suitable extracts. Or one could delete every word in a chosen category, say every technical term (sometimes helpful as a revision exercise), or every adjective (a method used at least once, and with considerable success, by an imaginative English teacher working with the project). However, when the object is to maximise learning, it is usually best for the teacher to hand-pick the words and phrases to be deleted, using just two criteria:

1. there should be sufficient clues left in the passage to make a completion task challenging, but not insoluble;

2. the clues that are going to be used in choosing the right word(s) should be as relevant as possible in terms of the desired learning goals.

Both these points can best be illustrated with reference to a particular passage. The following extract dealing with the expansion of metals is presented in two versions. Following on the opening section, version A has every fifth word deleted. By contrast in the case of version B every deletion has been individually chosen by the teacher.

Introductory Example

Subject Physics

Source C. Windridge 'The Expansion of Solids', *General Science*, Book 1

Passage Type Principle

Activities Text completion

The expansion of solids

Materials expand when they are heated. Most materials expand, or become larger, when they are heated, and contract, or become smaller, when they are cooled. The expansion of solid materials, like iron and brass, is so small that it is not noticed unless special apparatus is used to measure it and to show that it is, in fact, occurring.

The expansion of solids. Push the metal ball of a ball and ring apparatus through the ring. Heat the ball and, when it is red hot, lift it with tongs and place it on the ring. The ball does not fall through the ring. It has expanded. What happens when the ball cools and contracts?

Heat the bar of a bar and gauge apparatus. Try to push the bar into the gauge. It does not fit. Allow the bar to cool. It now fits into the gauge for it has contracted in length.

Lay a thick iron rod across two bricks. Use Plasticine to attach a straw to one end of a knitting needle. Place the needle, so that the straw is upright, on one of the bricks and underneath the rod. Then heat the rod. The straw turns. Why? Now allow the rod to cool. The straw now turns in the opposite direction. Why?

A Expansion and contraction can _____ a nuisance or even _____ damage. Therefore, engineers make _____ for expansion and contraction. _____ pipes are built with _____,

B Expansion and contraction can be a nuisance or even cause _____. Therefore, engineers make allowances for expansion and contraction. Steam pipes are built with loops, bends

bends and moveable collars
_____ that no damage is _____
when the pipes become __
and expand. Telephone
wires _____ power
cables are left _____ so
they do not _____ when
they contract in _____
weather. Large metal
bridges _____ loosely on
rollers or _____ pads
built into their _____.

Then expansion can take _
freely and no damage ____
done to the bridges. ____
tar-filled gaps are _____
made in concrete roads __
that cracking does not ____
when the concrete expands._____
rails on a railway _____
are welded together to _____
a single rail that _____
often more than one ____
in length. This rail _____
heated and stretched. It _____
then fixed down firmly _____
the expanded state so ____
it contracts only slightly _____
the weather becomes
colder. _____ pendulums
of clocks are _____
provided with wooden or
plastic bobs and adjustable
nuts. Wood and plastic do
not expand as much as
metals. The nut of a
pendulum is turned so that
the position of the bob is
altered and allowance made
for expansion and
contraction.

and moveable collars so
that no damage is done
when the pipes become __
and expand. Telephone
wires and power cables are
left slack so they do not
snap when they _____ in
cold weather. Large metal
bridges rest _____ on
rollers or plastic pads built
into their supports.

Then _____ can take
place freely and no _____
is done to the bridges.
Narrow tar-filled _____
are sometimes made in
concrete roads so that _____
does not occur when the
concrete expands. The rails
on a railway track are
welded together to make a
rail that is often more than
one kilometre in length.
This rail is heated and
stretched. It is then fixed
down firmly in the _____
state so that it contracts
only slightly when the
weather becomes _____.
The pendulums of clocks
are sometimes provided
with wooden or _____
bobs and adjustable nuts. _____
and plastic do not expand
as much as _____. The
nut of a pendulum is turned
so that the position of the
bob is altered and
allowance made for _____
and contraction.

From C. Windridge, *General Science*.

Table 9 is a listing of the words that have been deleted. Version A has 33 in all. Version B, 15 deletions.

To begin with version A, one might ask the following very simple question: how often can a gap be filled without looking beyond the sentence in which it occurs and the sentence immediately preceding and without reference to the principle of the expansion of solids? (If you are working on your own you are strongly recommended to arrive at your own answer before proceeding. If you are collaborating with a group you may wish to compare your answers with those of others.)

Table 9 Deletions made in 'Expansion of solids'

Version A			Version B	
1. be	12. cold	23. track	1. damage	9. single
2. cause	13. rest	24. make	2. hot	10. expanded
3. allowances	14. plastic	25. is	3. contract	11. colder
4. Steam	15. supports	26. kilometre	4. loosely	12. plastic
5. loops	16. place	27. is	5. expansion	13. Wood
6. so	17. is	28. is	6. damage	14. metal
7. done	18. Narrow	29. in	7. gaps	15. expansion
8. hot	19. sometimes	30. that	8. cracking	
9. and	20. so	31. when		
10. slack	21. occur	32. The		
11. snap	22. The	33. often		

Answers to this problem will no doubt vary a little, but almost certainly you will come out with a residual list of no more than ten gaps that can't be filled without reference to the passage as a whole and its principal theme. Our own list consists of just eight items: they are items 4, 5, 8, 10, 14, 16, 18, and 26. The remaining deletions may be thought of as trivial, and many of them are short grammatical words like 'is', 'in' and 'the' which can be supplied without any reference to content. Words like 'supports' (15) are more difficult to supply, but there is a sense in which the thinking they require is tangential to the main idea. The content on which one draws in finding the right word is encapsulated within the bridge example and the sentence that contains it. As to the items in our residual list, there are at least a few which cannot be solved without specialised knowledge which is not included in the text at all. For instance, how is the reader to know in advance that the writer has chosen to write about steam pipes (4) rather than some other pipes or that such pipes will include loops (5) as well as bends? In sum, when deletions are made in accordance with a mechanical formula, the problems they pose are often trivial or only marginally relevant, and they will sometimes be insoluble.

Version B is very different. Here the teacher has chosen each deletion separately, taking into account its relevance to the central theme and the clues that have been left in to help the solution.

The central theme is given in the second sentence: 'Most materials expand, or become larger, when they are heated, and contract, or become smaller, when they are cooled.' Both the fact of expansion and its direction, heat → expansion, cooling → contraction, are central. They are directly implicated in the solution of no less than six gaps: items 2, 3, 5, 10, 11 and 15. Almost equally central is the idea that expansion and contraction can cause damage (1, 6) by such effects as cracking (8). Differential rates of expansion make up yet another general theme which the science teacher takes to be crucial, and this becomes the focus of deletions 12, 13 and 14. The remaining deletions can all be justified by the way in which they highlight the significance of an example by focusing the pupil's attention on just how the expansion occurs or how it is taken up in such a way as to avoid damage.

Of course the exact number of deletions could have been extended or reduced a little without materially affecting the learning task. Here and there, one could have chosen to retain a deleted word (like 'wood' (13)) and delete the most important cue ('wooden' in the preceding line). So the teacher has a fair degree of latitude in arriving at a suitable list of deletions. That is a good thing in itself. The fact that the teacher has exercised judgement in devising the task gives one a sense of involvement as (s)he observes the pupils trying to solve it, and this means that the teacher too can be caught up in the excitement.

Such are the principal considerations governing the choice of deletion. Now that we have examined these and their application to a fairly difficult passage, we can turn to some of the remaining issues. These range from the choice of a suitable passage to the actual conduct of the lesson, and for the most part they are of a very practical nature.

Suiting the technique to the passage

As is evident from the preceding discussion, completion can be an excellent recipe for a worthwhile lesson based on an extract from a suitable text. But completion is not the only technique used by teachers on the project, nor is it equally suitable for all kinds of passage or for every teacher purpose.

As we have just seen, it is ideal for drawing attention to the principal threads in a very cohesive extract, eg a passage in which the same idea is followed through a number of instances, some positive and others negative, with similar considerations entering into each. 'The expansion of solids' states a principle and sets out some of its applications. Such a passage is well suited to learning by completing well-chosen gaps. So too are most of the other examples included in this book. For instance, 'Jumping waterfalls' (Example 2) describes the close adaptation of a behavioural mechanism (how salmon leap) to the cues and conditions of an environment (the play of light and water in the various parts of the waterfall). Similar considerations apply to 'After the Black Death' (example 3) which describes a historical situation and its contrasting effects on various classes of society. Like 'Jumping waterfalls', 'Coniferous trees' (example 5) describes an adaptive mechanism – how conifers regulate their need for water through the winter months – and the passage includes a number of contrasts between conifers and deciduous trees. Although not included in this section, simple classifications which set out the main differential characteristics of contrasted categories of things or of events are often well suited for a completion activity. Finally, we have found completion to be admirably suited to the appreciation of literary passages, whether of poetry as in 'My Grandmother' (Example 1) or in prose, as in 'Shardik' (Example 4). Here the pupils' attention will be drawn to issues of style as well as issues of fact, and to the connotations of words and phrases as well as their meanings.

There are also passages, however, where completion is not a profitable technique. It is especially inappropriate for use with passages that feature a series of rapid shifts in focus. For instance, there are passages that describe the phases in processing some manufactured commodity, or in a natural cycle of events like the formation of rocks. Since each phase is different in context and action, and outcomes differ likewise, all the most relevant clues will tend to be local, if indeed the problem can be solved at all. Such a passage might be suitable for sequencing but not for completion. Again, a text that consists of a series of instructions is not at all well suited to deletion and completion for the same reason. Finally, the decision whether to use deletion in a story setting can be a tricky one. It is an excellent technique for drawing attention to a few well-chosen and telling examples of style. But when used as a source of grammatical or even logical gap-filling exercises, it may well be that it helps to keep the pupils busy but does little to enhance their appreciation of literature.

Preparation of material

Preparing a passage for a completion lesson always involves time in selecting deletions, in making a master-copy incorporating these, and in printing further copies for class use. So it is as well to avoid unneccesary slips in the actual preparation of materials.

First of all, it is worth repeating that the passage should contain sufficient clues to allow the task to be completed successfully. Of course pupils will be drawing on their own existing knowledge as well as the version of the text prepared by the teacher – and this is what one wants. But since the text is likely to deal with new material, it is always wise to leave a substantial portion – usually the opening section – intact.

Next, one must consider the actual presentation of gaps. Leaving a gap without filling it can be confusing when one gets to the end of a line: is it a gap or just a short line? So we advise using a horizontal bar to signal a gap of one word. The bar should be of standard length regardless of the length of the word deleted. If more than one word is being deleted then one will usually want to show whether the missing portion consists of a simple phrase or a whole sentence. This can be signalled by P for a phrase or S for a sentence, thus:

Only rarely would you wish to signal the actual number of words, since this can easily have the effect of causing pupils to worry about grammar at the expense of content and/or style.

There is also an alternative layout which is sometimes preferable, especially if you want the pupils to write down one or more alternatives for each of the gaps. This is to use square brackets

[   ], [(P)   ], [(S)   ]

Amount of deletion

We have just hinted that there is no need for every deletion to be restricted to a single word. Work undertaken in the course of the project has included a number of lessons in which at least some of the completions amounted to more than one word, and several examples are included in this book. Indeed, the general feeling among those with most experience is that phrase and sentence deletions are more challenging and more likely to focus attention on the central themes in a passage. Others might argue that the same purpose can be achieved by careful selection of individual words. Here again, there is not sufficient basis either in theory or in experience to justify any firm rule. Teachers will want to try out a variety of deletions for themselves. But it is important to give the pupils a clear indication of what they are supposed to find: one word, two or three words, a short sentence, or a line of poetry. So long as the pupils know what is wanted, there is no need to stick to a single type, even within a given passage.

Initial guidance

Suppose the passage has been selected, the deletions have been made, and multiple copies have been prepared for distribution to the class. What are the points to watch for?

First, one has to make sure that everyone knows what to do and why. Is one word only needed for each gap or more? Should the word be written down or just kept in mind? Does it matter whether one has the exact word or phrase or is it sufficient to find something that gives the right sense? Should one try to offer more than one option for each gap wherever such alternatives are possible?

None of these is a question to which there is a universal answer. Each decision hinges on the purposes that the teacher has in mind. For instance, in a scientific or historical passage, the exact word(s) may be quite unimportant while in a literary passage the phrase may be crucial. What about alternatives? Let the teacher decide. However, this is not to say that things should be left entirely open. Every one of the above decisions needs to be made sooner or later for each lesson, and for the most part they can be communicated right at the start, since they will arise naturally out of an introduction in which the pupils are told why they are being asked to study the passage and what they should be looking for.

Group and class discussion

The most common formula has been to begin with a class introduction, then to have pupils working together in small groups of two to five, arriving at their own solutions and justifications, and to end the lesson with a class discussion involving speakers from these groups as well as the teacher. The introduction gives the teacher an opportunity to put the topic in its proper focus and to deal with the questions raised in the last sub-section. The small group discussion provides an opportunity for every pupil to find out not just how the gaps can be filled in a particular way but why – because each member of the group tends to be involved in searching the passage for relevant clues. The final class discussion gives scope to pull together the principal threads and to draw out some general implications. It also offers an excellent opportunity for pupils who have been won over to an idea to act as reporters for the group even though they were silent in the original discussion. It is surprising how often this happens.

It should be added that sometimes teachers prefer to take the first one or two completions as a 'class-together' procedure. This enables them to bring out some of the considerations which lead to the pupils completing the exercise adequately. This is especially likely to happen when a class has had little previous experience of this kind of work. While the groups are underway, the teacher is most likely to be busy listening in, ready to supply an important clue or to inject an extra suggestion, eg to consider alternatives, not to get too bogged down with inessentials, and so on. But as long as things are going well, the best course will be silence.

Examples
Example 1

Subject English Literature

Source 'My Grandmother' by Elizabeth Jennings

Passage Type Poem

Activities Text completion

Introduction

To appreciate fully what the teacher set out to achieve and how she realised this, you need to spend some 10–15 minutes trying to solve the completion problems as the pupils did.

If you are working with a group, you will no doubt wish to compare your choices and discuss the reasons that lay behind them.

In the end, you will wish to compare your reconstruction with the original. A list of deleted words is given on page 153. Needless to say, any discussion of whether your version or another might be better than the original, and how and why, would be beyond the scope of this book!

My Grandmother

(Elizabeth Jennings)

She kept an antique shop – or it kept her.
Among Apostle spoons and Bristol glass,
The _____ silks, the heavy, _____
She watched her own reflection in the _____
Salvers and _____ bowls, as if to prove
Polish was all, there was no need of _____.

And I remembered how I once refused
To go out with her, since I was afraid.
It was perhaps a wish not to be used
Like antique objects. Though she never said
That she was hurt, I still could feel the guilt
Of that refusal, guessing how she felt.

> Later, too _____ to keep a shop, she put
> All her best things in one long _____ room.
> The place smelt _____, of things too long kept shut,
> The _____ of absences where _____ come
> That can't be polished. There was nothing then
> To give her own _____ back again.
>
> And when she died I felt no grief at all,
> Only the guilt of what I once refused,
> I walked into her room among the tall
> Sideboards and cupboards – things she never used
> But needed; and no finger-marks were there,
> Only the new dust falling through the air.

Initial comment

In a poem such as this, every word must form a good fit, as can often be illustrated by substituting other words for those used by the poet. This can be shown using the deletions made by the class teacher. There are several constraints on each word, and many can be brought out by counter-example:

grammatical fit	rules out 'satins silks' (line 3)
local sense	rules out 'empty silks', 'laughing silks', etc;
rhythm	rules out 'soft silks, the heavy fur', there being exactly ten syllables to each line in the poem;
rhyme	rules out 'the pewter' (line 4, end);
sense of the whole	rules out 'too proud' (line 13).

But there are also more subtle considerations:

repetition	'. . . her own reflection in the brass Salvers . . . '. . . to give her own reflection back again' (lines 4, 18) '. . . guilt Of that refusal . . . . . . the guilt of what I once refused' (lines 11, 12, 20)
assonance	'. . . give . . . grief . . . guilt' (lines 18, 19, 20)
ambiguity	'. . . reflection . . .' (line 18)
multiple layers of meaning	last line of poem and, perhaps, lines 9 and 10.

Even with these additions, the list is not exhaustive, since it does not include such features as the balance of long and short words, the meta-phorical and the concrete, the striking and the expected, all things that go to make up individuality and felicity of style, as well as contributing to the richness of the communication. None of these can be illustrated by counter-example, because all are optional. Indeed their over-use would lead to unacceptably mannered writing as well as reducing their impact.

Now all of the above could have been made the object of an illustrated lecture by the teacher. Instead she chose to construct a group completion lesson. Nevertheless her objectives were the same: (a) to help her pupils to an appreciation of the poem which is both informed and, at least in part, their own and (b) to give them a knowledge and a feel of how a poet achieves a desired effect.

It should be noted that she could not have attained these two objectives without taking considerable care in choosing which words to delete and, especially, what to leave in. In particular, the decision to leave the second and fourth stanzas intact was quite deliberate. It was taken to give a double example of the form of the poem and at the same time provide an intact slice sufficient for pupils to gain a general feel of the poem: its message and its method.

Context

The class was a third-year, mixed ability class in a comprehensive school and the poem was one of several chosen for study as part of a theme: old age. One of the poems studied in a previous lesson was a violent protest against the indignities suffered by patients in a geriatric ward. The teacher refers back to this in her introduction.

The lesson as a whole falls into three parts: teacher's introduction, small group work (in pairs), final class discussion. What follows is a transcript of what was said during the first and third parts of the lesson.

Lesson transcript

Teacher's introduction

In this one [poem] the situation is totally different: it's about a human being, and it's about as gentle and non-violent a poem as I could imagine. It's called 'My Grandmother' and the poet's name is Elizabeth Jennings. What I am going to ask you to do is to go through verses 1 and 3 between the two of you and work out as we've done before what the words should be that fill the gap. But before you do that, remember it is a poem, and as such the poetry is written in certain ways obeying certain rules that she has set herself.

If you want to find the rules that you will need to know in order to work out the words that fit the spaces, you will have to look at the whole poem.

So let's read verse 2. It won't make sense because at this stage we are taking them in isolation, but look at the second verse there [she reads second stanza aloud] and at the last verse [she reads fourth stanza aloud]. Now I am not going to tell you anything at all about the rules that she has made for herself, but I will give you this clue: it's something to do with the length of the lines and it's got something to do with rhyme. If you can work out from the full verses, verses 2 and 4, what the rules are, then you will find it much easier to work out the words in the spaces.

Now remember: one word to a space and the word can be any length. The spaces are equal lengths; you can't judge from that how long the word is. And remember, you may not get the word that's in the original poem, but that doesn't matter. It's whether what you've worked out is a good word that works in the circumstances.

Right, you all know what you're doing – pairs, don't write them down, just work it out in your minds, you'll remember them when it comes to say them over again.

Small group work (pairs)
Not recorded.

Class discussion
A pupil (*unidentified and not always the same*): P
Two pupils: PP
Several pupils: Sev
Individuals: S, Ju, Jo, M, Sa
Teacher: T

T	Now first of all, what have you worked out about the rules? Simon, you arrived at the idea of what rhymes with what quite quickly by yourself. How – what does rhyme with what?
S	After each line, each second line after that rhymes with it and the last two rhyme.
T	Yes, and the last two rhyme, the last two rhyme with each other; can you put the other ones a little more plainly?
S	The first line rhymes with the third and the second with the fourth.
T	Wonderful, yes, in other words alternate lines rhyme. There is a

way of describing that when you are talking about poetry which I'll come on to later, but let's leave it out just now. Line 1 rhymes with line 3, line 2 rhymes with line 4, and the last two rhyme. Now that helps you to work out some of the words, particularly in the first verse. What about the length of the line? How long are the lines? Did you get anything there?

P   Ten beats.

T   Ten beats, ten syllables to the line. Yes, I agree with you there are, and that too helps you. Obviously if you've got six beats there, you know the missing words must account for four. Could be two and two, could be three and one, you know how many there should be. Right, let's just start looking at your answers! What did you think came before 'silks', Julie?

Ju   'Fine.'

T   'The fine silks.'

P   'Coloured.'

P   'Smooth.'

T   And you got the same as that – John?

Jo   'Heavy.'

T   'The heavy silks' – you thought she would use the same word twice; it's quite possible. Poets often do that to give the effect. 'The heavy silks, the heavy' something – Mark?

M   'The woven.'

T   'The woven silks', because they are a fabric – yes –

P   'The light silks.'

T   'The light silks' – now you've all worked that out presumably from what you know about silks: you said . . .

Ju   'Fine.'

T   'Fine' – because you associate silk with being fine. Somebody said 'woven', somebody said 'light', somebody said 'heavy'. You see, you do get silks in different qualities. They're both correct, but you've worked it out – you've all worked it out from that way round – what do I think silk's like? Now, in fact silk is like all these things but there is only one of the suggestions so far actually fits the line. What guesses have you got for the second one?

PP   Didn't get one.

T   Didn't get one at all, either of you?

PP   No, no.

P   We got 'fur'.

T   What '. . . the heavy fur'. Why did you say 'fur'?

Sev	Rhymes with 'her'.
T	You're absolutely correct – it does indeed. But if you had, say, '. . . the fine silks, the heavy fur', how many beats are you short?
P	Two.
P	Three.
T	Hm, you're three short. So both of those can't be right even if either of them is.
P	'Furniture.'
T	Right, Sandra, read it out then.
Sa	Which one?
T	That line, with 'furniture' at the end of it. Try it out.
Sa	'The . . .'
T	Try 'heavy', try Charles's one.
Sa	'The heavy silks and the heavy furniture.' That's what she said.
T	How does that sound to you from the length of the line?
P	You can't have 'heavy' silks and 'heavy' furniture.
T	But how did you like 'furniture' for the end?
Sev	Yes, that is all right.
T	You like it, yes?
Sev	Don't think the 'heavy' fits in. Not 'the heavy'. It's all right but not 'heavy'. Not 'heavy silks'.
T	But what about 'furniture'? You're quite happy with that, it would pass your approval? You don't like 'the heavy' for 'silks'?
Sev	No, no.
T	I think that's quite a good suggestion; the two 'heavies' together if you want to create that kind of effect.
P	'Bright.'
P	'Coloured.'
T	You are still coming back to 'coloured'. You now know how long it should be. 'Heavy' is the right length although you're not happy with it as a word. Let's leave that one, and think about it when we've said a few more things about the poem. What did you get for the end of the next line?
Sev	'Brass.' 'Brass.'
T	Universal shout of 'brass' – how did you find out if that was right?
Sev	Rhymed with 'glass'.
P	Also, you can polish it. Rhymes with 'glass' and also you see reflections in it.
T	Well, 'grass' rhymes with 'glass' too.
Sev	But you can't have grass . . . You can't see reflections in grass . . .

T   Quite so – it's got to be something you can polish and it's got to be something you can make salvers out of – what is a salver? There was a rush for dictionaries and I presume that was the word you were looking up.

Sev   A tray.

T   So clearly you could make a tray out of brass; and what did you reckon the bowls were made out of in that case?

Sev   'Silver.'

T   'Silver' – two metals both you can polish and both you can see your reflections in. ' . . . brass Salvers and silver bowls, as if to prove Polish was all, there was no need of . . .'?

P   Didn't know that one.

T   No tries at all? It's a difficult one because – how long must it be?

P   One beat.

T   One, right, and what must it rhyme with?

Sev   Prove.

T   Or not quite rhyme. And again this is where you've got to look elsewhere in the poem and you find words which don't quite rhyme. Can you find an example of that, somebody?

P   'Then' and 'again'. 'Room' and 'come'.

T   'Room' and 'come' – unless you come from a certain part of the country it wouldn't rhyme – what others?

P   'Guilt' and 'felt'.

T   'Guilt' and 'felt' don't quite . . .

P   'Then' and 'again'.

T   Yes and then some people say 'erg-én'. Depends where you come from really.

P   'Put' and 'shut'.

T   'Put' and 'shut' don't quite – so you're looking for a word of one syllable which almost rhymes with 'prove'. We'll come back to that one as well. Try the second verse: 'Later, too . . .'?

Sev   'Old'

T   'Later, too old to keep a shop' – could it be anything else? What apart from being old might prevent you from keeping a shop?

P   'Ill'

P   'Fragile'

P   'Disabled'

T   Who said 'fragile'? Can you think of a similar word with one syllable?

P   'Frail.'

T   That's the one the lady chose – she didn't choose 'old'. I agree with you it makes absolutely good sense, makes absolutely good

sense, 'old' – but the one the lady chose was 'frail'. 'Later, too
frail to keep a shop, she put All her best things in one long . . .'?

P	'Empty'.
P	'Lovely,' 'dark.'
T	'. . . in one long empty room', '. . . lovely room'?
P	Don't like 'lovely'.
T	You don't like 'lovely'.
Sev	No.
P	She would lock her antiques in a lovely room, wouldn't she?
P	Yes, just as well as in your dark rooms . . . if she was saving them.
T	What, in a lovely room?
P	Yes.
P	But she's storing them away, too frail to carry on with the shop, so she's picking out the best to store away. She wouldn't put them in a beautiful room, would she?
T	You don't think do you, she might be taking goods from the shop and using them to furnish her own house?
P	Yes; possible.
T	Look at the rest of it. At the moment you're guessing. You've taken up a position: one lot of you think she is making a lovely room, the other lot think she is storing it. What does the poem say?
P	It's empty and she's making it beautiful by putting all the best things in it.
T	Yes, I see what you mean '. . . in one long empty room', so she puts all the stuff in it. Go further in the verse and see if you can resolve this argument. Is she furnishing a room or is she storing furniture in it?
Sev	Storing, storing it.
T	Why do you say that so definitely?
P	Place'll smell musty.
P	A lovely room wouldn't smell musty, would it?
P	Smell nice and clean.
T	Might have some faded splendour about it, I suppose. You think 'musty' here?
P	Yes.
P	Could be 'dusty'.
T	'Musty' or 'dusty'?
P	No, we think it should be 'dusty' really.
P	No, no, it can't be dusty, can it? Can't smell dust. Can't be dusty 'cause she's always polishing things.

T	But not the room, it's the furniture she polishes.
P	You can't smell dust though, can you?
T	The reason I . . . I would say not 'dusty' or 'musty', but it's for another reason.
P	It's only got one syllable.
T	Which has? The word you need?
P	Yes.
T	Then what do you think?
P	The place smelt old.
Sev	Yes.
T	'The place smelt old, of things too long kept shut The . . .?'
P	That was hard.
T	The next one, 'The (something) of absences'
P	'The feel'
P	'The sense'
T	'The sense of absences . . .' [Bell rings for end of lesson.]
T	Well, we will be able to spend more time on this. In fact, in many cases you've got some very good ideas – and I'm interested in this discussion as to whether she is furnishing a room or storing it and I don't think you've quite got the answer to that yet.

Final comment

The teacher's introduction is a good example of how to avoid over-direction while at the same time giving pupils a clear indication of what they have to do and how they should go about doing it. All this is done right from the start.

The discussion transcript illustrates the degree of pupil involvement. It also shows that the members of this class were well able to discover and apply the obligatory constraints described on page 145. As to the remaining considerations, they were perhaps only part-way there. For instance all the children's contributions centre on what the room was like or would be like in fact, and what the old lady would or would not do in real life, as it were. They have yet to discover the part played by the poet's selection and bias. They concentrate on what is told and neglect the telling. However, because of the interest and enthusiasm generated by the lesson, the teacher was able to devote another lesson to the same poem, and now the class was able to discuss the mood of the poem and its style in a way which would not have been possible without the indirect learning which resulted from this completion exercise.

Single word deletion has been widely and enthusiastically employed by English teachers in the study of poetry. It can often encourage pupils to become involved with poetry where more traditional approaches may fail. When fully exploited, it motivates pupils to become involved in the writing of poetry by starting from the point of view of the original writer and then taking on the role of writer themselves.

Note

Following is a list of the words deleted from the poem 'My Grandmother': faded, furniture, brass, silver, love, frail, narrow, old, smell, shadows, reflection.

Example 2

Subject Humanities or Biology

Source 'Salmon-survival Problems', in *Man: A Course of Study*

Passage Type Behaviour Mechanism

Activities Text completion

Introduction

This exercise is designed for teachers, not children. The following is a short passage from the MACOS (*Man: A Course of Study*) material. Assume that you are designing a completion activity for first- or second-year pupils in a comprehensive school. Your primary objective is to ensure that they fully understand the adaptive mechanism which enables salmon to overcome the force of gravity when, swimming upstream to their spawning grounds, they encounter a waterfall. A secondary objective, as ever, is to get them to think while reading by continually asking themselves just what the text is saying, and whether it makes sense. We suggest you allow yourself 12–18 single-word deletions, and that no deletions are made to the first paragraph. What words would you delete? Teachers working in groups will doubtless wish to share their ideas.

Jumping waterfalls

When given a choice between several places to jump at a waterfall, salmon choose to jump where the most water is falling. A more difficult jump, perhaps, but a safer one.

Salmon aim at the top of a waterfall by sight. Swimming toward the waterfall the salmon can see the sun shining off the top of the water and they head toward this bright light. During the evening and on cloudy days, salmon will not leap.

A salmon may leap several times its height. It does this by letting the river help. Water comes plunging down, then rises strongly before heading downstream.

The salmon makes use of the upward force of the water. As a fish approaches a waterfall which it recognises by sound, it swims down until it reaches the upward-moving water. With the water giving an added push the salmon leaps.

Focus of deletions

There are two central ideas. The first is the use of the upward force of the water when it rebounds after striking the lower surface with the accumulated energy of its downward plunge. Several of the deletions should focus on this, although it would not do to delete all the key words in the last two paragraphs. In particular, the notion of upthrust is conveyed at four points:

'rising strongly' (third para)
'upward force' (fourth para, first sentence)
'upward-moving water' (penultimate sentence)
'water giving an added push' (last sentence)

Because only single-word deletions were suggested, you could delete one word at each of these points and still be confident that the remaining text should provide enough clues for their successful replacement either by the original word or by an acceptable synonym.

The second main idea is the mechanism that enables the salmon to achieve this objective: it uses the play of light on water to guide it to a point below the greatest drop. This is brought out in the second paragraph, and you could concentrate several deletions in this one paragraph. What you hope is that the pupils will retain the idea because of the effort expended in the completion task. The idea itself is a much simpler one than the first, and reducing the number of deletions to two or three could easily trivialise the exercise.

As to the remaining deletions, we return to the fourth paragraph. Here there is a third idea, subsidiary in this extract: although salmon aim at the top of a waterfall by sight, the initial orientation of the fish is a response to the sound of the waterfall. Unfortunately, it is not easy to see what clues will be left for the pupil if the key word 'sound' is deleted, unless they have prior knowledge about the subject. In point of fact, the present extract is taken from a booklet that is largely concerned with the way in which both the visual and the audial systems of the salmon incorporate quite specific innate recognition mechanisms that are especially adapted to regulate migratory behaviour. So pupils who are studying the passage in the context of that curriculum would be able to draw on knowledge acquired in previous lessons.

When comparing your own deletions with those presented in the next section, you should bear in mind:

1. that the list we present is not the one true answer; it is one of several possible answers, but one that has been arrived at by consensus of a group of teachers and tried in practice with several classes of pupils;

2. there may well be too many deletions for a class that has less relevant experience or knowledge.

Context

As we have just noted, the passage is taken from a booklet, but that booklet is itself part of a complete Humanities package, *Man: A Course of Study* (MACOS). The package consists of written materials (of which several were produced by researchers in the field of animal behaviour and anthropology) supplemented by visual aids, video-films, and teacher materials.

Amongst the teacher groups following the MACOS course is a group in the East Midlands of England. In the first year of the 'Reading for Learning' project this group collaborated with the project team in designing reading activities for the MACOS material. Since a number of the teachers were involved in team teaching and all met regularly to discuss the MACOS programme, there was an opportunity for alternative activities and variations of activities to be tried and compared.

For all pupils following the MACOS course, however, there was substantial support for this and other texts. This was provided in part by means of a video-film on salmon, and in part through the teaching style which characterises the MACOS course. Pupils are encouraged to adopt a problem-solving approach to learning, to make first-hand observations and to draw inferences from data.

Thus, for all the pupils concerned it was a familiar experience to be faced with a task which requires inferences to be made from textual data. However, some classes had the opportunity to see the film with or without narrative and/or natural soundtrack before coming to the text, while other groups worked on the text before seeing the film.

Not surprisingly, pupil response to the task varied with their prior experience, and although only one deletion pattern was rated by the teachers as non-productive (this was a regular one in six pattern of deletion), a variety of lists of deletions were developed for different circumstances.

The following version is one that was designed for pupils who had already seen the film.

Jumping waterfalls

When given a choice between several places to jump at a waterfall, salmon choose to jump where the most water is falling. A more difficult jump, perhaps, but a safer one.

Salmon aim at the top of a waterfall by _____. Swimming toward the _____the salmon can _____ the sun _____ off the top of the _____ and they head toward this bright _____. During the evening and on _____days, salmon will _____ leap.

A salmon may leap several times its _____. It does this by letting the _____help. _____ comes plunging _____, then _____ strongly before heading downstream.

The salmon makes use of the upward _____ of the water. As a fish approaches a _____ which it recognises by _____, it swims down until it reaches the _____-moving water. With the water giving an added _____ the salmon leaps.

When the task was presented to pupils working on the text without the previous experience of the film, the key words 'sight' and 'sound' were left in, so as to help pupils build a conceptual framework for completing the remaining deletions. That too would be the version used by teachers and classes studying animal behaviour without the support of the MACOS programme.

Comment

In this activity, the deletions are designed to get pupils to focus on the content of the text rather than its language. The words chosen must represent the concepts of the text as accurately as possible. This does not mean that the language of the text can be ignored altogether. Every gap must be completed with a word that fits in both with the grammar of the text and with its conceptual framework. But it is the conceptual fit that is the more important criterion and this means that, in general, alternatives should be acceptable.

It is difficult to think of an alternative to 'not' at the end of the second paragraph, but most of the remaining deletions do allow several acceptable variations. For instance, the words 'force' and 'push' in the last paragraph are clearly interchangeable and for either one might substitute such words as 'thrust', 'pressure', 'movement', etc.

It is important to note that in this passage most of the discussion in groups was relevant discussion, concerned with the adequacy of a particular word for conveying the intended meaning. This may have something to do with the simplicity of the language used. Whatever the reason, here at least is a case where single-word deletion achieved the right objective and where deletion of a whole phrase might well have failed. This is not true of the next example, as we will see.

Example 3

Subject History

Source R.J. Cootes, 'After the Black Death', in *The Middle Ages*

Passage Type Historical Situation

Activities Text completion
            Underlining

Introduction

The passage used in this example is one of seven extracts that together constituted a chapter in the basic text-book used by second-year, mixed-ability pupils in a comprehensive school. Thus, for each extract, the text-based lesson was an integral part of the curriculum. Because there were several groups involved in these activities, one of the project officers was able to make at least an informal comparison between the effectiveness of a completion task and that of an analysis activity on the lines described in Part I of this book.

The extract shown below is a version of that used by the two classes concerned. Words that were deleted in the version given for completion are shown *in italics*.

It is the opinion both of the observer and of the teacher that the lesson was only partly successful. The object was to focus attention on how the circumstances of the common people had changed following the Black Death, how they reacted to these changed circumstances, the consequences of their own actions, and how in the end the relations between the powerful and the common people came to be materially altered.

After the Black Death

Before the Black Death, going as far back as the twelfth century, many villeins had been freed from their labour services to the lord of the manor. Instead of having to work part of the time on the lord's

---

land they paid him rent for their cottage and strips. With this money the lord hired free labourers to work for wages. Most lords found that wage labourers worked harder than villeins who were always anxious to get back to their own strips.

After the plague, however, workers were scarce. Labourers realised their increased *value* and *demanded* more wages than before. Many lords paid up, rather than let their crops rot for lack of hands to gather them in. The same happened in the towns. Masters had to pay higher wages to get enough journeymen to work for them.

Parliament tried to put a stop to these demands. Laws were made ordering that wages remain as they had been before the plague. Men who travelled in search of higher wages were to be branded on the forehead with a red hot iron!

At the same time Parliament asked for more and more taxes to pay for unsuccessful wars in France. Angrily, working men ignored the laws and tried to *avoid* the taxes.

Meanwhile, those who were still villeins saw the increased *advantages* of being free-men, now that wages were rising. So they tried to *exchange* their labour services for money rents. Some lords agreed, but others refused to give villeins their freedom. They strictly enforced all labour services, and made sure the slackers were fined in the manor court. Villeins became bitter and *restless*. The adventurous ones gathered their few possessions and *fled* with their wives and children. They could easily find *work* in a town or on another manor. Men were so hard to get that good wages were paid to *newcomers* and no questions asked about where they came from.

The common people of England, seeing the chance to better themselves, grew *discontented* with their lords and masters. There were threats of violence against some lords, including a number of abbots and bishops who refused to free their villeins. Because their estates belonged to the Church, many abbots and bishops claimed they should not rent them out or interfere with the old customs in any way. Villeins no longer *accepted* such excuses. They had lost *respect* for wealthy, pleasure-loving Church lords. So had many poor priests, who were firmly on the side of the peasants.

While the task for the completion group proved to be absorbing, it was noted that much of the discussion centred on linguistic considerations. For instance, pupils realised the workers wanted more money but they couldn't think of the one abstract noun 'value' for the first gap and wasted an inordinate amount of time in search of it.

Could it be that the list of words selected for deletion was not the best for the teacher's objective? Try to make up an alternative list which would stand a greater chance of success. The number of deletions should be broadly similar. If you can, do this before proceeding.

Course of the lesson

A copy of the text with deletions was provided for each pupil and pupils were asked to work with one or two partners. They were told that the extract dealt with the relationships between rulers and peasants and how these began to change after the plague. In their study of this extract, however, they were being asked to concentrate on the effects on the peasants: how things changed for the peasants, how they felt about these changes and how they responded to these changes.

Because there were two teachers in the classroom there was considerable support while pupils were working in small groups and it was not necessary for the class teacher to speak to the whole group. Nevertheless it soon became apparent that teacher support was necessary, especially to begin with.

The first two deletions created problems for many pupils. They could think of words that fitted the sense of the passage but did not fit grammatically. They could also do the opposite, but they couldn't do both.

For the first deletion a noun is required – and it is important to note that it is an abstract noun like 'value' or 'worth' which will fit the sense of the passage. The most common completion was 'work'. For the second deletion a verb is required. In the original it is 'demanded', but this is not obvious if the clue is taken from 'and'. 'And' can lead to the expectation of another noun. 'They' is of course implied by the text, but is not there in print.

Of course the trouble arises out of the close juxtaposition of these two particular gaps. Many pupils worried away at these two deletions until the teachers helped them with clues and/or encouraged them to go on. Others were content to put in 'increased *work* and *a lot* more wages' or 'increased *taxes* and *demand* more wages', but they too had spent an inordinate amount of time on this section.

Thus a deletion pattern which was intended to focus pupil attention on a specific aspect of content had the effect, initially, of directing attention to grammar. For this reason, despite the obvious involvement and enjoyment shown by pupils in this lesson, both teachers agreed that their objectives were not fully achieved.

The alternative lesson proved more successful. Pupils in the parallel class had the same introduction but they had been given the text straight and were asked to underline with different colours or symbols those parts of the text which described:

1. how the peasants felt about the changing conditions;
2. what action they took;
3. what effects the changes had on them.

This activity was actually finished sooner than the completion task, which meant that pupils had enough time to go back over the text and mark those parts that described the effects of the plague on the rulers. When the two classes were tested for recall of content one week later, the performance of the analysis group was significantly better than that of the completion group.

The observations of the two lessons suggest that pupils undertaking the analysis task had no need to worry about irrelevant linguistic detail and could go straight to the meaning of the text. They were therefore at an advantage.

Nevertheless, despite differences in recall according to the type of activity, there were positive outcomes of the lesson for all pupils. First, both groups went on in a second lesson to a close study of the remaining text – working either at a completion or an analysis activity, so that all pupils read the complete chapter in considerable detail and discussed it in depth. A final oral reading of the last few paragraphs, by a boy previously reluctant to read or to study, concluded the second lesson. In the view of the class teacher, the chapter would have been too difficult for these classes had there been no support for the reading. With the support of the directed activities, every pupil was willing and keen to study it. This he thought was the most valuable outcome of both lessons and he said so to his pupils. For their part, they said quite spontaneously how much they enjoyed the lessons.

Possible improvements

Given this class, and given this pattern of deletions, pupils spent too much time trying to find the right word to fit in with the immediate context and grammar. An analysis activity was more successful. Does this mean that single word completion is not appropriate for the study of this passage and others like it? Perhaps. But perhaps the main fault lay in the choice of the first two gaps. Or in the teacher's failure to deal with the difficulty more promptly. Or maybe the pupils were so wrapped up in tackling what eventually turned out to be the wrong problem that it was difficult to spot the difficulty and diagnose it.

Nevertheless, it was suggested at the beginning that teachers might try to devise an alternative pattern of deletions. Here is one:

Before the Black Death, going as far back as the twelfth century, many villeins had been freed from their labour services to the lord of the manor. Instead of having to work part of the time on the lord's land they paid him rent for their cottage and strips. With this money the lord hired free labourers to work for wages. Most lords found that wage labourers worked harder than villeins who were always anxious to get back to their own strips.

After the plague, however, workers were _____. Labourers realised their increased value and demanded _____ wages than before. Many lords paid up, rather than let their crops rot for lack of hands to gather them in. The same happened in the _____. Masters had to pay higher wages to get enough journeymen to work for them.

Parliament tried to put a stop to these demands. Laws were made ordering that wages should remain as they had been before the plague. Men who travelled in search of higher wages were to be branded on the forehead with a red hot iron!

At the same time Parliament asked for more and more taxes to pay for unsuccessful wars in France. Angrily, working men ignored the laws and tried to avoid the taxes.

Meanwhile, those who were still _____ saw the increased advantages of being _____, now that _____ were rising. So they tried to exchange their labour services for money rents. Some lords agreed, but others refused to give _____ their freedom. They strictly enforced all labour services, and made sure the slackers were fined in the manor court. _____ became bitter and restless. The _____ ones gathered their few possessions and fled with their wives and children. They could easily find work in a town or on another manor. Men were so hard to get that good ____ were ____ to newcomers and ____ questions asked about where they came from.

The common people of England, seeing the chance to better themselves, grew _____ with their lords and masters. There were threats of violence against some lords, including a number of abbots and bishops who refused to _____ their villeins. Because their estates belonged to the Church, many abbots and bishops claimed they should not rent them out or interfere with the old customs in any way. Villeins no longer accepted such excuses. They had lost _____ for wealthy, pleasure-loving Church lords. So had many poor priests, who were firmly on the side of the peasants.

The above deletions were arrived at with the knowledge of hindsight. They deliberately avoid the linguistic traps of the original deletions, and they focus attention on the following points:

1. a reduced labour pool increases the bargaining power of the labour force remaining (the word 'value' is a difficult one for children to supply when applied to human beings since it implies the idea that labour is itself a commodity and that value is something that can be measured by price);

2. this means that it now paid villeins to become free-men more than it did before;

3. some did so, against the law, and got away with it while others were disgruntled and expressed this by violence and 'insolence'.

The above list is not the only one possible. Your own lists may be as good as this or even better. Maybe none is any better than the first. But they should be, since they were arrived at with some knowledge of the snags encountered by the first set of deletions.

There is another alternative and this would be to use longer deletions. Here is such a version, focusing on the same essential ideas. (P = phrases, S = sentences)

Before the Black Death, going as far back as the twelfth century, many villeins had been freed from their labour services to the lord of the manor. Instead of having to work part of the time on the lord's land they paid him rent for their cottage and strips. With this money the lord hired free labourers to work for wages. Most lords found that wage labourers worked harder than villeins who were always anxious to get back to their own strips.

After the plague, however, workers were scarce. Labourers realised their increased value and _____ P _____. Many lords paid up, rather than let their crops rot for lack of hands to gather them in. The same happened in the towns. Masters had to pay higher wages to _____ P _____.

Parliament tried to put a stop to these demands. Laws were made ordering that wages remain as they had been before the plague. Men who travelled in search of higher wages were to be branded on the forehead with a red hot iron!

At the same time Parliament asked for more and more taxes to pay for unsuccessful wars in France. Angrily, working men ignored the laws and tried to avoid the taxes.

Meanwhile, those who were still villeins saw the increased advantages of being free-men, now that _____ P _____. So they tried to _____ P _____. Some lords agreed, but others refused to give villeins their freedom. They strictly enforced all labour services, and made sure the slackers were fined in the manor court. Villeins became bitter and restless. The adventurous ones gathered their few possessions and fled with their wives and children. S _____. Men were so hard to get that good wages were paid to newcomers and no questions asked about _____ P _____.

The common people of England, seeing the chance to better themselves, grew discontented with their lords and masters. There were threats of violence against some lords, including a number of abbots and bishops who _____ P _____. Because their estates belonged to the Church, many abbots and bishops claimed they should not rent them out or interfere with the old customs in any way. Villeins no longer accepted such excuses. They had lost respect for _____ P _____. So had many poor priests, who were firmly on the side of the peasants.

It goes without saying that when one has deleted whole phrases and sentences, what one is after is a completion that makes just about as good sense as the original. But for the task to be successful it may well be necessary to go through at least one of the deletions as a class-together exercise, so that pupils get to know what is wanted. Even then, we cannot say for certain that this exercise would achieve each teacher's objective. But there is a good chance that it would. The next example provides very clear support for the potential of larger deletions.

Example 4

Subject English
Source Richard Adams, *Shardik*
Passage Type Narrative
Activities Text completion

Introduction

There are just four deletions in the following passage. Three of them are short sentences while the fourth is a part of a sentence. The actual length of these deletions varies but the gaps in our text have been deliberately kept standard. Try to fill each gap in such a way as to complete the sense of the passage while keeping to the style of the writer. Then see if you can list the main considerations that led to your selections. As always, teachers working in groups should compare notes with one another.

Shardik

The enormous bear wandered irresolutely on through the forest, now stopping to glare about at its unknown surroundings, now breaking once more into a shambling trot as it found itself still pursued by the hiss and stench of burning creepers and the approach of the fire. It was sullen with fear and bewilderment. Since nightfall of the previous day it had been driven, always reluctant yet always unable to find any escape from danger. Never before had it been forced to flight.[

]Now with a kind of angry shame, it slunk on and on, stumbling on half-seen roots, tormented with thirst, and desperate for a chance to turn and fight against this flickering enemy that nothing could dismay. Once it stood its ground at the far end of a patch of marsh, deceived by what seemed a faltering at last in the enemy's advance, and fled just in time to save itself from being encircled as the fire ran forward on either side. Once[

]Yet still it paused and paced about, looking for an opportunity to fight; and as often as it turned and went on, slashed the tree-trunks and tore up the bushes with heavy blows of its claws.

Then slower and slower it went, panting now, tongue protruding and eyes half-shut against the smoke that followed closer and closer. It struck one scorched foot against a sharpened boulder, fell, and rolled on its side, and when it got up became confused, made a half-turn and began to wander up and down, parallel to the line of the on-coming flames.[

]Choking in the enveloping smoke, it could no longer tell even from which side the fire was coming. The nearest flames caught a dry tangle of quian roots and raced along them, licking across one fore-paw. Then from all sides there sounded a roaring as though at last the enemy were coming to grips. But louder still rose the frenzied, angry roaring of the bear itself as it turned at last to fight.

Swinging its head from side to side and dealing tremendous, spark-showering blows upon the blaze around it, it reared up to its full height, trampling back and forth until the soft earth was flattened under its feet and it seemed to be actually sinking into the ground beneath its own weight. A long flame crackled up the thick pelt and in a moment the creature blazed, all covered with fire, rocking and nodding in a grotesque and horrible rhythm. In its rage and pain it had staggered to the edge of a steep bank. Swaying forward, it suddenly saw below[

]Then it plunged. A moment later there rose the sound of a heavy splash and a hissing, quenching after-surge of deep water.

Objectives

The initial task here is exactly the same as that given to the pupils. It focuses on the style of the writer, on the techniques used to portray both the bear's strength and power and its vulnerability in the face of a new situation. The objective was to focus attention on how this contrast is achieved. Deletions were made at points in the text where the writer:

presents the background of the bear (first gap);
describes its competing reactions to the fire (second gap);
summarises the state of the bear (third gap);
introduces a new element into the story (fourth gap).

Would the pupils produce sentences which served these same functions? Would they use some of the same devices as those of the writer?

In particular, we find that several devices have been used to achieve contrast:

1. longer sentences are used to carry the action of the story; shorter sentences summarise the state of the bear;

2. the rhythm reflects the varying pace of the bear's flight from the fire;

3. repetition is used to contrast the bear's opposing reactions to the fire: 'now stopping to glare . . . now breaking into a shambling trot', 'always reluctant . . . yet always unable', 'Once it stood its ground . . . Once, in a kind of madness'.

Phasing of the lesson

This lesson did not form part of the ongoing work in an English course. It was prepared in order to explore the possibilities of sentence deletion. Sentence or line deletion was being used by a number of teachers in the study of poetry and increasing numbers of teachers were reporting on the potential of sentence deletion for the close study of longer stretches of prose.

The project team decided to try out these techniques for themselves. The class was a mixed-ability, third-year class in a comprehensive school.

In the introduction to the lesson, pupils were told that they would read with the teacher an extract from a book. The book was called *Shardik* and was written by the author of *Watership Down*. The extract they were to hear came from the beginning of the book. Shardik was the name of a bear, and later in the story it would turn out that he was no ordinary bear. Just the same, the bit they were to study could be read as a straightforward description of a bear's reaction to a forest fire. The pupils were warned that when the extract had been read they would be asked to make up sentences to fill the gaps in such a way as to keep both the sense of the passage and its style.

Every pupil had a copy of the text. Following the introduction the teacher read the extract aloud, and this was followed by an initial class discussion dealing with what was actually 'going on' in the very long sentences, especially in the sentence immediately preceding the second gap.

After this, pupils worked in twos or threes making up the sentences to fill the gaps. Both the class teacher and one of the project officers were available for help if needed, but in fact pupil involvement in the task was so high that they acted as observers for most of the lesson. There was time enough at the end of the lesson for a full discussion in which each pupil grouping made at least one contribution. These contributions were listened to very attentively by all the other pupils, and criticism was always constructive and positive.

Pupils' response

First deletion

Original sentence:

'For years past no living creature had stood against it.'

Sample of sentences offered by pupils:

'There was no other man or beast that could frighten him.'
'Always before it had been on top.'

Second deletion

Original sentence:

'Once in a kind of madness, it rushed back on its tracks and actually struck and beat at the flames, until its pads were scorched and black, singed streaks showed along the pelt.'

Sample of sentences offered by pupils:

'Once it nearly broke through the wall of blazing heat but was induced to retreat by an avalanche of roaring flames.'

'Once by instinct, the bear dug a deep trench to stop the fire but the raging inferno leaped over it like a kangaroo.'

'Once the large bear had got encircled by the scorching fire there was nothing it would do but try and fight back.'

'Once removed from the presence of the roaring flames it turned to scrutinise it.'

Third deletion

Original sentence:

'It was exhausted and had lost the sense of direction.'

Sample of sentences offered by pupils:

'Moving bewildered, it trudged alongside the flames.'
'Enshrined in a volt of dense smoke and fog.'
'Never before had it been so confused.'
'It was tired and didn't know which way to go or what to do.'

Fourth deletion

Original sentence:

'. . . in a lurid flash, another bear, shimmering and grimacing, raising burning paws towards itself.'

Sample of sentences offered by pupils:

'. . . its burning fur in the reflection of the water.'
'. . . in the lurid flash, the bear was in a ferocious state – as it saw itself in the stream.'
'. . . an extinguisher, it was a mass of still water and relief, with its life in the hands of the water.'
'. . . its burning face in the reflection of the water.'

These are representative samples and not all of them are perfect. Some of the responses to the third deletion were not complete sentences. One is surprised by the instinct which guides a bear how to dig a trench, although one may also admire both it and the child who thought of it. The grammar of one of the suggestions for the fourth gap is rather irregular. There are some strange aberrations in spelling, like 'volt' for 'vault'.

Yet one is bound to note how well most of these suggestions mirror the function of the original, in the sense that they convey an idea which is similar even if it isn't exactly the same. Also noteworthy is the deliberate variation in length of sentence: short for the first and third deletions, long for the second and fourth. Finally, note the choice of wording in almost every suggestion: a mixture of long words and short ones, rare words and common. This too was caught from the original and faithfully transposed.

Final comment

For a passage like this, there had to be a highly supportive introduction. The high percentage of embedded sentences makes for very difficult reading, and so do such rare items of vocabulary as 'quian' and 'grotesque'. The teacher did not tell the class the meanings of such words at the beginning of the lesson but she did explain how these could be worked out from their context.

Given the right kind of support, it is clear from this example that sentence deletion has considerable potential for the study of style and of meaning in literary prose. The pupils are required to be faithful to the style of the passage and preserve its sense, and this means they have to pay very careful attention both to the meaning of the text and to the language in which it is couched. What is more, the fact that pupils are being asked to write complete sentences in a given style can be used to further their own creative writing.

It could be that where single word deletion is ideal for getting pupils to focus on the criteria which govern the creation and appreciation of poetry, we should more often think of sentence or phrase deletion to achieve the same purpose in relation to prose. Certainly, as we saw in example 1, in poetry one finds many constraints in the choice of each single word. So thinking about an individual missing word is likely to alert pupils to many aspects of poetic structure. In prose the constraints on each word are generally fewer and the writing is correspondingly less 'economical' or 'tight'. Both sense and style remain important but, because of the lesser constraints, one is perhaps more likely to get a feel for these considerations when one is asked to consider the shape of longer units like phrases and sentences instead of focusing on the choice of single words.

We conclude this example with a piece of prose produced by a pupil in the course of a follow-up lesson. The boy in question was a member of a 'special English' class consisting of pupils not considered able enough to study French. He decided to write a description of Shardik's reactions to the fire in his own words. Here it is (spellings corrected):

> The bear is the most powerful creature in the forest and never before had it experienced a forest fire or its abilities. The fire is able to beat the bear, this fills the bear with bewilderment and fear. The bear can't explain to himself how the fire operates the only thing it knows is that the fire is unstoppable and does not give the bear a chance to fight something that he did not experience before. Also the inability of the bear to do anything about the fire this makes the bear feel helpless. Also on top of this the bear is not in his own territory which gives him a disadvantage straight away.
>
> Another creature might have packed in. But the bear has got that incredible will to live to survive and to fight which makes him go on, fight against something that can't be beaten.

Example 5

Subject Geography

Source E.W. Young and J.H. Lowry, 'Coniferous Trees', in *People Around the World*

Passage Type Biological Adaptation

Activities Text completion

Introduction

Complete each of the gaps in the following passage with a suitable phrase. You will need to study the whole passage before tackling the first deletion and you are warned that the first deletion may be the most difficult one of all!

> **Coniferous trees**
>
> No plants or trees make much growth until the mean air temperature is over 6°C, so the growing season in Northern Russia is very short. Anything that does grow must adapt itself to these short cool summers and also, of course, to the bitter winters.
>
> The best answer to the problem has been found by the coniferous trees, and it is these – chiefly pine, spruce, fir and larch – that make

up most of the taiga, as the great forest of Northern Europe and Siberia is called. In some areas the lighter green of the silver birch makes a graceful contrast with the sombre masses of dark-green coniferous trees; but the latter are everywhere in the majority.

A tree lives mainly by the food dissolved in water that it draws in through its roots. When the ground is frozen the tree cannot take in water, so that coniferous trees _____. Our own broad-leaved deciduous trees – oak, elm, etc, do this by shedding their leaves and 'dying' for the winter; but summer in the taiga is too short for the deciduous trees' leisurely life cycle of budding – leafing – flowering – fruiting – seeding. To _____, most coniferous trees keep their leaves all through the winter. These leaves, to avoid being _____, are very thin (the pine 'needle' is our most familiar example) and thus offer very little resistance to the wind. In addition they have a waxy surface with very few pores – two points that help to _____. The trunks and branches of coniferous trees are covered with thick resinous bark that _____. Many such trees carry their branches sloping downwards. This allows the snow _____ _____.

When spring comes the tree again picks up the business of living, but even by keeping its leaves it has now saved enough time to be able to produce fruit and seeds in one season. Accordingly it has adjusted itself, over millions of years, to live without _____; instead it carries its seeds on the outside of 'cones' which take about one and a half seasons to ripen. In early summer the second-season cones begin to cast their seeds, and some of these form the next generation of the forest.

Comment

The passage is one of several that we have encountered which deal with adaptation in one form or another, usually with an instance of biological adaptation. Such passages tend to have a common form. There is a statement of the adaptation problem in general terms (here the way in which plants cope with long harsh winters) followed (or sometimes preceded) by a general introduction to the life forms which typify the adaptation (here the coniferous trees). Following this introduction, we find a listing of adaptive features, each of which comprises a specific problem together with a particular adaptive response. Not infrequently, the individual feature affects one part of the organism and its response, and this helps to determine the order in which things are mentioned – here many of the features relate to leaves, and these are dealt with before other features of conifers. The discussion of such adaptive features can of course vary in length, depending on how far the writer chooses to detail the relevant descriptions and mechanisms. Here they are all quite brief.

Unfortunately, despite the concentration of features relating to leaves, there is some confusion in the order of this passage and we will come back to this later.

There is one more point to be made about these sorts of passages, and this has to do with contrast. If a particular life form is adapted to certain unusual conditions, its appearance and behaviour will differ from some more typical norm, and this will apply to each adaptive feature. Here deciduous trees are taken to represent the typical norm; they are the forms with which we are most familiar. Sometimes there will be explicit reference to the contrasting normal feature, or to the normal condition, but sometimes it will be implicit. The present passage has instances of both.

At this point we list the phrases that were deleted from the passage as presented on pages 169–70:

1. have to be dormant (asleep) in the winter
2. save time each spring
3. withered by the biting winds
4. prevent their precious moisture from being evaporated away
5. protects them, too, from the cold, drying winds
6. to slide off before its weight is heavy enough to break the branches
7. bearing fruit

Needless to say, you were not expected to re-invent these phrases word for word but rather to find a form of words that made sense.

Context

There are many pupils in the age range 11–14 for whom the concept of adaptation is not an easy one. This passage was chosen by a teacher in a comprehensive school to introduce the concept to a second-year, mixed-ability group. The initial task was not the completion task as presented above, but an analysis activity very similar to the one which was so successful for example 3. Pupils were given the passage without deletions. The first three tasks involved underlining:

1. underline those sections of the passage that refer to particular parts of coniferous trees;

2. now, using a different colour, underline those sections that tell you about the effects of the weather on these parts;

3. now, using a third colour, underline those sections that tell you how the part is modified to cope with the harsh weather.

After completing the underlining, the class were asked to produce a table with three columns. The first column was to refer to successive 'features' dealt with in the text, ie the life cycle of the tree and its parts; the second was to contain adaptations; and the third was to show the effects of these adaptations.

In the event, the class needed a great deal of help in completing these tasks and the tables they reproduced were a little disappointing. Here are three examples:

Table 10 Example of pupil work 1

	Examples of adaptation	*Effects*
Life cycle: 1) 2)	it carries its seeds on the outside of cones they keep their leaves	It saves time
leaves – shape	very thin	little resistance to wind
trunks	thick resinous bark	protects from wind
branches	the branches slope down	so the snow falls off so the branches don't break
fruit	cones	
seeds	able to produce fruit and seeds in one season	

Table 11 Example of pupil work 2

	Examples of adaptation	*Effect*
Life cycle		
1)	it needs $1\frac{1}{2}$ years to regenerate itself	
2)	Coniferous trees lie dormant in the winter and do not shed their leaves as the summer is to short to grow them back	

	Examples of adaptation	Effect
Leaves, shape	very thin	Little resistance to wind
Surface	waxy with few pores	Prevents moisture from escaping
Trunks + Branches	Have very thick resinous bark	This protects them from the cold drying winds
Branches	The branches slope downwards and are very flexible	This protects them from heavy snow that would break the branches off, taking away its moisture stores
Fruit	The time to grow fruit is very short so it does this in $1\frac{1}{2}$ seasons	

Table 12 Example of pupil work 3

	Examples of adaptation	Effect
Life cycle	keep leaves in winter it also lives without bearing fruit	it saves time
		saves time
	carries seeds	
Leaves shape – surface	very thin	little resistance to winds
Trunks	covered with resinous bark	protects them from cold drying wind
Branches	the branches slope downwards	it allows the snow to slide off before heavy enough break them
Fruit	fruit and seeds cannot be grown in the same season	It has learnt to live without bearing fruit
Seeds	They are carried on outside of the cones	

The first pupil is clearly a weaker student than the other two. But all three are fairly successful in the first two colums and a little uncertain about the third.

Knowing how much verbal support had been given to the class, the teacher and the project officer were unconvinced that the central idea of adaptation had been properly grasped. For instance, very few pupils gave evidence that they understood how seed-bearing cones offered an adaptive solution to the problem of summers which are too short for flowering and fruiting.

As often happens, there are several possible reasons to account for the children's problems. The topic is not an easy one; the notion of 'feature' is abstract; it might have been better to ask for problems and adaptations rather than adaptations and effects. Above all, however, the passage itself is confusing because a number of more specific adaptive features are buried inside the principle mechanism referred to as the life-cycle. In effect, the last two sentences refer back to the beginning of the previous paragraph, and this is not obvious.

The completion exercise was conceived as an alternative that avoids some of these problems. The first two deletions and the last are closely related. These all refer to the life-cycle. What is more, the best clue to the second deletion 'to save time each spring' is in the final paragraph 'even by keeping its leaves it has not saved enough time'.

Because the task is well defined, the completion exercise makes one look for any relevant cues wherever they are to be found in the passage. So provided that:

1. the deletions have been carefully chosen to focus on whatever is most significant in the passage;

2. there is enough information left undeleted to allow the student to solve the problem,

completion is a good introduction to the ideas one wants to put over.

For the future, the teacher decided to use the completion task in conjunction with the present passage, but to follow this up with a text-analysis task to be used in connection with another passage, also concerned with adaptation.

2 SEQUENCING

Introduction

Like all text-based activities that we have worked on, sequencing is designed to make pupils read a passage carefully, to consider the implications of what is said, and above all to think about the coherence of the passage – how it all fits together. In some ways, sequencing does this more openly than completion, since the whole job is to re-assemble the scrambled sections in whatever way makes the best possible sense. There is one sure way to appreciate the challenge of sequencing and its potential. Try it.

Below is an extract from a school text. It has been cut into eight sections, and the author's order has been altered.

Read through all the sections. In the context of the whole passage decide which order makes the best sense to you from reference to evidence in the text.

Introductory Example

Subject History

Source A. Darlington 'The First Revolution and the Second', in *Pollution and Life*

Passage Type Evolutionary process

Activities Sequencing

The First Revolution and the Second

A Just as the Neolithic Revolution happened in the Stone Age, so the Industrial Revolution produced the machine age. From it sprang large towns.

B Although the craft of weaving had been practised as early as 5000 B.C. it only became mechanised in the middle of the 18th century. This is what marked the beginning of the Industrial Revolution.

C This meant that still more machines and factories were needed to make more goods. Towns grew where there was materials for the machines and suitable conditions for working them.

D Indeed, some argue that the Industrial Revolution has not yet ended. Their opinion is that it cannot end until the problems which come from it have been solved. There is something to be said for this point of view.

E Man started depending for his living more upon trade than upon his farm animals or the crops he himself could grow.

F It was five thousand years before the next big change – the Industrial Revolution of 1760–1840. This is so recent that elderly men and women, still alive today, can remember speaking to people who were alive at the end of that period.

G They had begun as the villages man built when he settled down to farm, but they were not necessarily near his farms any longer.

H One thing is certain. There could have been no Industrial Revolution had not the Neolithic Revolution come first. Changes carried out by factory owners two centuries ago were based on the ideas and methods of their Stone Age ancestors.

Comments

Before going on, you will wish to confirm the original order of the segments as given by the writer of the passage. You will find this printed upside down at the foot of this page.

Ordering the segments is a puzzle, and often quite a fascinating one. But although it is obviously a good thing that it does have entertainment value, this alone would not justify its use as an aid to learning and understanding. The point is that the problem can force the solver to read over each segment several times to see what clues might relate it to any other segment, then to build up sequences of segments, and finally to consider how these go together to make up the whole. In other words, one is led to rehearse both content and structure:

The passage contains two main themes each of which includes subsidiary points:

1. An analogy is drawn between the Neolithic and Industrial Revolutions; the main point of similarity: that change in technology produces great social change; the main point of difference: a vast time difference. Total: three points;

2. The Industrial Revolution gave rise to big towns; the towns had their origin as villages; the villages expanded because of two factors: expansion of trade reduced the pull of the land; mechan-

isation and its needs created the conditions for cumulative expansion. Total: five points.

Now there are several ways of ordering these eight points. But it wouldn't do to mix in a statement about towns with a discussion of the first theme, or to alter the order of the three subsidiary things said about towns (G, E, C). The sequencing problem brings one face to face with these constraints, which derive from the sense of the ideas. What is more, it does this indirectly in a game-like setting.

It is less important to establish the original order than it is to establish the coherence of what is said. Sometimes several orders are possible, and this may actually be a good thing if it leads to disagreement and alerts pupils to the need to justify their sequencing.

It is of course true that logical coherence is not the only clue to sequencing. There are linguistic cues besides: 'This meant . . .', 'They had begun . . .', 'Indeed . . .', 'large towns . . . Towns grew', '5000 B.C. . . . five thousand years' (a slip?). However, this is almost certainly a good thing in two ways. In the first place, such linguistic clues provide confirmatory evidence, thus making the activity more rewarding. In the second place, they have been put in more or less deliberately by the author to help the reader to make sense of the passage, so there is good reason to hope that students who have been alerted to their role in the context of a sequencing problem will continue to exploit them in their independent reading.

When to scramble

It goes without saying that because sequencing a scrambled passage is a matter of establishing a coherent order, the task would not work for a passage that consisted of a set of points which were arranged in an arbitrary order to begin with.

In practice, teachers have tended to adopt this technique when most of the segments are of a kind and their order is more or less crucial. For instance, when a passage tells you how to set up an experiment and the segments are successive steps, as in 'Making a constellation viewer' (Example 6). Or when each of the segments represent a distinct step in a process, as in 'Building a polder' (Example 13).

However, sequencing can be used to advantage with a wide variety of passages. Although the ordering of information in the original should not be arbitrary, there is no need for all the segments to be of a piece. The passage about the two revolutions is a good instance to the contrary. 'During Wind and Rain' (Example 7) shows how the technique can be used to bring home the subtle thematic development underlying the construction of a poem.

Preparation

The text needs to be broken up and printed on separate pieces of paper or card each of which must be identified by a letter or number which is deliberately chosen at random. The letters will then be used to describe alternative arrangements offered in the course of group and class discussion. Ideally the size of each piece of paper should be the same irrespective of the amount of print on it. The easiest way to achieve this is to take the space covered by the biggest segment of print as the unit size for that particular sequence.

Pupils will tend to use physical clues to the sequence given a chance. Matching up irregularly cut edges between segments, or using fade lines left by the printing process are both favourite quick routes to completion.

There are no fixed rules for the size of segments. Often they will be three or four lines long, but we have also used much longer segments (cf 'Transmission of sound', Example 8), and sometimes shorter (cf 'During Wind and Rain', Example 7). But it is important to make sure that each segment makes a distinctive contribution to the whole.

If the material is going to be used many times over, it is worthwhile reproducing the segments on durable card. You may, however, want the pupils to retain a copy of the ordered segments in their notebooks. Some teachers have chosen to do this when dealing with an experimental procedure in science or with the key stages in a historical event. The proposed segments are printed on paper and stuck or stapled in pupil notebooks.

This system also has the virtue that for major items of information in the course, the teacher has a firm control over what is put into pupil notes. Time spent on the sequencing activity and the ensuing discussion can be balanced against the time that would have been spent in pupil notemaking or taking.

Class management

Pupils should be organised into discussion groups of two or three. It is difficult for more than three to consider a set of segments together. An increase in group size also increases the possibility of reduced involvement by any one member of the group.

The distribution of the segmented text in the classroom can be a problem, but there are many ways round it. Putting the segments in envelopes can help, especially where using paper clips or rubber bands may present some pupils with unwanted diversions.

Once the task has started, the teacher's main role is to see that the decisions the pupils make as to the reordering of the text can be justified either from the evidence in the text or from existing knowledge related to cues in the text. How this is done is partly a matter of teaching style. However, as the pupils gain in experience, teacher intervention should be greatly reduced, unless the task is especially difficult.

Where a correct order is wanted, for example in a description of a process or experiment, approaches vary. Some teachers will not accept a sequence until it is fully correct. Others will verify correct sub-sequences and indicate areas of error. It may be necessary to give pupils additional clues as they are working, eg establish the first step in a sequence of instructions; provide the rhyme scheme for a poem; or draw attention to some critical feature which will help in determining the right sequence.

Methods of checking the final order vary. With some texts there will not necessarily be a final correct order. The class may, during discussion, come to a concensus as to which they prefer. This may or may not be in agreement with either the author's version or the teacher's version. When your pupils are confident enough to reject these, you may feel you're winning!

Examples

Example 6

Subject Physics

Source C. Windridge 'Making a Constellation Viewer', in *General Science 2*.

Passage Type Instructions

Activities Sequencing

Introduction

The following set of instructions is listed in scrambled order. In order to share the experience from the pupil's point of view, you should do two things:

1. decide on an appropriate order for the instructions;
2. consider what additional instructions or explanations would need to be added in order to make the instructions usable by first-year, secondary-school pupils.

Making a constellation viewer

1. Hold the central part of a card against one end of the tube.

2. Make a card for each constellation.

---

3. Make a card tube about 20 cm long and 4 cm in diameter.

4. The constellation appears to you as it would do at night.

5. Make a list of the constellations which you can recognise.

6. You should look at the sky at night, however.

7. Use a needle to prick holes to represent a constellation on an 8 cm square of card.

8. You can use this viewer during the day, when the night sky is not available.

9. Hold the other end against your eye and point the tube towards a bright light or a window.

Context of lesson

This activity was designed by a member of the project team in collaboration with the class teacher. The class consisted of first-year pupils in a 10–13 high school. The topic of the solar system had already been initiated by the class teacher in a previous lesson in the course of which pupils had learned something about the origins of the solar system and constellations. The pupils had been told that they would be making constellation viewers, and right from the start there was a high degree of commitment and enthusiasm.

The first objective was to show the pupils how to make a constellation viewer and to do so by following the instructions in the text. But there were also two additional objectives: (a) to use the opportunity to get pupils to predict the logical and practical order of steps in an activity before undertaking it, and (b) if possible to get them to anticipate the snags they might meet with and how they might overcome these.

The text-book from which the passage is taken does give its readers information about constellations before instructing them to make a constellation viewer. But pupils are not told how to make a card tube 20 cm long and 4 cm in diameter. Similarly, they are not told how to make an 8 cm square of card. In so far as these things are not obvious to them, the list of instructions has to be extended, and this is in fact what happened.

Conduct of lesson

The pupils were presented with the cut up segments of the text and they were told that these were the only instructions that could be found. However, they were warned that some important details about how to

Correct order of instructions: 5, 7, 2, 3, 1, 9, 4, 8, 6.

proceed were missing and that the order of the steps was not given. Their task would be first to decide on the best order in which to do things, and second to discover in detail how each step should be carried out. Thus, when they had ordered the segments, they were to work out how to do things and then write the additional instructions on extra slips of paper.

Rough paper was provided to allow the pupils to try out their ideas about making the tube. Throughout the lesson both teachers were available to help as and when needed.

Pupils worked seriously at ordering the instructions and formulating additional steps. As in all mixed-ability classes some were much more equal to the problems than others. At one end of the ability range, several pupils applied their knowledge of geometry to the task of constructing the tube and circle on the card. But creative solutions were also worked out by pupils with less mathematical knowledge. Amongst these was the solution of making the square card first, and then marking a circle of 4 cm diameter on the card. The diameter of the unfixed tube could then be adjusted to match the circle and finally glued at the right diameter.

While solutions were being worked out by small groups, the class teacher brought the whole class together several times to discuss possibilities and evaluate them. But although there was much free borrowing of ideas, the final solutions varied.

After they had ordered the instructions, all the pupils were successful in making their viewers. When they had made these, they soon asked to produce their own set of instructions for making a constellation viewer in the light of their experience. This is not an easy task and they did so with varying success. Here are some representative examples. They show that nearly all of these writers had come to grips with the problem.

A Making a constellation viewer

First we got a piece of blue paper. Then we drew a square in the middle of it. We cut the square out with the rest we made a roll. We sticky taped the square on. But to hold the roll together we put some more sticky tape round the hole. Going back a little we drew the circle with a compass, we made a little dot to show where to put the needle. We pricked a hole in the circle to make a constellation viewer.

B Making a constellation viewer

1. First cut out a 20 cm long piece of card.
2. It is best to have black paper so that the stars stand out more clearly.

3. Then roll the card round so that you have a tube 4 cm across.

4. Put a mark where the paper meets and then glue it together.

5. Next cut out another piece of card, 8 cm square.

6. Set a compass at 2 cm and draw a circle in the centre of the card. It should be 4 cm across.

7. Next trace the stars of a constellation and draw them inside the circle.

8. Use a needle to prick holes where the stars are.

9. You can make a card for each constellation.

10. Hold the central part of the card against one end of the tube.

11. Hold the other end against your eye and point the tube towards a bright light or a window.

12. The constellation appears to you as it would do at night.

13. You can use this viewer during the day, when the night sky is not available.

14. You should look at the sky at night however.

15. Make a list of constellations which you can recognise.

C Making a constellation viewer

1. You take a piece of card and measure an 8 cm by 8 cm square.

2. Find the centre of the square by folding the opposite sides to meet each other.

3. Draw a circle with a compass measure 2 cm on your compass and draw your circle, it should be 4 cm in diameter.

4. With the rest of the card measure a 20 cm long piece of card and twirl it around until it matches the circle on the card.

5. You then stick it, to make sure the tube is 4 cm in diameter then measure it with a ruler.

6. You take the square with the circle in the middle and trace a constellation which will fit into the circle and poke a pin through the tracing paper and onto the card.

7. Fix it onto the tube and look up to the light it might look like a night sky.

Example 7

Subject English Literature
Source 'During Wind and Rain' by Thomas Hardy
Passage Type Poem
Activities Sequencing

Introduction

This example consists of a lesson conducted with a fifth-year group of 28 pupils, forming an upper band within a comprehensive school. Readers who wish to tackle the task for themselves may like to use the five 'clues' provided for the class. The complete poem in its original order will be found on page 189.

As part of their work for 'O' level literature the pupils were required to study a selection of the poems of Thomas Hardy. They had been engaged in this for two months prior to the lesson described here. The teacher reports as follows:

> 'It became clear to me from their writings on the poems that, while reasonably happy to comment and show understanding of the meaning of Hardy's words, they were markedly less confident where rhyme and rhythm were concerned. They were having difficulty in grasping how these two aspects of a poem could contribute to its meaning and its effect on the reader. Teaching scansion and rhyme schemes has never seemed to me to be a very satisfactory way to lead pupils towards a more sensitive response to poetry and tends to produce an ability to label and classify rather than to think and feel. The lesson described here was an attempt to go some of the way in tackling this problem.'

Essentially the lesson took the form of a sequencing task, the whole of the selected poem being presented in 16 scrambled segments each consisting of a couplet or a single line.

During Wind and Rain

1. And they build a shady seat
   Ah, no; the years, the years;
2. How the sick leaves reel down in throngs!
3. Treble and tenor and bass,
   And one to play;

---

4. Under the summer tree
With a glimpse of the bay,

5. Down their carved names the raindrop ploughs.

6. They change to a high new house,
He, she, all of them – Aye,

7. Making the pathways neat
And the garden gay;

8. They sing their dearest songs –
He, she, all of them – yea,

9. Clocks and carpets and chairs
On the lawn all day,

10. And the rotten rose is ript from the wall.

11. They clear the creeping moss –
Elders and juniors – aye,

12. And brightest things that are theirs
Ah, no; the years, the years;

13. With the candles mooning each face
Ah, no; the years O!

14. While pet fowl come to the knee
Ah, no; the years O!

15. See, the white storm-birds wing across

16. They are blithely breakfasting all –
Men and maidens – yea,

Clues

1. The poem is in 4 stanzas of 7 lines each.

2. Shortly before she died, Emma wrote an account of her childhood in Plymouth. Hardy read this book and the above poem is based on memories he found in it.

3. The poem tells how happy times are gradually overtaken by change and decay.

4. Hardy's sense of structure can be felt very strongly in this poem.

5. Pronounce 'Aye' like the first letter of the alphabet.

'Most of the 'units' on the sheet are couplets. It seemed to me much too difficult to sequence 28 separate lines. Lines which have been given separately are the final lines of each stanza. I was aware that this constituted a clue as to structure, both the punctuation of the line and its tone having a 'finality' which the pupils would recognise from earlier studies of Hardy.

The clues given at the foot of the sheet were intended to give the pupils both a general framework within which to work and in one instance, no 5, a specific piece of advice.'

Conduct and progress of lesson

The following account was provided by the teacher and is reproduced in full, without comment.

The lesson occupied one double period of 1 hour and 10 minutes. The class was divided into normal working groups ranging from three pupils in a group (two instances) to five in a group (one instance).

Pupils were told that they were about to receive a sheet on which was printed a poem of Hardy's. The lines of the poem had been re-arranged into 'units' so they were now in the wrong order. All punctuation given was strictly correct. Each 'unit' was numbered.

One sheet was issued to each pupil.
It was pointed out to the pupils that:

1. the title of the poem was given;
2. they had 16 'units' to re-arrange;
3. there were five clues given at the foot of the page which might prove useful;
4. at regular intervals new pieces of information might be offered to them if I deemed it necessary.

They were told that they might make any marks which were necessary on the printed sheet and asked to bring the poem to me for checking on completion.

Fifteen minutes after the lesson started the whole class was given the following piece of information:

Supplementary clue 1

The rhyme scheme of this poem is A, B, C, B, C, D, A.
What under normal circumstances would have been regarded as the most dry and irrelevant piece of information was seized upon with great glee. Groups who had become listless and frustrated were reactivated; some had ideas confirmed, others saw the need to re-think. One group didn't have a clue how this could be any help at all.

Apart from the last verse of the poem, there is no particular logic about where the verses come in relation to each other, and so the next clue was given five minutes later:

Supplementary clue 2

The following words relate to the poem and are in order:
'singing'   'gardening'   'eating'   'moving'

Clue 3 was given five minutes later, largely to allow groups to check their progress so far, but also to assist the slower groups. I felt it to be important that a high degree of success be achieved by everyone.

Supplementary clue 3

They sing by candlelight;
They eat out of doors;
The last line of the poem is very grave.

Five minutes later the final clue was given. The information in it seemed to confirm rather than surprise:

Supplementary clue 4

The first word in each stanza is the same

The first completely correct entry was handed to me 35 minutes after the lesson had begun; the rest within the next ten minutes.

Feedback

I then asked everyone to jot down for me:

1. the sort of methods they could remember using in completing the exercise;
2. the clues on the sheet which they found most and least useful;
3. which supplementary clues they had found most useful;
4. what they thought they had learned from the exercise.

Here are some examples of the replies:

In response to 1

1. 'First we tried to find the last line of each verse.'
2. 'We looked at the punctuation to see where the full stops were and then tried to establish whether those were the last lines of the verses. Then we looked to see which of the lines

sounded most final and regarded these as the end of the poem. I also tried to find a couplet in which the last word of the first line rhymed with the supposed last line of the stanza. Here the rhyming scheme helped.'

3. 'We tried to discover a rhyme scheme. We looked for first and last lines. We tried to put couplets together.'

4. 'We tried to organise our own rhyme scheme before you gave us one.'

5. 'Looking for subjects that go together and fit in with the rhyming scheme.'

6. 'First of all we looked for single sentences and then decided whether they came at the beginning or the end of each stanza.'

7. 'Associating actions with words.'

8. 'We tried different lines together in verses to see how they sounded. We then tried to group the lines into themes.'

9. 'Picking out two lines which rhyme together and have similar meanings.'

10. 'Looked at diction and found which couplets had to go together according to meanings.'

In response to 2

Clue 1 on the sheet was thought by everyone to be the most useful and clue 2 the least. Clue 5 was rated second in value, then clues 3 and 4.

Comments included

1. 'We used clue 3 at first to pick out the 'happy, rosy bits' and the 'old souring bits'.'

2. 'The clue that it's about Emma was useless.'

3. 'The one about its sense of structure was useful.'

4. 'Clue 2 was no use at all.' (Repeated many times).

In response to 3

1. 'The three points given in supplementary clue 3 helped very much in confirming the order of the lines.'

2. 'The rhyme scheme was very helpful.' (Repeated many times.)

Generally, all of the supplementary clues had their champions. Obviously, it depended how much of a breakthrough each clue allowed.

In response to 4

1. 'I learnt that there was a very complicated structure, regular, but complex.'

2. 'Structure and how many different rhyme schemes you can have.'

3. 'I think that this approach to the poem was useful, because it helped me to understand the rhyming scheme and the form of his poems. It also made me study the poem more closely and able to become familiar with it.'

4. 'Learn the structure of the poem and helps you remember quotations. Helps you to understand rhyming scheme in much more detail and makes the poem more familiar to you than just answering questions.'

5. 'It makes you look a lot closer at the rhyme scheme, you have to really try to analyse each line to fit it in.'

6. 'Learnt more about rhyme structure, much more aware of it.'

7. 'Learnt how Hardy feels when putting the poem together, get closer to the meaning while you think.'

8. 'This approach to Hardy's poetry makes me concentrate in much greater detail in the structure and diction of each poem. I recognise and learn quotations more easily and the whole poem seems much more clear after discussion and such depth of thought.'

Conclusion

I found it both interesting and exciting to eavesdrop on the sort of talk which took place during the lesson. Perhaps the 'sensitive' response I was hoping for was rather lost in the debating and conferring, but as individuals, they will take with them a far greater awareness of rhyme and rhythm than they had before. With this knowledge I think they stand a better chance of getting nearer to the truth of how form relates to content in poetry. Perhaps the most gratifying thing I observed in the whole exercise was watching a pupil reading out loud to the others in his group what they had produced half-way through the task. The listeners were concentrating on the sound as well as the meaning and making comments like 'No, that just doesn't *sound* right.'

During Wind and Rain

They sing their dearest songs –
He, she, all of them – yea,
Treble and tenor and bass,
And one to play;
With the candles mooning each face
Ah, no; the years O!
How the sick leaves reel down in throngs!

They clear the creeping moss –
Elders and juniors – aye,
Making the pathways neat
And the gardens gay;
And they build a shady seat
Ah, no; the years, the years;
See, the white storm-birds wing across!

They are blithely breakfasting all –
Men and maidens – yea,
Under the summer tree
With a glimpse of the bay,
While pet fowl come to the knee
Ah, no; the years O!
And the rotten rose is ript from the wall.

They changed to a high new house,
He, she, all of them – aye,
Clocks and carpets and chairs
On the lawn all day,
And brightest things that are theirs
Ah, no; the years, the years;
Down their carved names the raindrop ploughs.

Example 8

Subject Physics
Source 'Transmission of Sound' in *Children's Britannica*
Passage Type Process
Activities Sequencing

Introduction

The following extract was chosen to introduce the topic of sound transmission as one of three elements in a sequence of lessons dealing with hearing and sound. The passage is given below in scrambled order. Readers may wish to experience the appropriateness of scrambled presentation for alerting the reader to the key concepts in the description of a sequential process. The correct order of segments is shown at the foot of page 191.

Transmission of sound

1. It can be shown that something is needed to carry the sound from the vibrating object to the ear. An electric bell is placed in a tightly sealed jar with wires connecting it to a battery outside. An air pump is connected to the jar so as to pump the air out of it. As the air is pumped out, the ringing of the bell becomes fainter and fainter, but when the air is allowed to re-enter the jar the ringing becomes louder and clearer. This shows that sound cannot travel through a vacuum, or empty space containing no air. In this it differs from heat, light and radio waves which can and do travel through all space. The substance through which sound travels is called the sound medium.

2. When the particles are crowded together by the string pushing them, the air pressure is slightly increased. As the string moves back the particles spread out again and the pressure decreases. These movements produce sound waves which travel outwards from the string in all directions, affecting the particles farther and farther away. The pressure variations caused by the waves strike the ear-drums and enable the sound to be heard.

3. The air particles move only to and fro, but the sound wave itself travels through the air. At some distance the particles move so slightly that the sound cannot be heard, and farther away still there is no movement at all.

4. Most of the sounds we hear travel through air, but sound can also travel through solid and liquid substances. The North American Indians made use of the earth as a sound medium. By putting their ears to the ground they could detect the approach of animals or enemies, and could receive, over long distances, signals made by striking the ground. A swimmer under water hears very clearly sounds such as those made by clapping stones together. Two tins with string stretched between them can be used as a crude form of telephone, the string acting as the sound medium.

5. A violin string, or other vibrating object, is surrounded by tiny particles of air. As it vibrates, the string pushes the particles next

> to it outwards so that they collide with neighbouring particles and so on. With each movement of the string a fresh impulse, or push, is given to the air. Hundreds of these impulses are caused every second, and in between the impulses the string moves back. As a result, the air particles move to and fro in time with the vibrating string.
>
> 6.   Anything that can be heard is a sound, whether it is made by speaking, by striking a note on the piano or by dropping a bucket. All sounds are produced by a vibrating object; that is, by one moving rapidly to and fro. In the case of a violin string which is plucked, or the wings of a buzzing bee or wasp, this vibration can actually be seen. If a finger is placed on the violin string the sound ceases because the string can no longer vibrate. In the same way, when the bee stops moving its wings the buzzing ceases.

Comment

As indicated earlier, this was one of three lessons designed with a common set of objectives: to introduce a number of key ideas in general science and to act as part of a study skills programme for first-year pupils in a comprehensive school. The remaining two tasks are included in this book as example 12 (pages 218–222). All of these tasks were designed by the Head of English in consultation with members of the Science department.

Before the class were asked to sequence the extracts, each of the segments was read aloud. This was important because of the vocabulary load ('substance', 'impulses', 'vibrates', etc).

The sequencing itself was done in groups of two or three pupils with support as needed by one of the two teachers who were present throughout the exercise. In general, only the weaker pupils needed help in deciding on the correct order.

It is almost superfluous to point out that the sequencing task is very appropriate for helping conceptualisation of a sequential process, here the transmission of sound. On the principle of 'what you do you remember' the task is ideally suited to the ideas conveyed by the text.

Correct order of segments: 6, 5, 2, 3, 1, 4.

PART II

3. PREDICTION

Introduction

Everyone must have had the experience of reading a story and stopping to consider what might be coming next, or how it will all end. It is almost unavoidable if the story is too long to read at one sitting. The creation of suspense is central to the art of narrative and there can be no suspense without anticipation. We may not know what will happen, but we know what might or what will, we hope, be avoided. We form questions and we frame tentative answers.

An accomplished writer will seldom allow the story to develop in strict chronological sequence. Instead, there will be interruptions. There are many devices for introducing these, from descriptive passages, through reflective interpolations to the subtle interweaving of plot and sub-plot. The interruptions are what makes suspense, and it is these that provoke the anticipation. A narrative that lacks any such elements is often plain boring.

Appreciation is partly a matter of experiencing anticipation and suspense, while critical appreciation involves recognising the devices used by an author to create suspense and to channel anticipation.

To predict is to put anticipation into words. Prediction is therefore an almost essential component in the teaching of literary appreciation. It appears in many forms and goes back a very long time.

So it is not surprising to find that teachers of English made quite extensive use of prediction techniques in the course of their association with the project. In some cases what they did was little different from what they had done before they learned about the project and its ideas. In others, there was some modification of previous practice: a greater use of oral discussion in small groups without any written output, or a closer study of one or two paragraphs to use as a basis for prediction instead of a less probing perusal of several pages. Or again, there were many examples of teachers combining prediction with some other technique based on analysis of the extract that was made available to begin with. A favourite technique here was to ask the pupils to underline those parts of the passage that featured certain key ideas, these being the ones that formed the basis for subsequent prediction. The first example of work that we offer in this opening section is essentially of this kind. It did call for a written output, a possible 'ending', but in that respect, too, it is far from atypical.

Still in the realm of narrative, a second category of activity derives from the ideas of Stauffer and Walker. This was used extensively in the course of the earlier project, on The Effective Use of Reading. It consists of presenting an entire passage or story one paragraph at a time and asking for interpretations and predictions at each paragraph. Often this is done with the teacher leading the discussion, but it can also be done using small group discussion, thereby achieving greater participation. Our second example is of this kind.

A problem that we have faced repeatedly has been how to use prediction techniques as an aid to learning from expository text. The problem is that the learner may seem to have insufficient knowledge to make useful predictions until after the work has been covered. However, this is not always an insurmountable obstacle. At least some of the time, one finds that pupils know a good deal more than one suspected (cf example 11, page 210). Or one can vary the paragraph by paragraph prediction by asking leading questions at each stage. Or one can ask the group to frame their own questions at each stage. Of course none of these should be taken to exclude any other. Just the same, we are bound to acknowledge that experience in the use of prediction is limited outside the field of English.

Introductory Example 1

Subject English Literature
Source Conan Doyle *The Hound of the Baskervilles*
Passage Type Narrative
Activities Prediction

Here now is a fairly typical example of prediction following a single quite substantial extract. You are invited to go through the same preliminary steps as the pupils and at least think about the sequel. We do not imagine that teachers' groups would want to parody Conan Doyle.

Instructions to pupils were:

   1. Read through the extract carefully.

The initial silent reading was followed by a brief class discussion about how the writer had built up a feeling of suspense. The next task was:

   2. Discuss in pairs what we can gather about the character of the narrator. Underline all those passages in the text that give us these clues. What are his most distinctive qualities?

Here the discussion in pairs was followed by a class discussion, in the course of which agreement was reached about the most distinctive qualities. The lesson was rounded off by:

3. Write a paragraph for homework, continuing the story where it left off and keeping to the style of the writer.

The extract, from *The Hound of the Baskervilles*, is reproduced here, followed by three typical 'endings'.

The Hound of the Baskervilles

The sun was already sinking when I reached the summit of the hill, and the long slopes beneath me were all golden on one side and grey shadow on the other. A haze lay low upon the farthest skyline, out of which jutted the fantastic shapes of Beliver and Vixen Tor. Over the wide expanse there was no sound and no movement. One great grey bird, a gull or curlew, soared aloft in the blue heaven. He and I seemed to be the only living things between the huge arch of the sky and the desert beneath it. The barren scene, the sense of loneliness, and the mystery and urgency of my task all struck a chill into my heart. The boy was nowhere to be seen. But down beneath me, in a cleft of the hills, there was a circle of the old stone huts, and in the middle of them there was one which retained sufficient roof to act as a screen against the weather. My heart leapt within me as I saw it. This must be the burrow where the stranger lurked. At last my foot was on the threshold of his hiding place – his secret was within my grasp.

As I approached the hut, walking as warily as Stapleton would do when with poised net he drew near the settled butterfly, I satisfied myself that the place had indeed been used as a habitation. A vague pathway among the boulders led to the dilapidated opening which served as a door. All was silent within. The unknown might be lurking there, or he might be prowling on the moor. My nerves tingled with the sense of adventure. Throwing aside my cigarette, I closed my hand on the butt of my revolver, and, walking swiftly up to the door, I looked in. The place was empty.

But there were ample signs that I had not come upon a false scent. This was certainly where the man lived. Some blankets rolled in a waterproof lay upon that very stone slab upon which neolithic man had once slumbered. The ashes of a fire were heaped in a rude grate. Beside it lay some cooking utensils and a bucket half-full of water. A litter of empty tins showed that the place had been occupied for some time, and I saw, as my eyes became accustomed to the chequered light, a pannikin and a half-full bottle of spirits standing in the corner. In the middle of the hut a flat stone served the purpose of a table, and upon this stood a small cloth bundle – the same, no doubt, which I had seen through the telescope upon the shoulder of the boy. It contained a loaf of bread, a tinned tongue, and two tins of preserved peaches. As I set it down again, after having examined it, my heart leaped to see that beneath it there lay a sheet of paper with writing upon it. I raised it, and this was what I read, roughly scrawled in pencil: 'Dr Watson has gone to Coombe Tracey'.

If there was one report there might be others, so I looked round the hut in search of them. There was no trace, however, of anything of the kind, nor could I discover any sign which might indicate the character or the intentions of the man who lived in this singular place, save that he must be of Spartan habits, and cared little for the comforts of life. When I thought of the heavy rains and looked at the gaping roof I understood how strong and immutable must be the purpose which had kept him in that inhospitable abode. Was he our malignant enemy, or was he by chance our guardian angel? I swore that I would not leave the hut until I knew.

Outside the sun was sinking low and the west was blazing with scarlet and gold. Its reflection was shot back in muddy patches by the distant pools which lay amid the great Grimpon Mire. There were two towers of Baskerville Hall, and there a distant blue of smoke which marked the village of Grimpen. Between the two, behind the hill, was the house of Stapletons. All was sweet and mellow and peaceful in the golden evening light, and yet as I looked at them my soul shared none of the peace of Nature, but quivered at the vagueness and the terror of that interview which every instant was bringing nearer. With tingling nerves, but a fixed purpose, I sat in the dark recess of the hut and waited with sombre patience for the coming of its tenant.

And then at last I heard him. Far away came the sharp clink of a boot striking upon a stone. Then another and yet another, coming nearer and nearer. I shrank back into the darkest corner and cocked the pistol in my pocket, determined not to discover myself until I had an opportunity of seeing something of the stranger. There was a long pause which showed that he had stopped. Then once more the footsteps approached and a shadow fell across the opening of the hut.

Samples of pupil completion 1.

. . . It seemed like hours and the pistol grew heavier every second but at last with my heart in my mouth I stepped out into the fading light of the day and glanced up at the man's features, my eyes came to a halt at his face. The nerves that had once been iron were shattered at one look at his face.

Both our expressions changed his was of fright, and mine of bewilderment. Immediately, he picked up a stick and hurled it at me, calming myself down I managed to dodge the swirling stick.

The man who had probably been in an accident which had result of the mutation of his face, made a dash for cover. I fired a salvo of shots in his direction two of which wounded him in the leg. I walked over to him, hands shaking a little and nerves tensed.

There was no fight left in him now and three days later he was in court being tried.

2.

Then once more footsteps approached and a shadow fell across the opening of the hut. My heart leapt within me as a dark figure entered the room with my pistol cocked, I advanced towards the stranger. My heart sank as a well known voice broke the silence it was Sherlock.

The news which he brought was extremely depressing. It appeared that the boy had left this habitation some days earlier and was found dead on the moors. In the postmortem it was found that the boy had died from exposure.

3.

The shadow was sillouhetted against the rapidly decreasing sunlight which made it look even more menacing and dark. I could hear faint echoes of breathing and by now the shadow was reminiscent of a gaping black hole. It was obscuring everything and the breathing was going on monotonously. I crouched low with my gun poised precariously on a stone beside me and with my heart in my mouth. Then suddenly everything went dark and I knew no more. After a while I re-awakened and felt another blow. My life swam around me and drowned me in its own existence. I woke once more and paused but felt nothing. Then I glanced round and saw a book with the title 'Autobiography'. I looked inside and found not a life story but the key to the whole thing: I went to the nearest telephone and phoned the police. I waited for a few minutes and then heard a sound just audible. When I met the police I told them everything. They said how they were hot on the trail of the criminals who had apparently been wanted for a while.

The class was drawn from an upper band in the third year of a comprehensive school. Following the lesson, the teacher commented on the insightful understandings shown in all aspects of the work and the high level of motivation. The written work, too, reached a commendable level, sometimes approaching parody. There is little to be added, and perhaps all that distinguishes this lesson from many other good lessons in English is the use of underlining in pairs to precede discussion and written work. However, the teacher concerned regarded this as a worthwhile addition to standard practice.

Introductory Example 2

Subject English Literature
Source Isaac Asimov, 'The Fun They Had' (adapted) in *Earth is Room Enough*
Passage Type Narrative
Activities Prediction

The second example was a deliberate attempt to use paragraph by paragraph prediction without excessive reliance on class discussion. The class was a fourth-year junior group and the passage selected (by the class teacher) is an extract from a story by Isaac Asimov.

In order to facilitate oriented discussion without teacher intervention pupils were presented with a list of descriptive generic labels for the kind of way in which the story might develop:

action	*argument*
event	*someone's thoughts*
conversation	*description*
explanation (reason)	

Discussion, in fours, centred on two things: what was in the paragraph being examined and what one could expect to find in the next paragraph. Within each of these, pupils could think about the actual things that were described or they could decide about the form of the story as indicated by the set of possible labels.

You may find it instructive and amusing to go through the extract paragraph by paragraph, so we have presented it in segments to enable you to cover up those parts of the passage beyond the section you are working on.

The lesson proved enjoyable, and discussion in groups was lively and task-centred. Nevertheless, there is a good reason to believe that the cues for discussion of each section could be improved. For instance, the list of questions featured in Table 13 (page 200) is appropriate for a great many story extracts including this one, and is more clearly related to the impact of the story. (The list as given was useful to introduce the somewhat similar set of discussion points used for prediction with an expository text (Example 9).) It should be noted that if such a table is used, it must be available to the pupils when they are working in small groups. Copies of such a list could be produced as a set mounted on card and would be re-usable.

The fun they had

So you don't like school! Well, you never know – your great-great-grandchildren might actually envy you.

Margie even wrote about it that night in her diary. On the page headed May 17, 2157, she wrote 'Today Tommy found a real book!'

It was a very old book. Margie's grandfather once said that when he was a little boy his grandfather told him that there was a time when all stories were printed on paper. They turned the pages, which were yellow and crinkly. It was awfully funny to read words that stood still instead of moving the way they were supposed to – on a screen, you know. And then, when they turned back to the page before, it had the same words on it that it had had when they read it the first time.

"Gee," said Tommy, "what a waste. When you're through with the book, you just throw it away, I guess. Our television screen must have had a million books on it and it's good for plenty more. I wouldn't throw it away."

"Same as mine," said Margie. She was eleven and hadn't seen as many textbooks as Tommy had. He was thirteen. She said, "Where did you find it?"

"In my house." He pointed without looking, because he was busy reading. "In the attic."

"What's it about?"

"School."

Margie was scornful. "School? What's there to write about school? I hate school."

Margie always hated school, but now she hated it more than ever. The mechanical teacher had been giving her test after test in geography. She had been doing worse and worse until her mother had shaken her head sorrowfully and sent for the County Inspector.

He was a round little man with a red face and a whole box of tools with dials and wires. He smiled at Margie and gave her an apple, then took the teacher apart. Margie had hoped he wouldn't know how to put it together again. But he knew how all right! After an hour or so, there it was again, large and black and ugly, with a big screen on which all the lessons were shown and the questions were asked. That wasn't so bad. The part Margie hated most was the slot where she had to put homework and test papers. She always had to write them out in a punch code they made her learn when she was six years old. Then the mechanical teacher calculated the mark in no time.

The Inspector had smiled after he was finished and patted Margie's head. He said to her mother, "It's not the little girl's fault, Mrs Jones. I think the geography sector was geared a little too quick. Those things happen sometimes. I've slowed it up to an average ten-year level. Actually, the over-all pattern of her progress is quite satisfactory." And he patted Margie's head again.

Margie was disappointed. She had been hoping they would take the teacher away altogether. They had once taken Tommy's teacher away for nearly a month because the history sector had blanked out completely.

So she said to Tommy, "Why would anyone write about school?" Tommy looked at her with very superior eyes. "Because it's not our kind of school, stupid. This is the old kind of school that they had hundreds and hundreds of years ago." He added loftily, pronouncing the word carefully, "Centuries ago."

Margie was hurt. "Well, I don't know what kind of school they had all that time ago." She read the book over his shoulder for a while, then said, "Anyway, they had a teacher."

"Sure they had a teacher, but it wasn't a regular teacher. It was a man."

"A man? How could a man be a teacher?"

"Well, he just told the boys and girls things and gave them home-work and asked them questions."

"A man isn't smart enough."

"Sure he is. My father knows as much as my teacher."

"He can't. A man can't know as much as a teacher."

"He knows almost as much, I betcha."

Margie wasn't prepared to dispute that. She said, "I wouldn't want a strange man in my house to teach me."

Tommy screamed with laughter. "You don't know much, Margie. The teachers didn't live in the house. They had a special building and all the kids went there."

"And all the kids learned the same thing?"

"Sure, if they were the same age."

"But my mother says a teacher has to be adjusted to fit the mind of each boy and girl it teaches and that each kid has to be taught differently."

"Just the same, they didn't do it that way then. If you don't like it, you don't have to read the book."

"I didn't say I didn't like it," Margie said quickly. She wanted to read about those funny schools.

They weren't even half-finished when Margie's mother called, "Margie! School!"

Margie looked up. "Not yet, Mamma."

"Now!" said Mrs. Jones. "And it's probably time for Tommy too."

Margie said to Tommy, "Can I read the book some more with you after school?"

"Maybe," he said nonchalantly. He walked away whistling, the dusty old book tucked beneath his arm.

Margie went into the schoolroom. It was right next to her bedroom, and the mechanical teacher was on and waiting for her. It was always on at the same time every day except Saturday and Sunday, because her mother said little girls learned better if they learned at regular hours.

The screen was lit up, and it said, "Today's arithmetic lesson is on the addition of proper fractions. Please insert yesterday's homework in the proper slot."

Margie did so with a sigh. She was thinking

about the old schools they had when her grandfather's grandfather was a little boy. All the kids from the whole neighbourhood came, laughing and shouting in the schoolyard, sitting together in the same classroom, going home together at the end of the day. They learned the same things, so they could help one another on the homework and talk about it.

And the teachers were people . . .

The mechanical teacher was flashing on the screen: "When we add the fractions $\frac{1}{2}$ and $\frac{1}{4}$ –"

Margie was thinking about how the kids must have loved it in the old days. She was thinking about the fun they had.

Ten talking points for use with short story extracts presented one section at a time. Do not feel obliged to discuss every question for each section!

Table 13

A. What's going on?

1. Is there something puzzling at the moment?
2. Is there something frightening the reader?

B. Well, well

3. Is there something here that we had expected?
4. Is there something unexpected? A fresh turn?
5. Does this section explain something that was puzzling before?

C. What next?

   6. How will it end?
      What are the clues in the passage so far?
      Anything else we have to go on?
   7. What about the very next section – can we guess what
      that will be about?

D. Looking back

(These questions are worth discussing right at the end,
following the last section)

   8. Was there a turning point in the story?
   9. Was the ending 'right'? How else might it have ended?
      Would that have been worse or better?
  10. Was the story gripping? Why?

Preparation and Conduct of Lessons

We have already noted that we have inadequate experience of the use of prediction for expository material. Following this introductory note, the reader will find three examples of such lessons. Each is instructive in its own way, but they are still more or less isolated examples, and should not be thought of as models that have been tried and tested many times. That has seemed to us a good enough reason not to include any in these notes.

One might add that even using narrative passages teachers have often tended to rely on class discussion rather than small group discussion when asking pupils to extrapolate ahead. Just the same, there is enough evidence to say with some confidence that text-based lessons can be conducted using prediction as the sole technique while still retaining all three of the characteristics of directed reading activities as urged in this book: curricular relevance, prior analysis of the passage, and discussion in small groups related to carefully designed assignments using the text as an aid to learning.

What then are the points to watch for when designing a lesson of this kind? As with other techniques, the teacher needs to decide what are the things that can be learned using that text and how they can be brought out most sharply.

Arising out of this is the question: what will the pupils be asked to predict? Enough has been said already to show that 'what's coming next' is not a good enough answer. When many segments are presented in succession (as for the Asimov example), the groups should have a set of questions or prompts to refer to as appropriate after reading each successive section. Such a list has been suggested for narrative passages and the reader will find a similar list usable with at least some expository material in Example 9. But neither of these sets is definitive and we would encourage teachers to devise alternative lists and try them out.

The next point concerns administration. When many segments are used, the format in which the text is presented is very like that used in sequencing. As in sequencing, it is important that each of the slips is numbered, but since the presentation is not scrambled the numbering is in order. When the lesson is under way, ie following the class introduction, each of the pupil groups should be able to collect the next segment when they have finished with the one they are discussing.

Of course, that means a certain amount of movement. But movement is not always a bad thing and what it does ensure is that there is a distinctive break between each section. This in turn can make for a less perfunctory discussion than there would be if the whole passage were available from the start.

Finally, the report-back section of the lesson is an opportunity for discussing the key features of the passage. In a narrative: what were the turning points, how satisfactory was the resolution, was the tale well-built to hold the reader's attention, and so on. In an expository passage: what were the questions raised, were they all resolved, what questions remain and how these might lead into the next lesson – whether or not this too will be text-based.

Example 9

Subject Geography (physical)
Source Haydn Evans, 'The Air', *The Young Geographer*, Book 2
Passage Type Process
Activities Prediction

Introduction

The passage is reproduced below in eleven distinct sections of uneven length. These were presented to pupil groups on separate slips of paper with instructions to read each in turn, then discuss it before moving on to study the next section. They were also given a list of functional descriptions to help them to realise how each section contributed to the sense of the passage as a whole. This list is shown immediately above the passage. You are asked to consider two questions in relation to each section:

1. Can you (and your colleagues) agree about which of the labels is best suited to the section in hand?

2. Are you able to predict what the next section is going to deal with?

Useful ways of thinking about 'factual texts'

Explanation of how . . .
Example of . . .
What happens when . . .
Rule: something (else) we know about . . .

Evidence: you can tell because . . .
Continuation: what about when . . .
Expansion: More about . . .

The air

1. The sun gives us light and heat and helps to make the weather. The sun also shines on the moon but the moon has no weather. This is because the moon is airless and waterless.

2. The earth has a layer of air around it like a blanket. This is called the atmosphere. We need air in order to live, and so do all animals and plants. Although air is invisible, we know it is there and that it has many effects.

3. If you turn a tumbler upside down and plunge it straight into a bowl of water, the tumbler will not fill with water. The air in the tumbler keeps the water out, so we know that the tumbler was not empty but full of air. Air can fill different shapes. When you blow up a balloon and squeeze it you can feel the air inside. We can feel the air when we run against it and when it is windy. Wind is air moving.

4. The air also has weight. It presses down on everything – about fifteen pounds to every square inch (one kilogramme to every square centimetre). We should not be able to withstand this pressure but for the fact that the air in our bodies is pushing outwards at the same time.
Air pressure is always changing.

5. It changes at ground level from time to time, but the higher we go the colder, thinner and lighter the air gets. The tops of high mountains may be covered in snow while the valleys below them are warm and pleasant. The snow remains on the tops of very high mountains throughout the year. The line on a mountain slope above which the snow never melts is called the snowline and nothing grows above it. The snowline is not at the same height on all mountain ranges.

6. In the hot lands near the equator the snowline is much higher than on the mountains in colder countries.

   The sun causes movements of air. It heats the land and the land heats the air.

7. When air is warmed it gets lighter and rises. Its pressure is low. Cooler, heavier air has high pressure and moves to take the place of the low-pressure air when it rises. If the difference between the low pressure and the high pressure is small then the movement of air is a breeze.

8. A big difference causes a wind.

9. When there is low pressure over land we have breezes blowing in from the sea. This usually happens during the day because the land warms up more quickly than the sea.

10. At night it is often the other way round. The land loses its heat faster than the sea, and so the cooler land breezes blow towards the low-pressure areas over the sea. These are called offshore breezes.

11. Changes in the direction of the winds help the weather men to tell us what kind of weather to expect.

    The instrument used for measuring the pressure of the air is the barometer. By watching the barometer we can tell what sort of weather we are likely to get. When the pressure is rising it usually indicates that fine weather is on the way, but if it is falling we can expect rain.

Two lessons on 'The air'

The lesson was devised in the first instance for a fourth-year primary class as a deliberate experiment to discover whether multiple section prediction could be usefully applied to expository as well as narrative material. The passage was selected by the teacher as part of the geography programme, but the lesson was devised and conducted by a member of the team with the teacher present and assisting as seemed appropriate. The class were used to working in groups and had some previous experience of text-based lessons, but none of prediction or labelling – until the week before this lesson took place.

It is this class who were then given the lesson 'The fun they had', so as to provide at least some preliminary experience of prediction. 'The air' offers more of a challenge to the teacher than Asimov's tale and is quite difficult for several reasons. The title is a little misleading, since the chapter is really about wind. Nevertheless, the writer has assumed that the reader must be reminded about air and its properties and should also be told something about the weight of air and air pressure. It is for this reason that we are introduced to the effects of altitude although, within the context of the chapter as a whole, that is an intrusion. So, taken as a whole, there could be a lot to learn.

To begin with, the class were told that the passage would tell them something about the wind as well as the air and they were reminded about the way in which they would be asked to come to some decisions about each section in turn before proceeding to the next.

Each pupil had been given a copy of the text sectioned off in slips that were clipped together and each pupil had a copy of the set of labels given on page 203. In addition they had sets of pro forma sheets as shown below.

Table 14 Form for sectioned story *The Air*

	What this bit says	What's coming next	Our guess	Questions we'd like answered
1.				
2.				
3.				
4.				
5.				
6.				
7.				
8.				
10.				

The instructions were to fill in the pro forma as they went along, section by section, by doing the following things:

1. Read the section.

2. Decide what it is about and whether it will fit one of the labels.

3. Can you guess which label will fit the next bit? If so, put that in the second column.

4. Can you guess what you will actually be told in the next bit? If so, put that in column 3.

5. Is there anything you feel you want to know which has been suggested by what you are reading? If so, put that in the last column.

The first three sections were dealt with in class, ie the reading and preliminary discussion was done in groups but the discussion was taken up as a teacher/pupil interchange following each section. Thereafter, the pupils worked through the material in their own groups.

At the end of the lesson, which lasted an hour, few of the groups had got through the whole of the assignment. They were asked to read through the rest at home, to produce a marked diagram on the basis of their reading to illustrate why there are onshore breezes in the daytime, and to make up a sentence explaining the diagram.

The lesson proved very successful on a number of counts: the pupils were hard at work throughout; there was task-oriented discussion; there was clear evidence of enjoyment and also of useful learning – particularly as judged by the diagrams and accompanying sentence, one of which is reproduced on page 50 of this book.

Nevertheless, there were also grounds for satisfaction to be tempered with criticism. Inspection of the pro formas showed that the pupils put in a good deal of work, but understanding of the task was far from adequate.

The final column, 'Questions we'd like answered' ('expect to be answered' would be an improvement) was usually completed very sensibly: 'why air moves', 'why we have rain', 'why some countries are warm and others are cold', etc. The first three columns showed evidence of thinking, since the entries in each sheet were all pertinent and different, implying that the pupils had thought about them. But on the whole they failed to use the labels appropriately even for the first column. (Our own suggestions would be: *1.* rule *2.* evidence (or examples) *3.* new rule *4.* expansion *5.* new rule *6.* expansion *7.* continuation *8.* explanation *9.* continuation *10.* new rule (summary).) They were clearly unused to categorising information in the manner intended and were therefore finding the task difficult.

The same lesson was repeated by another member of the team with a group of first-year secondary pupils who had had a good deal of experience with text-based work but again had done no work on prediction and no labelling along the lines indicated. The results were broadly similar: a good level of work, but difficulty with generic labels. However, this group went on to a second lesson, in which they read the text again and discussed which of the labels provided the best fit for each successive section of the text. This turned out to be a useful and interesting lesson. Nor was the time wasted since in the end the group were able to show good under-standing and memory for structure as well as detail. Nevertheless, it seems clear that for this work to be most effective, it needs to be thought of as a programme of three or four lessons based on at least two passages with different content but similar structure, ie passages of the same type.

Final comment

The method and ideas featured in this example are still at an exploratory stage. Their potential strength is that they challenge the reader to a thoughtful and insightful style of reading. They demand that readers formulate their own questions and anticipate the material as they go along. What is more, it is generally possible to apply these headings to a wide range of texts. Therefore, despite the fact that the method is relatively untried, it is worth bringing to the notice of teachers. There are four provisos:

1. For the method to be fully effective, both the teacher and the pupils should have adequate previous experience of text-based lessons including text analysis. It is not recommended as a first foray into directed reading activity work.

2. Different text types require different sets of labels, although there may be some overlap. For instance the labels used for 'The fun they had' (*narrative*) are different from those suggested for 'The air' (mainly *process*). For a lesson based on an account of the develop-ment of printing (not included in this book) we suggested the labels: *development, problem, expansion, reason, example, solution, application, inventor, background, what he did.*

3. Pupils need to be taught the relevant set of labels in an analysis lesson (with the whole passage present, using a different text of the same type) before proceeding to prediction using multiple sections and generic labels.

4. Teachers should feel free to experiment for themselves and improve on these suggestions in the light of their own experience. For instance, the breaks between sections in this example do not coincide with the main breaks within the text. This was deliberate, because prediction is a little easier after a new theme has been introduced. But it is also a little misleading since the sections sometimes require two labels to do them full justice. So there is scope for further experimentation to discover the most effective ways of breaking the passage.

Example 10

Subject History

Source P. Grayson, 'Stonehenge', in *Derbyshire Antiquities*

Passage Type Structure

Activities Prediction
            Sequencing

Introduction

The following extract on Stonehenge was used as the basis of a lesson which took the form of a cross between prediction and sequencing. The passage was first divided into segments and these were handed out for discussion at intervals. Pupils worked in pairs, their task being twofold:

1. to decide what the passage was about;

2. to establish the relative position of each segment of text within the passage as a whole; did it belong at the beginning, in the middle or at the end; whereabouts in relation to segments they had received already?

To enable you to get the feel of the task, the passage is presented here with a gap after each section, and in the order in which these were presented to the pupils. The original order is given below.

---

1. A mound was then erected around it to give protection and enable sightings to be taken at any time of the day.

2. The next stone would be erected at a certain distance from the table in line with the setting sun on the longest day of the year, when it is set at its most northerly point. Another was set up diametrically opposite.

3. Other large stones may once have stood along this mound forming an avenue. By placing smaller stones at other strategic places the moon could be studied and when the two systems crossed an eclipse

---

Correct order of segments: 8, 2, 4, 7, 1, 6, 3, 5.

would occur. A special stone erected due south showed when the sun was at midday. This was called the Heel Stone or King Stone.

4. The next would be erected on the shortest day along with its opposite number.

5. The circle was used for sun worship, as an observatory, and for other happenings such as marriages and funerals, coronations of new chiefs, summer and winter festivals and possibly a court house. Similar ceremonies are still carried out by the Indians in Patagonia.

6. Two gaps were left in the mound to serve as entrances. There is evidence of a long mound stretching for a hundred yards to the south of the circle at Arbor Low to the very top of the hill.

7. The spaces between these four stones were then filled with others at regular intervals, each representing a 'month' between the summer and winter solstice stones.

8. The system used for erecting a circle was quite simple, depending on certain natural phenomena. Three blocks were erected in the form of a table almost on the crest of a hill.

The class was the same as that which participated in the second presentation of the prediction lesson on 'The air' (first-year comprehensive). Discussion was lively and insights were good. Most of the pupils realised that *4* should immediately follow *2* and that both should precede *1*. Several guessed correctly that the passage was about Stonehenge after seeing two or three segments. Most were able to tell this after they had seen *5*. All arrived at something like the original sequence by the end of the lesson, the only variation being the location of *5* which could be placed right at the beginning, albeit a little less well.

Comment

Although the above account is very short, it should be apparent that the method is potentially very powerful. It is challenging and elicits a very strong element of prediction as well as reflection about the placement of the sections already available at any stage. Also, unlike the technique illustrated in the previous example, it does not pre-suppose much previous experience on the part of teacher and class.

Example 11

Subject History

Source D.B. O'Callaghan, 'The Roaring Twenties', in *Roosevelt and the United States*

Passage Type Historical

Activities Prediction

Introduction

The accompanying text is a section of a chapter from a book which was used as set reading material by the history teacher concerned, and had been so used for a number of years. There are four sections in all, and these deal respectively with industrial prosperity, the consumer-oriented economy (instalment plans and the pursuit of pleasure), gangsters and the KKK, and the plight of the farmers. The last of these sections is reproduced in Part I of this book, Example 4. That lesson too was contributed by the same teacher.

From the start this teacher had determined to use the text as a basis for discussion, with the aim of getting the pupils to build their own mental picture of the central themes and thereby come to an understanding of what were the main issues and their causal structure. One way of going about this was to ask them to pick out selected categories of ideas (description of a state of affairs, action taken to overcome a problem, outcomes of such action, and so on), and then go on to produce or complete a flow diagram depicting the events and their causal structure. This is the method discussed in Part I. A year later, the teacher thought such a method might be too directive: why not draw on the pupils' existing knowledge? If comprehension is a matter of comparing what you read with what you know, why not start with what the pupils already know?

In order to get the most out of the activity, the teacher devoted several lessons to the chapter and its themes. Later lessons involved notemaking, diagrammatic representation, and discussion of wider issues. What we are presenting here is an account of the first two lessons in which the emphasis was on prediction. The text shown on page 211 is a part of the chapter under discussion, but this was not introduced until half way through the second lesson. On the other hand, the teacher had assembled a number of period pictures, and these were made available in the course of the first lesson to help to stimulate ideas.

One of the co-ordinators associated with the project had been closely involved with all these activities, and he was able to sit in on the first lesson and comment on it.

Conduct of lessons

We have extensive notes on the conduct of these lessons both from the teacher and from the co-ordinator. The best way of conveying something of the feel of the lesson is to use these notes for describing it. So this section consists of the following:

1. A brief description of the first lesson in the teacher's own words.

2. A part of the observer's minute by minute written observations on the lesson, with occasional comments by the teacher himself.

3. An extract from the observer's written comments addressed to the teacher.

4. Examples of pupils' work produced in the first lesson.

5. A description of the second lesson, again in the teacher's words.

6. Examples of work produced in the second lesson.

Prosperity for industry

Throughout the 1920s the United States was ruled by a succession of Republican Presidents – first by Warren Harding, then by Calvin Coolidge, and finally by Herbert Hoover. In Congress, too, the Republican party was strongly represented.

The main reason for the popularity of the Republicans at this time was that by the middle of the 1920s many Americans were better off than they had ever been before. The United States was prospering and the Republicans claimed that much of the prosperity was the result of their policies. These were based upon the simple belief that if the Government did all that it could to help business men to prosper, then everyone would be better off. A business man whose firm was doing well would not only make higher profits for himself and his shareholders, he would also be able to employ more workers and to pay them higher wages. In this way a share of the increasing wealth of factory owners and investors would trickle down and benefit people at all levels of society.

Believing this, the Republican governments which ruled the United States in the 1920s tried to create the most favourable conditions they could for American business men. High tariffs, or import taxes, were placed upon goods from abroad, so that American manufacturers would not have to face competition from foreign manufacturers in selling their products: the taxes on high incomes and company profits which had been imposed during the war were drastically reduced to give rich men more money to invest: and attempts such as those made by Theodore Roosevelt and Woodrow Wilson to limit the power of industrial corporations and trusts were almost entirely given up. Why bother? If the growth of trusts caused industries to be run more efficiently, thought most people, then let them grow.

Such favourable government policies as these helped American industry to grow rapidly. Leading the way was the motor industry. In 1910, when Franklin Roosevelt used the Red Peril in his New York Senate campaign, motor cars and trucks were still novelties to many people. By the 1920s this was no longer so. In 1920 there were already over nine million motor vehicles registered in the U.S.A. The number continued to rise and by 1929 it was calculated that there were enough cars in the United States to have sent the whole population of the country speeding along the roads at the same time.

The leading figure in the car-making industry was Henry Ford. The son of a farmer, Ford built his first car in a backyard shed in 1896. It was ten years later, however, that he produced the car that was to make his fortune – the Model 'T', affectionately known to millions of Americans as the 'Tin Lizzie'. Between 1908 and 1927, when the model went out of production, more than fifteen million of the high-backed, antique looking Tin Lizzies rattled out of Ford's factories on to America's roads. It became the highest-selling car in world history.

The spectacular increase in motor vehicle manufacturing stimulated the growth of other industries. Steel was needed for car and truck bodies and engines; glass for windscreens; leather for seats; rubber for tyres and inner tubes; and petrol (known as gasolene or gas to Americans) for power. The industries producing these things all benefited from the motor boom.

Lesson 1: Teacher's description

I asked the students to work in groups of four and to predict what the chapter on the Roaring Twenties was all about. I had intended this activity to take up about half the lesson, but it immediately developed into diagramming for one group, and I suggested to others that they might adopt a similar approach. I introduced photographs after about fifteen minutes. It was soon evident that a vast amount of knowledge existed on this topic and the lesson allowed recall and reorganisation to take place. Misconceptions appeared to surface and were dealt with in groups. Confidence was boosted and the results genuinely pleasing to the students.

Lesson 1: minute by minute observation (extract)

1.49 Teacher has put on the board 'The Roaring Twenties', enclosing it in a jagged outline. He has asked the class to speculate what's going to be in a chapter of that title and jot a brief list of their joint ideas on paper. They get straight to work generating words to do with gangsters, illegal booze, and jazz and so on.

1.50 Just as they are nicely under way teacher arrives with a 'new' idea that, though good, seems, to me at least (already well aware of where the group were getting to), strictly superfluous. His new idea is that they might like to work by producing a diagram rather than a list. With his help they settle for producing both lists and diagram/drawings.

Teacher comment: I'd thought this too ambitious at first, but one of the other groups spontaneously started a diagram, and I thought this would give the idea more credibility. It did.

1.54 Things have slowed down but are going well. It's certainly the writing that is slowing things down.

Teacher comment: Yes, this worried me, even when I suggested the group might make more than one response.

1.55 My group hears another group calling out about speakeasies. Shall they use it? One of them is not sure it might not be a trick to mislead them. Others are more enthusiastic.

1.56 There are some disadvantages in that everyone has now some kind of writing or recording task; it is splitting the group into four individual workers who occasionally talk themselves back together again. On the other hand it seems to be steadying the activity in a not wholly undesirable way.

1.59 I have been surprised at some of the ideas that seem to have spontaneously come up – for example, 'Wall Street Crash' and 'illegal immigrants'.

Teacher comment: Previous study of Germany. Quite evidently a productive use of *knowledge* gained in class. Most comforting!

Lesson 1: Comments to teacher by the co-ordinator

As to the business of discovering in action what it is that learners must do, I feel you and they were similarly successful here – though, in this case, the matter being more complex, much of the picture is likely to emerge more clearly at later stages (when, for example, they get on to generating their own questions, the activity scheduled for the second half of the lesson but which you decided 'on the run', and wisely, I think, to postpone until tomorrow's double period). In the meantime they were deep into searching the memory bank, selecting relevant items, interrelating and re-presenting these, checking against the response of fellow-workers as to whether convincing selections, inter-connections and re-presentations were being made; hypothesising and putting simple suppositions to the test; laying bare misconceptions and putting them right; admitting mistakes; asserting possibilities and adducing evidence in support; collaborating with fellow-learners, keeping them up to the mark and seeing them through some awkward moments.

. . . .

The experience was not entirely without its 'other edge' and a part of me was seriously worried about the pace of it all, the time it was taking, and how you had not pressed on with what had seemed in advance a very sensible schedule.

. . . .

Perhaps the answer to this problem of space and pace (if there is a problem – I'm not really sure) would be to schedule sessions of this kind on even larger chunks of the syllabus with even broader scope. It is after all both a furrow-turning and synthesising process, ideally suited to opening up or pulling together large sweeps of knowledge. It would probably only raise serious deadline-meeting problems if used for picking up and processing one at a time a string of small, detailed pockets of information (a job, I feel sure, it could support mightily but to less full advantage than in creating and focusing up a suitable wider view).

Figure 19 Lesson 1 – example of pupil work 1

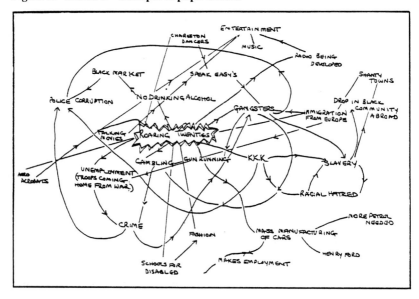

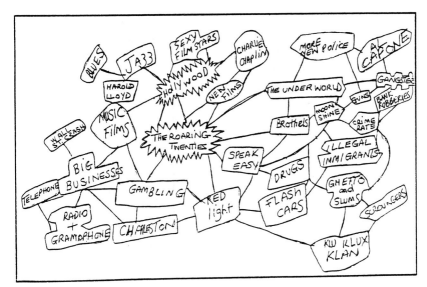

Figure 20 Lesson 1 – example of pupil work 2

Figure 21 Lesson 1 – example of pupil work 3

The Roaring Twenties
1. Crime rate bad
   Murders
2. Inflation
3. Street battles
4. Gangsters
5. Gambling casino
6. Speak easy
7. Unemployment
8. Black marketing
9. More police
10. No police cars
11. Prostitutes
    Lots of entertainment
12. Big film stars
    President
    Fashion
    Crystal sets
    Important people

Schooling not compulsory
More kids
More manufacturing
More factories
Cheap gas
Less popular towns
Silent movies
Black and white

Ku Klux Klan

Lesson 2: Teacher's description

I asked the students to think of questions they would like to ask on the four sections of the book. I suggested they might like to use 'who', 'why', 'what' etc to get started. The generating of the questions would hopefully help them to read the text more carefully.

The introduction of the text was eagerly welcomed and the search for answers took up the second half of the lesson. Mostly they kept to the

---

The Roaring Twenties

Prosperity for industry
1. Industry became prosperous because the Republican Government put high taxes or import taxes were placed on imports from abroad.
2. It means that they were making more and they were selling more.
3. The parts of industry that become prosperous was the film industry and the car industry and radio manufacturing.

Instalment plans and pleasure
1. What is meant is that installment plans is higher purchase.
2. They were important because the more you spent the faster went the wheels of industry.
3. They had motion pictures, theatres, and listening to the radio as pleasures and dancing.
4. It was used to help people buy things that they couldn't at the moment.

Gangsters and Klansmen   (unfinished)

Figure 22 Lesson 2 – example of pupil work 1

Figure 23 Lesson 2 – example of pupil work 2

The Roaring Twenties

Prosperity for industry
Why did industry do so well in the 1920s and not after or before?

Instalment plans and pleasure
What does this mean?
It means that people's standards of living went up.

Gangsters and Klansmen
Why were Klans like the KKK so rife in the 1920s?
Why were there so many gangsters in the 1920s?

Hard times for the farmer
Is this because of natural disasters?
Or is it because at around this time industry was booming?

The Roaring Twenties

Prosperity for industry
Why did industry become prosperous?
What does it mean for prosperity for industry?
What parts of industry became prosperous?

Instalment plans and pleasure
What is meant by instalment plans?
Why were instalment plans so important?
What pleasure did they have?
How were the instalment plans used?

Gangsters and Klansmen
Why did the Klansmen start up again in the twenties?
Why was it so difficult for the police to put down the gangsters
and Klansmen?
How did the gangsters become so powerful?

Hard times for the farmer
Why was it hard times for the farmer?
How did the farmer cope?
Did it affect all farmers?
If so, which ones did it affect more?

Figure 24 Lesson 2 – example of pupil work 3

questions, but it was interesting to see how some students still insisted on
trying to answer their questions from their existing stock of knowledge –
why not? – the questions were to some extent questions they already knew
the answers to.

Comment

It is clear that this approach can provide pupils with the greatest freedom
since it builds on their own knowledge more obviously than any other
method.

However, it is well to remember that:

1. successful prediction presupposes a good deal of pre-existing
    knowledge and this may not always be there;
2. open-ended prediction takes a great deal of time and even then
    you will probably need one or more follow-up lessons, as were
    given here, if you're interested in teaching a specific content as well
    as a general method.

PART II

4. FURTHER POSSIBILITIES AND EXTENSIONS

Introduction

Text-based lessons should all share certain features (clear objectives, group work, and emphasis on the main ideas in the passage and their structure), but they do not constitute a programme or an end in themselves. Teachers should feel free to adapt the ideas offered in this manual to suit their own needs and the passages they have chosen to support their own teaching. This means that many of the rules we would wish to lay down are negative rules:

1. deletions need not be single words;
2. segments for sequencing need not all be the same length; etc.

To these we would add:

There is no need to adhere to a single type of activity for each text-based lesson; still less for a series of related lessons.

This rule may help to suggest the way in which the field can be opened further in the sense that the techniques available to the teacher are a sort of open-ended set. In this final section, we would like to stress this element. We saw in Part I that the typical lesson involving analysis of an unaltered passage requires more than one technique, eg underlining or labelling followed by tabulation or diagrammatic representation. That is certainly less true of text reconstruction, and most of the previous examples are either of completion or sequencing or prediction. The following examples show, however, that one can also combine several of these techniques with one another, or one can incorporate analysis and reconstruction within the same lesson.

Examples

Example 12

Subject General Science
Source D.M. Desoutter, 'The Ear', in *Your Book of Science*
Passage Type Mechanism
Activities Diagram labelling. Comparison of text and diagram

Introduction

The lessons in this example are a continuation of the one described in Example 8. One lesson involved comparing a passage with a diagram. Figure 25 was prepared by removing the labels from the original. Copies were then made both of the diagram and of the text, and the pupils' task was to study the passage carefully and use it as a basis for restoring the labels to the diagram.

The ear

Sounds would not be sounds if we had no ears. They would simply be unnoticed and useless vibrations of the air.

Fortunately, our ears are excellent instruments for the detection of these vibrations, with the result that we can talk to each other, listen to music, and hear a car coming in time to jump out of the way.

This sketch shows the main parts of a human ear. The outer part which we can see collects the sound, and when sounds are very faint you can collect a bit more by cupping your hands so as to make a bigger 'ear'.

The part that we can see is called the outer ear, and it is divided from the middle ear by the eardrum. This is rather like a minute drum skin, and it is vibrated by any sound waves which come in from the outer ear.

Attached to the eardrum is a little bone, or ossicle, called the hammer. There are three of these little bones in all, and movements of the hammer are transmitted to the anvil and to the stirrup, which then vibrates another tiny 'drum skin' called the oval window.

All this space in the middle ear is filled with air, but the vibrations are transmitted by the movements of solid bones at this stage. On the other side of the oval window there is a liquid-filled system called the cochlea, and this in turn picks up vibrations from the oval window.

The cochlea, with its coiled-up tubes or passages, is made of bone, and there are three tubes in all. Inside one of them is the basilar membrane on which grow many thousand tiny hairs. These hairs pick up the vibrations of the fluid and send tiny electrical signals to the main auditory nerve. Here, all that can be said about the auditory nerve is that it is like an electrical cable sending very small voltages through to the brain. It is when these voltages arrive inside the brain that we get the sensation we call sound. The vibrations are something outside: sound is something inside.

You will notice that there is a tube leading down from the middle ear. This tube is closed for a good deal of the time, but when you swallow or yawn it opens so that air can get in or out. This is a necessary safety precaution, otherwise your eardrum would suffer whenever there was a change of air pressure. You can notice the effect sometimes if you are coming quickly down a steep hill in a car, or perhaps coming down in an aeroplane.

The atmospheric pressure becomes greater and pushes in on your eardrums. It is only when you swallow or yawn that these 'Eustachian' tubes open and air gets into the middle ear to balance up the pressure. The opening end of the Eustachian is at the back of the throat.

Figure 25 How the ear works

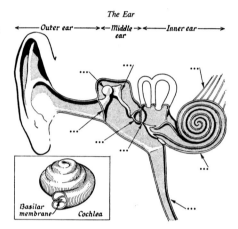

The final lesson in the series involved both texts (Examples 8 and 12) as well as the diagram. Pupils were asked to go over the two passages they had already studied and use them as a basis for completing Figure 26. The actual instructions they were given were as follows:

The diagram illustrates how we actually hear sound. You will notice, however, that it is incomplete. You must discuss with other members of your group how it should be completed and, when you have agreed, fill in the empty boxes. The following method may help you:

1. Refer back to the two texts (Examples 8 and 12), underlining groups of words which explain a separate stage in the production of sound.

2. Compare each group of words you have underlined with the diagram (figure 25) and, where the stage it explains has been included in the diagram, label it with the appropriate box number.

3. Use the information you have outlined but not allocated a number to fill in the remaining boxes.

Comment

It would not be difficult to devise a lesson consisting of a series of charts with a verbal commentary dealing with the physical characteristics of sound

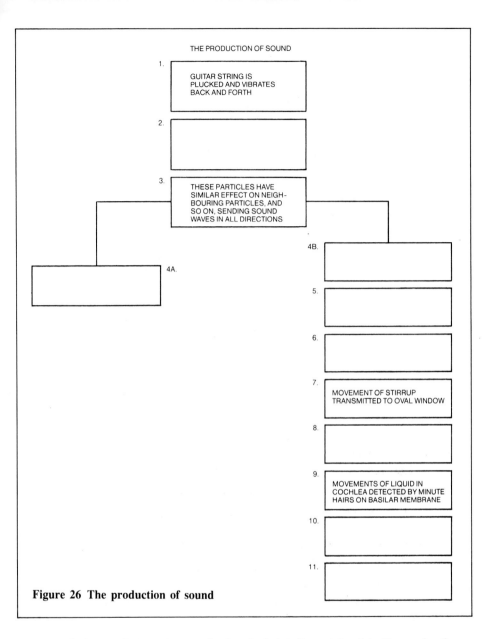

THE PRODUCTION OF SOUND

1. GUITAR STRING IS PLUCKED AND VIBRATES BACK AND FORTH

2.

3. THESE PARTICLES HAVE SIMILAR EFFECT ON NEIGH-BOURING PARTICLES, AND SO ON, SENDING SOUND WAVES IN ALL DIRECTIONS

4A.

4B.

5.

6.

7. MOVEMENT OF STIRRUP TRANSMITTED TO OVAL WINDOW

8.

9. MOVEMENTS OF LIQUID IN COCHLEA DETECTED BY MINUTE HAIRS ON BASILAR MEMBRANE

10.

11.

Figure 26 The production of sound

transmission and reception at the level of detail contained in Examples 8 and 12. If it were well put over, and the visual aids were well chosen, then such a lesson would lead to adequate comprehension at a certain level. But since there are a great many new ideas implicit in it (vibration, causal chain of events, wave movement and wave transmission, physical events and their physiological correlates, the notion of the brain as mediating between mind and a physiological stimulus), it is safe to assume that the lesson about the ear would have made a fair impact but would have gone in one ear and out the other. What we have instead is a well-designed series of tasks, with adequate support – including the underlining of

significant sections and subsequent sifting of the bits that have been underlined – leading to a finished product (the completed Figure 26) which
embodies all the central ideas at a level appropriate to the pupils
concerned. What is more, the reasoning and discussion called for in all
three lessons help to make the diagram not only meaningful but
memorable.

Example 13

Subject Geography

Source C. Rowe *et al.*, 'Building a Polder' in *European Patterns* Oxford Geography Project Book 2

Passage Type Process

Activities Matching text and diagram. Questions

Introduction

Both diagrams and text are scrambled. Match text segments to diagrams
and then arrange each section in order. As you work, make a note of the
cues you found most useful. If you can, discuss your ideas with a colleague.

The enclosing dam shuts off the bay from the sea to form a lake of fresh water. Gates in the dam let water out into the sea at low tide but do not let sea water in.

The Zuider Zee is a shallow bay open to the North Sea and its tides.

After five years the soil has formed. The polder is ready for farming and settling and forms new land for the Netherlands.

Part of the lake is separated from the rest by a dyke. The water is pumped out of this part into the Ijsselmeer. As the lake floor behind the dyke dries out it is sown with reeds to protect the surface and help the soil to form. Drainage ditches and canals are dug, leading to the pumping station.

Context

You will have taken only a few minutes to complete the activity. None-
theless, the simple task required concentration when comparing text and
diagram.

The exercise was originally designed for a small first-year remedial class
studying geography. The teacher's objectives were: to get pupils to study

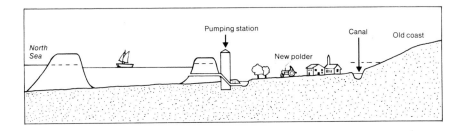

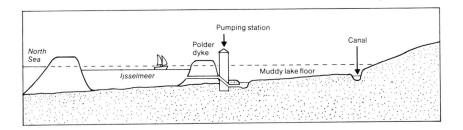

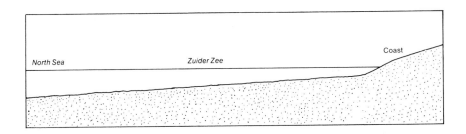

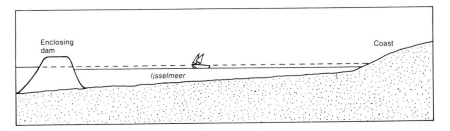

Figure 27 Building a polder

both text and diagram to work out what was basically involved in building a polder, and to provide a practical activity to reinforce previous work. The work was undertaken in the context of a topic on 'Farming in Holland'.

Pupils were given the text and diagram segments, cut up, together with the accompanying worksheet.

Worksheet 'Building a polder'

Now we have discussed what a polder is and how one is made in the Netherlands we shall finish with a small exercise of putting events in their correct order.

On your desk you have four small pictures and four pieces of writing.

Stage 1 Match the correct piece of writing with its picture.

When you have all four pictures with their correct writing go on to stage 2.

Stage 2 Place the four paired pieces in the order you would put them in if you were going to build a polder.

When you have the pictures and writing in their correct order read the pieces of writing to see if they follow the right pattern.

Next underline carefully in coloured pencil or ink all words to do with water,
    eg, shallow, bay, sea, tides.

Next underline carefully in another colour all words to do with land,
    eg floor, soil, farming.

If your pictures and words are in the correct order the water underlining should be in the first part of the sequence and the land underlining towards the end.

Read the four pieces of writing and answer the following questions in sentences:

1. Into which sea does the Zuider Zee open?
2. What is the depth of the water in the Zuider Zee?
3. What is the name of the lake formed by the enclosing dam?
4. What do you think is the Dutch word meaning 'lake'?
5. Is the water level in the lake higher or lower than in the sea?
6. What is one feature about the water in the lake?
7. What is used to separate the lake into smaller parts?
8. Give two reasons why reeds are planted on the lake floor?
9. What sediment lies on the lake floor?
10. How many years does it take for new soil to form?
11. What is a polder?
12. Why are polders needed in the Netherlands?

The worksheet was read aloud with pupils following. After a brief question and answer session, pupils were set to work, in pairs, with support from the teacher as needed.

Comment

The teacher considered that the lesson was the most successful of the term. Pupils worked hard and those who were slow were so anxious to complete the task that they insisted on doing so during the next available period. Above all, they were successful. This is a clear illustration of the effectiveness of the approaches for weaker pupils in eliciting a higher level of reasoning than that normally expected of them.

It is worthwhile, too, to ponder over the design of questions at the end. They are not mere invitations to scan text and diagram for 'the answer'. Instead they invite careful comparisons and often additional thinking too.

Example 14

Subject Physics

Source How the National Theatre Silenced its Critics

Passage Type Problem: solution

Activities Completion
Prediction
Diagram construction

Introduction

In this example there are a number of activities. The text is presented in three sections, each of which requires a different type of response.

In the first section certain words have been deleted with the intention of revising information already familiar to the pupils.

As the deletions chosen are specific and in some instances technical, you may not be able to produce completions to fill the gaps. However, sufficient text remains for you to make an attempt to pinpoint the gist of the first section of text. The task will be easier if you have a colleague with whom you can discuss the passage. The deletions are given on page 227.

Extract 1

The money problems of Britain's National Theatre may multiply, but the much publicised complaints from members of the audience at the Olivier Theatre that they could not hear the actors are now being stemmed.

During construction of the National Theatre's South Bank complex, the _____ consultant for the architects decided that because it is impossible to design a large structure with _____ acoustics the NT's architects should veer toward too much rather than too little _____. This would make the _____ of the hall theatre slightly too 'live', with a few too many _____, rather than too _____. Fine tuning, by installing sound _____ panels to cure isolated trouble spots, would achieve the ideal sound.

The deletions were chosen specifically by the teacher to generate discussion among pupils of the following ideas: 'acoustics', 'acoustically dead' and 'acoustically live'.

The next section of the text is given complete.

Extract 2

When it opened the National Theatre (NT) received complaints from the audience, especially those in the front row of the gallery, that speech from the stage was unintelligible. Late echoes of the stage sound were converging on the gallery front, muddling the sound coming direct from the stage, making the actors' words unclear.

A quick and simple solution would have been to damp the theatre acoustics drastically with an abundance of sound-absorbing panels. But this would have ruined the acoustics in those areas where they were fine to begin with. Instead, the offending sound-reflecting surfaces were tracked down one by one and individually damped.

Context

This material was used with a Physics group early in their 'O' level course. Towards the end of the first term of the course there is a topic on 'Waves and sound'. The pupils had previously discussed the control of sound and also watched television programmes on 'Waves and oscillations' from the BBC 'Physical Science' series. Accordingly, they were divided into groups of two or three and invited to discuss two questions:

1. What was the exact nature of the problems posed by the acoustics of the National Theatre?

2. How did they overcome these problems?

To deal with the first question, they were asked to produce a diagram by studying Extract 2. This helped them to offer suggestions in dealing with Question 2: how to track down the sound-reflecting surfaces.

Only after completing these tasks were the pupils offered Extract 3.

Extract 3

To speed up this time-consuming work, two separate techniques were adopted. By good fortune an 8th scale model of the Olivier Theatre, built by the Building Research Establishment, existed at Cambridge. Light beams and mirrors were used in this replica to plot the reflective paths converging on the gallery front. Meanwhile at the theatre, between performances, a high-voltage spark created a vicious crack on stage which was picked up by directional "gun" microphones placed round the auditorium and pointed at each possible offending surface in turn. Whenever a peak showed on an oscilloscope fed by the microphone the surface was identified as a positive offender. In practice it emerged that most of the unwanted reflections came from roof areas high above the audience.

The results obtained with light from the model and with sound from the auditorium were then compared. They tallied, so further work has continued mainly with the model.

Most of the unwanted reflections have now been killed by cladding the offending surfaces – this has reduced the overall reverberation time of the auditorium from 1.5 to 1.3 seconds. A further small reduction, to 1.1, is now planned. This, along with mild electronic reinforcement of the desirable early echoes arriving at the balcony front, should do the trick, and the complaints should, like the echoes, diminish to less than a whisper.

Pupils read the final part of the text and in discussion with their colleagues compared their solutions to the acoustic problem with those given in the article.

Comment

It may be noted that the material and tasks used are a good illustration of the practical use of some ideas met during the course. It was seen as a good opportunity to use material similar to that from a prominent scientific journal with an age group which does not normally come into contact with such publications.

Deletions from Extract 1

These are in the order in which they appear:

    acoustic, ideal, reverberation, sound, echoes, dead, absorbing.

Appendix 1

TEXT ANALYSIS FOR TEACHERS

Throughout this book we have referred to the importance of analysing a passage as a necessary preliminary to designing an effective text-based lesson. Again and again we have found that it is only in the process of making decisions about the boundaries of the principal segments and what they contribute to the argument that one discovers exactly what it was the writer had to say and what emphasis s/he wanted. Of course, one is free to disagree with the content or with the emphasis, but understanding must precede criticism.

It would have been possible to draw up a set of rigorous rules for splitting the text into its main segments. Also, we might have provided a full set of labels like 'comment', 'example', 'effect' and so on with strict instructions about how to choose between them. But the procedure would have been complicated and the rules would have been arbitrary.

There is a case for drawing up such rules for use by research workers, but they would probably not be helpful to teachers. On the other hand, experience suggests that the analysis one can do in one's head is not enough. The compromise we have suggested is an informal breakdown into segments combined with a search for labels that are appropriate and useful, regardless of whether there might be others that would do equally well.

On page 61 of this book, we presented such an analysis for one fairly characteristic passage. There we used obliques to mark off segments. In addition we used two sorts of labels to bring out the information in the passage and how it cohered. On the left of the passage we used specific labels, these being summaries, similar to the subtitles in newspapers; on the right we provided what we have termed generic labels, these being descriptions of the function of each segment within the passage as a whole. Generic labels are common to passages of a similar type while specific labels are not.

This method proves particularly effective for designing lessons around the chosen passage. Can some or all of the information be usefully presented in the form of a table? What should be the headings for the columns of such a table? What would one be representing by a separation into rows as well as columns? Would it be useful to require pupils to begin by searching for the several categories of information (underlining)? What sort of a diagram would one use to bring out the structuring of the ideas in the passage? All these are questions which can most easily be resolved after a written analysis along the lines of that on page 61, even if it is in some respects rough and ready.

For these reasons, teachers may find it useful to have a few additional examples they can study, as a guide to making up their own.

The first three passages, 'Building a nation', 'Cycles of reproduction', and 'Railways today', are introduced for the first time in this appendix.

Railways today (Figure 28, page 230)

'Railways today' is similar in structure to 'Hard times for the farmer' (page 61) and, like it, is of the type we have called 'situation'. It is instructive to note the coincidence of most of the generic labels: problems, effects, action taken, outcome. It would be possible to make up a table contrasting roads and railway transport from the information in the passage. However, if the teacher prefers to adhere to the structure of the passage itself, then a diagrammatic representation, like that shown in figure 11 (page 99), would probably be more appropriate. Only the barest outline of the diagram need be supplied, or the group could be asked to devise their own, especially if they have previous experience of such work.

Building a nation (Figure 29, page 231)

'Building a nation' is clearly a classification. It should be added that the two complementary criteria – privileges and obligations – have some generality in historical passages and are also representative of a much wider class including advantages/disadvantages, gains/losses, etc. It is therefore a particular kind of classification and one which is quite common. Like all such passages, it is ideally suited for tabular representation. A diagram like that on page 236 would be less good, since it would not easily be made to bring out the parrallelism of the column headings (privileges, obligations, comments).

Cycles of reproduction (Figure 30, page 232)

The second passage, 'Cycles of reproduction', is also a kind of classification, but its structure is a good deal less tidy. The most information-rich section is that we have labelled 'examples of group 2' and here again the central information could be brought out as a table with columns headed 'cycle', 'seasons' and 'relation to mating'. Rows could be the animals discussed.

It is clear, however, that the passage also raises a number of other questions but to these it gives only a very partial answer. The teacher may wish to deal with them in some other way, eg by asking pupils to generate unresolved questions and to suggest ways of finding the answers to them: where could we look them up, what kind of research would they rely on?

River basins (Figure 31, page 235)

Finally, readers will recognise 'River basins' as example 9 on page 127.

Figure 31 is one way of representing the organisation of this passage. It has two advantages: it shows the general form of structure which is common to this passage and others of its kind, and it brings out the peculiarities in the structure of this passage, some of which are inelegant and anomalous.

(*Continued on page 234*)

Figure 28 Railways today

Railways met with competition	In the twentieth century use of the motor car and aeroplane grew rapidly and soon began to compete with the railways. //	INTRODUCTION
Lorries	Lorries were used for short journeys between factories/	PROBLEMS 1-3
Cars	and people started using cars for personal transport./	
Motorways made things worse	Motorways enabled greater distances to be covered quickly and more traffic switched from using the railways to the roads.//	
Railways lost money	Railways therefore (apart from the profitable inter-city routes) started to lose money./	EFFECTS
Closures	This loss in railway traffic has led to the closure of many small lines, causing considerable hardship to the people who would still use them, chiefly those living in rural areas. //	
Protest *to no avail; no money*	They have fought campaigns to resist these closures but the arguments have always revolved around the problem of who should pay to keep the railway lines open – the taxpayer at large, the railways, or the people who wished to keep the line open.//	ACTION OUTCOME
Things not as bad as they seem	At first sight the future of the railways might appear gloomy, but closer study shows this to be untrue. /	INTRODUCTION
Railways can be quick	Railways still have one great advantage – that is the ability to transport large amounts of freight quickly over long distances. /	POTENTIAL, 1-2
and uncongested	They are rapidly gaining another advantage, for roads are now becoming very congested with more and more lorries, in spite of the construction of new motorways; and the railways are relatively under-used.//	
Modernisation plans	As a result the railways plan to modernise and attract more traffic back to their under-used lines.	PLANNED ACTIONS
Containers	The use of containers /	1
Freightliners	and freight-liners has to some extent revolutionised the carriage of freight. /	2
Description of containers	Containers are in effect very large standardised packing cases. They are taken ready-packed from the factory by road, rail, or ship to their destination and there is no need to unpack and repack the contents once their journey has started./	COMMENT ON 1
use of freightliners (example)	Each day 3000 Renault cars leave the Flins delivery centre on special Freightliner trains./	COMMENT ON 2
use of containers (example)	In West Germany alone the railways handle almost 2000 containers daily./	COMMENT ON 1
fast passenger trains	Among other attempts to bring traffic back to the railways is the planned introduction of inter-city services with 150–200 kph passenger trains./	3
Increased services	Not only will the services be quicker but the number of trains will be increased, so although the railway network itself may have less track it should be used by more trains and passengers than before.	4

PHASE 1

RE-ASSESSMENT

PHASE 2

From C. Rowe *Railways Today* (Oxford Geography Project 2, European Patterns)

Figure 29 Building a nation

Annotation (left)	Text	Annotation (right)
Romans ruled from afar / Saxons came to live here	The Romans ruled what was to become England for nearly 400 years as a Roman province, but few native Romans settled here. / When the Saxons conquered the country they did more than merely occupy it – they became part of it. //	CONTRAST / SETTING } SETTING
These were kings, trusted helpers, freemen and slaves.	The nation was gradually built up on the basis of loyalty. / The kings of the small countries within Britain needed trusted helpers and free workmen who would fight for them and also slaves who would do the hard farmwork. //	COMMENT / LIST OF GROUPS } GROUPING
Thegns had land to spare / Required to enforce law / Required to fight for king	The kings gave their noblemen or THEGNS enough land to support at least five families / who in return saw that the people knew and obeyed the king's law. / They also fought so loyally in battle that they would much rather die defending their leader's body than escape home safely to their families. / These powerful thegns were the elite of each king's army. //	GROUP 1 / PRIVILEGE / OBLIGATION 1 } GROUP 1 / OBLIGATION 2 / COMMENT
Freemen also required to fight / Had some land / Called Ceorls	but plenty of ordinary loyal infantrymen were needed who would fight to the death for him. / He gave these ordinary freemen, upon whom he relied so much, about 40 hectares of land which was enough to support one family. / These freemen, or CEORLS, served their thegns loyally just as the thegns served their king. /	GROUP 2 / OBLIGATION / PRIVILEGE / COMMENT 1 } GROUP 2
Some Ceorls grew richer / Most grew poorer / Thegns taxed Ceorls	As time passed some ceorls gradually increased their wealth and became thegns, but usually the richer thegns became richer and more powerful whilst the ordinary ceorls became poorer. This difference grew when the thegns were allowed to raise taxes from the freemen. //	COMMENT 2 + CONTRAST / COMMENT TO COMMENT 2
	The thegns, who needed plenty of farm workers, overcame this problem by using half-free workers and slaves. /	GROUP 3
Geburs half-free had some land / also worked lord's land	The half-free, or GEBUR, workers were given a small piece of land (between nine and twelve hectares), a few animals and some farm tools. In return they had to work on their lord's land two or three days every week. During busy seasons they had to work even longer. //	PRIVILEGES } GROUP 3 / OBLIGATION
Slaves were last group / Prisoners of war or children sold.	The cheapest labour of all was the slave labour which the Saxons gained by capturing prisoners of war or by using the children of the slaves. / Some people even sold themselves or their children into slavery to pay their debts.	GROUP 4 } GROUP 4 / COMMENT

From R. Pitcher & A. Harris, 'The Developing World', History One, Man Makes His Way

Figure 30 Cycles of reproduction

	Main text	Structure
Eggs produced in ovaries	You have seen that inside the body of a mammal such as the female rat, there are two ovaries in which the egg cells are produced./	INTRODUCTION — BACKGROUND AND GENERAL SUMMARY
Regular intervals	The eggs of all mammals ripen in the ovaries and are released at regular time intervals./	MAIN PRINCIPLE
Frequency in mice and pigs	Thus mice produce ripe eggs every 4 days and pigs every 21 days./	EXAMPLES
Called cycles	This regular occurrence of an egg or eggs developing and being released is called a cycle./	LABEL
Frequency and label (human)	A woman normally produces one egg every 28 days and the events concerned with this are called 'the menstrual cycle'.//	EXAMPLE
Chemicals control cycle	Chemical substances produced in the body have some effect in controlling the cycles of egg production/	MECHANISM
In rabbit mating necessary for ovulation.	but in the doe rabbit, eggs are only released from the ovary *after* mating has occurred.	COMMENT (RESTRICTION)
Some animals have frequent cycles.	//Some animals, such as mice, rats, and hamsters, have these cycles of egg production at all times of the year./	CONTRASTED GROUPS — GROUP 1
Others have definite seasons	Other animals have a definite breeding season and it is only then that eggs are released from the ovary and it is only during this time that the female will mate with the male.//	GROUP 2
Bitches season	Bitches, for example, have two breeding seasons a year, sometime in the spring and the autumn, when they are said to be on *heat* and bleeding from the uterus occurs./	EXAMPLE 1 — PROPERTIES 1–3
Bitches cycle	During this period of heat there is one cycle of egg production/	
Bitches relation to mating	and this is the time when mating occurs. In between these times the bitch will not mate.//	

N SECTION

EXAMPLES OF GROUP 2

PROPERTIES 1-3

EXAMPLE PROPERTIES 1-3

EXAMPLE PROPERTIES 1-3

PROBLEMS OF MECHANISM

SOLUTION, OBJECTION

ADVANTAGE CONTEXT

rutting season. There is one cycle of egg production and this is the only time that mating occurs./

The time of the breeding season normally occurs so that the young are born at a favourable time of year, usually in the spring. Thus when deer mate in the autumn it means that the embryos will develop in the female and will be ready to be born in the spring.//

Bats mate in the autumn/ but their embryos only take a short time to develop in the female's body and the sperms do not fertilise the eggs until early spring.

Badgers mate in July or August in southern England and although the eggs are fertilised the embryos are not implanted in the uterus wall of the female until December or early January.

The embryo then grows rapidly and the young are born eight weeks later.//

Just what controls when the breeding season will occur is not easy to explain./

The seasons and the length of day may have an effect although animals living where there is little change in the length of day will still have a definite breeding season.//

It is obviously important that when only one or two cycles of egg production occur during the year, there should be a good chance of the eggs being fertilised./

A definite breeding season, when mating occurs and coincides with egg production, makes reproduction much more likely.

From Nuffield Biology, *Introducing Living Things*

and cycle

Relation to mating

Bats season
Cycle and relation to mating
Badgers
Seasons and relation to mating cycle

Length of day may affect breeding but not sole cause

If only a few cycles

coincidence with mating essential

The diagram (Figure 32) looks forbidding, but is quite easy to follow:

1. At any rank, each segment consists of all the lower-ranking segments that it 'dominates' – and nothing more. The numbering of segments simply makes this fact explicit, because each segment below the first rank bears the number of the segment which immediately dominates it (however many figures this may require), followed by its own number.

2. The break up of segments into units of the next lower rank represents the functional relations between the things that are said. For the present, this is done on an intuitive basis: one knows lots of other similar passages, and one knows the sorts of things that can reasonably be said. In principle, the set of fundamental relations could be described and criteria could be derived for this recognition. But that's a job for the future.

3. The labelling of segments (in block capitals) shows their function in the whole. For the present, such labelling is informal but – we hope – informative.

4. Ordinary lower case type is reserved for specific content.

Figure 31 shows how these segments are nested in the passage itself. To avoid cluttering the presentation, the figure is restricted to segments of the first three ranks.

We now note the following points:

1. The major segments: (1) (2) and (3) show a very common structure: BACKGROUND, MAIN STATEMENT, ADDITIONAL INFORMATION. In this case, the main statement is a catalogue and a specific sort of catalogue at that: one might call it USES OF A NATURAL RESOURCE. Given that specification one will not be surprised to find MECHANISM (or HOW IT IS HARNESSED) either as part of BACKGROUND or as part of ADDITIONAL INFORMATION.

2. There can be little question that (13) and in particular (132) belong where they do. They are part of the introductory section. A section which provides a context (as 131) and a summary statement (as 132) is exceedingly common in texts of this kind. These are the key part of (1) forming what we have called an ANNOUNCER. (We are grateful to Mr S. Munslow for the insight.) You cannot go boldly into your MAIN STATEMENT without some kind of ANNOUNCER. What is somewhat strange is the irrelevant information (12) intruding at this point, and keeping the reader away from (2).

3. Within (2) itself there are some obvious anomalies. For instance the homes and buildings (2111), (2112) are introduced as part of a definition (the one violation of our rule 1), unlike the list of industries (22). Some of these are subordinated (CASE 3, CASE 4) and others

(Continued on page 237)

Figure 31 River Basins

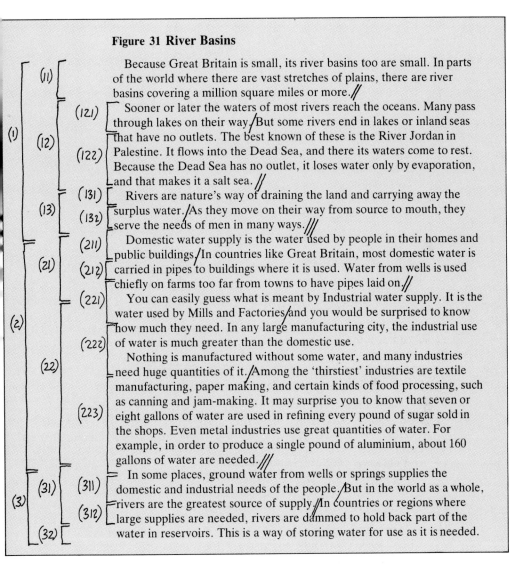

Because Great Britain is small, its river basins too are small. In parts of the world where there are vast stretches of plains, there are river basins covering a million square miles or more.//

Sooner or later the waters of most rivers reach the oceans. Many pass through lakes on their way./But some rivers end in lakes or inland seas that have no outlets. The best known of these is the River Jordan in Palestine. It flows into the Dead Sea, and there its waters come to rest. Because the Dead Sea has no outlet, it loses water only by evaporation, and that makes it a salt sea. //

Rivers are nature's way of draining the land and carrying away the surplus water./As they move on their way from source to mouth, they serve the needs of men in many ways.///

Domestic water supply is the water used by people in their homes and public buildings./In countries like Great Britain, most domestic water is carried in pipes to buildings where it is used. Water from wells is used chiefly on farms too far from towns to have pipes laid on.//

You can easily guess what is meant by Industrial water supply. It is the water used by Mills and Factories/and you would be surprised to know how much they need. In any large manufacturing city, the industrial use of water is much greater than the domestic use.

Nothing is manufactured without some water, and many industries need huge quantities of it./Among the 'thirstiest' industries are textile manufacturing, paper making, and certain kinds of food processing, such as canning and jam-making. It may surprise you to know that seven or eight gallons of water are used in refining every pound of sugar sold in the shops. Even metal industries use great quantities of water. For example, in order to produce a single pound of aluminium, about 160 gallons of water are needed.///

In some places, ground water from wells or springs supplies the domestic and industrial needs of the people./But in the world as a whole, rivers are the greatest source of supply./In countries or regions where large supplies are needed, rivers are dammed to hold back part of the water in reservoirs. This is a way of storing water for use as it is needed.

Figure 32 Structure of the extract River Basins

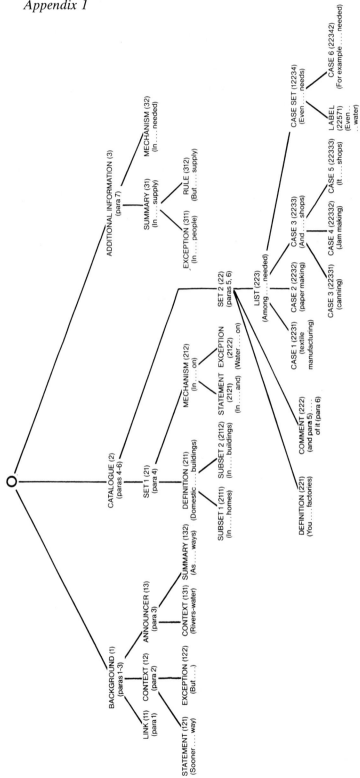

are not (CASE 1), (CASE 2), while (CASE 6) is introduced indirectly. However, all these may be normal and permissible variations which do not greatly impede the flow of comprehension.

4. There are two major anomalies, one being the CONTEXT (12) which is patently irrelevant to the main theme. It cannot be argued that this is really a separate entity, on a par with (2), because in terms of sheer length, nearly all of it is an EXCEPTION (122). The Dead Sea is a red herring!

5. The second major anomaly is the EXCEPTION in para 7 (311). This has the effect of making the whole section sound like an ANNOUNCER (with the form CONTEXT + RULE). What is more this ANNOUNCER would be entirely appropriate.

6. Both anomalies are spotted by our young readers, which is why they discard (11) and (12) and elect to substitute (31) in the ANNOUNCER role. (32) is still quite acceptable as a parenthesis, and if there is no CODA or SUPPLEMENTARY INFORMATION, the anomaly is still less than that in the passages as it stands.

7. There is a moral for writers: Beware of parenthetic statements, especially when they are tangential to the main theme.

Appendix 2

ORGANISING A COURSE

There is little doubt that an understanding of the design and use of text-based lessons is best attained by working with a study group. Whilst it is possible for one person to read about the techniques, and to apply them in a classroom, a group studying together profits from the ability to simulate classroom discussion, share ideas and gain independent feedback. Therefore, where possible, initiation into the use of directed reading activities should be through a study group.

The notes that follow are designed for the guidance of a study group leader and are based on the experience of working with study groups over a period of four years.

Kind of group

During the project, study groups were formed both from areas within an LEA and from individual schools. The advantage of the school-based group is that day-by-day feedback is possible, efforts can be co-ordinated with pupils, and results assessed across the curriculum. Hence, the school-based group is desirable when possible.

Sometimes a decision has to be made between a subject area group and a mixed subject group. In this instance it is difficult to give precise advice. A single subject group can study examples from a single area of the curriculum; the issues raised in discussion are liable to be relevant to all the members of the group; and the group will have a unity of experience. On the other hand, a cross-curriculum group is made aware of language issues in a variety of texts; often, subject teachers are brought face to face with examples of 'ignorance' among their colleagues, which serve to highlight the ease with which false assumptions can be made about the knowledge of pupils; and teachers are made aware of the form and content of texts outside their own subject.

The subject group may, therefore, gain something in efficiency, but the cross-curriculum group generally comes to grips with wider educational issues.

Kind of course

Over the past four years many patterns of course have been attempted. They have ranged in time from a single day to a school term, and have varied in content from the straight talk to the activity workshop.

It can be said immediately that one day combining talk, discussion and workshop is the least satisfactory. Indeed, it is just not enough. A minimum of four sessions is necessary, and these need to be spread over, say, four weeks. These four sessions allow at least the main structure of the activities to be introduced, whilst the space of four weeks gives sufficient time for activities to be planned and implemented with pupils. Course organisers would normally select examples for workshops from the main body of this book.

Four-session structure (2-hour session)

Session 1   Principles and example

Session 2   Text analysis. Teacher workshop using 1–2 examples

Session 3   Text reconstruction (as above)

Session 4   Text analysis and text types
ie discussion of text types woven around a workshop based on an example

More satisfactory is a six-session structure spread over a term. Various timing structures are possible, such as a weekly meeting for three weeks followed by three meetings spread over six weeks to allow more time for classroom trials.

Six-session structure

Sessions 1–3   As above

Session 4   Analysis of activities prepared by group

Session 5   As session 4, above

Session 6   Analysis of examples used by group including discussion of text types

In addition, the group will need one or two sessions for discussion of wider issues of preparation, management and planning reading development within a school. The ideal short course should also include ample opportunities for members to carry out their own original activities with a class and to discuss issues arising from trial lessons. To include these in a timetable would entail about eight meetings spread over a term, with provision for follow-up after one term working with pupils.

Using the experience of the group

It cannot be overemphasised that learning about directed reading activities is achieved best by actually carrying out lessons with pupils and by discussing outcomes. Hence, a possible plan, which is offered as a guide, and not as a prescription, might be:

1. Before the first meeting, the group should read the Introduction.

2. At the first meeting, emphasise main features of the activities then proceed immediately to an analysis activity. The choice of this first activity is important. It should be at secondary-school level,

possibly a text that describes a process, not longer than 300 words, and worked *by the group in pairs*. This may be the group members' first experience of intensive reading and discussion. Use the example to stress the role of the directions in forcing attention, the role of discussion in arriving at meaning, and invite the participants to examine the effect of the activity on their own reading.

3. From this point encourage the group to devise simple activies of their own, and to report back on their results. Encourage them, too, to read the introductory sections to Part I and, later to Part II as well as to browse through selected examples. It may be wise to ask them *not* to look at any examples that will be made the basis of a later workshop.

4. Allow as much time as necessary for members to discuss their own work as well as the ideas and examples in the book.

Appendix 3

OBTAINING PERMISSION TO USE COPYRIGHT MATERIAL

Copyright in a work lasts until 31 December 50 years after the author's death or fifty years after publication, whichever is the later. It is always necessary, therefore, to seek permission to make copies of extracts from text or illustrations which fall into this category. Usually the publishers concerned will give permission freely if such copies are for classroom use and not for a wider circulation.

Before granting permission, publishers will usually need the following information:

1. Length of extract (ie approximate number of words).

2. Precise details of any diagrams or illustrations (ie figure and page numbers).

3. Author, title and series if there is one (title of articles and author in a newspaper or journal).

4. Date of publication (or issue of newspaper or journal).

5. The number of copies you intend to make.

6. The use to which you intend to put the copies. (It would probably be helpful if you were to state whether you wished your students to underline or in any way annotate the copies.)

7. The intended readership (ie your own class, other classes in the school, other schools, etc).

8. The format (ie single sheets, folders, bound booklets).

9. Whether or not the material is to be for sale, and the price if it is to be sold.

Note

Where you wish to reproduce an item from an anthology, the anthology's acknowledgements list should give the name of the publisher or other copyright owner to approach for permission to reproduce such an extract.

Sources for further reading

The lessons and discussions contained in this book draw on ideas in several fields, especially reading comprehension, structure of text, study skills and group dynamics. A proper bibliography over so large a field would be very long and not particularly helpful. The following list is short and deliberately selective. Its purpose is to open doors for those who want to advance their understanding of any of the ideas that we have touched on. The references have been divided into three headings (although some have relevance to more than one of these) – reading and the structure of text, study skills, and learning in groups.

Reading and the structure of text

1. Department of Education and Science, *A Language for Life*, Report of a Committee of Enquiry under the Chairmanship of Sir Alan Bullock, HMSO, 1975. Authoritative discussion of the role of oral and written language in education from pre-school to adulthood. Especially relevant are Chapters 8, 'Reading: the later stages', 12, 'Language across the curriculum', and 15, 'The secondary school'.

2. Eric Lunzer and Keith Gardner (eds), *The Effective Use of Reading*, Heinemann Educational, 1979. This sets out the background to the present project in some detail. Chapters 4, 'Incidence of reading in the classroom' and 9, 'Improving reading through group discussion', are of special interest.

3. Frank Smith, *Reading*, Cambridge University Press, 1978. A short and untechnical, yet authoritative, introduction. Covers the whole field of the relation between reading and existing knowledge and hence brings out the problem of learning by reading. Contains no references or bibliography and therefore insufficient by itself.

4. A. K. Pugh, *Silent Reading*, Heinemann, 1978. A very short book which yet deals with many aspects of reading that are central or marginal to our concern, including comprehension and readability, speed reading and alternative ways of improving reading efficiency. Useful references.

5. Open University Courses in Educational Studies, Language in Use, Block 5, *Talk and Text*. Prepared by A. K. Pugh, Open University, 1981. The second part of this work bears the title 'Analysis of text and the reader'. This is particularly helpful as a first introduction to the variety of approaches to the study of text, its organisation, and how this facilitates or impedes the reader's task.

6. A. J. Sanford and S. C. Garrod, *Understanding Written Language*, Wiley, 1981. A text-book for more advanced students covering the same ground as the last two references. Up-to-date, authoritative and clearly presented.

7. H. G. Widdowson, *Teaching Language as Communication*, Oxford University Press, 1978. This book (like the companion volume. *Explorations in Applied Linguistics*) is primary addressed to those concerned with the teaching of English as a second language for students of science. However, the author stresses the role of content in determining what is said and how it is said. The work is therefore particularly relevant to the idea of text type.

Study skills

8. David Wray, *Extending Reading Skills*, Centre for Educational Research, University of Lancaster. Brief discussion of a number of recent studies dealing with the improvement in reading for study and its evaluation. Covers the whole age range. Useful references.

9. Michael Marland, *Information skills in the secondary curriculum*, Schools Council Curriculum Bulletin no. 9, Methuen Educational, 1981. Important as background to the issues covered in the present book; contains suggestions for teaching children how to find out, especially from library resources. Good bibliography.

10. Ralph Tabberer and Janet Allman, *Introducing Study Skills at Sixteen Plus*, NFER Nelson, 1983. Teaching study skills is rare in the lower secondary schools, more common at A level. This is an analysis of such courses with detailed consideration of a smaller set of case studies. One of the findings that emerges is the need for curriculum relevance.

11. Janis Burnett, *Successful Study*, Teach Yourself Books, Hodder and Stoughton, 1979. There is an abundance of books on how to study addressed to the older student, many of doubtful value. This one has much to recommend it.

12. R. A. Carson and W. R. Adams, *Study Skills: a Student's Guide for Survival*, Wiley, 1972. An American manual which is outstanding both for content and method.

Collaborative work

13. Douglas Barnes, *From Communication to Curriculum*, Penguin, 1976. Decribes what happens when children are asked to discuss things in small groups. Gives examples, some of which are successful and others less so. The issues that are raised are then analysed and discussed in the light of insights drawn from psychology, sociology and linguistics. Matter-of-fact and free from technical jargon.

14. Terence Brake, *The Need to Know*, British Library Research and Development Reports, Report No. 5511, British Library Board, 1980. Describes a school project on finding out. The chosen topic was 'leisure'. The method is reminiscent of the ideas used in our project in the reliance on group work, but goes far beyond in its exploitation of a wide variety of information sources.

15. Eric Lunzer and Tony Gibson, *Decision Making and the Language of Manipulative Display*, School of Education, University of Nottingham, 1979. A brief discussion of how and why interaction works better when there is something one can talk about actually present and capable of being handled. Examples are taken from several different contexts.

16. Graham Gibbs, *Teaching Students to Learn: a Student Centred Approach*, Open University Press, 1981. Although this book is addressed to the problem of improving study skills, the method is to get students to learn from one another. The students concerned are older than school-children, but the ideas are stimulating and have some general applicability.